The Anvil of Civilisation

Diadem of Princess Sit-Hathor-Unet (12th Dynasty)

THE ANVIL
OF CIVILISATION

*An Outline of the Birth, Development
and Inter-relationship of the Ancient
Civilisations of Western Asia
and the Mediterranean
4000–400 B.C.*

by

LEONARD COTTRELL

FABER AND FABER
24 Russell Square
London

First published in mcmlviii
by Faber and Faber Limited
24 Russell Square, London WC1
Printed in Great Britain by
Ebenezer Baylis and Son Ltd
Worcester and London

To

my Mother

BEATRICE MARTHA COTTRELL

Contents

	PROLOGUE	*page* 15
I	THE BEGINNINGS	19
II	EARLIEST EGYPT	34
III	'LORD OF THE TWO LANDS'	44
IV	THE TWO RIVERS	59
V	EGYPTIAN RELIGION	68
VI	EGYPT TO THE MIDDLE KINGDOM	75
VII	SUMER AND BABYLON	93
VIII	THE ISLAND KINGS	106
IX	CLASH OF EMPIRES (1)	119
X	CLASH OF EMPIRES (2)	137
XI	THE END OF THE EIGHTEENTH DYNASTY	158
XII	THE IRON AGE REVOLUTION	173
XIII	'BABYLON, THE MIGHTY CITY'	186
XIV	THE DAWN OF WESTERN CIVILISATION	201
XV	MYTHS AND MORALS: LITERATURE AND ART	213
XVI	'THE KING WITH HALF THE EAST AT HEEL'	227
XVII	ATHENS: GLORY AND DECLINE	246
	EPILOGUE	262
	GLOSSARY	267
	BIBLIOGRAPHY	271
	INDEX	277
	COMPARATIVE CHRONOLOGICAL TABLE	*at the end of book*

Illustrations

Diadem of Princess Sit-Hathor-Unet (12th Dynasty) (*Photograph by courtesy of the Metropolitan Museum of Art, New York*)
frontispiece

PLATE 1 (a) Narmer (Menes), Founder of the 1st Dynasty (3200 B.C.) with a kneeling captive. Slate palette commemorating his victories. (*Photograph by Lehnert and Landrock*)   *facing page* 48

      (b) King Djoser (2800 B.C.) in running posture (*Photograph by courtesy of the Department of Antiquities, Cairo*)

      (c) Ancient Egyptian quarry showing method of quarrying stone (*Photograph by the author*)   49

      (d) Egyptian writing tablet used by schoolboys, showing 'hieratic' script (*Photograph by courtesy of the British Museum*)

PLATE 2 (a) Impressions from Sumerian cylinder seals (*Photograph by courtesy of the British Museum*)   64

      (b) The Egyptian Goddess Sekhmet (*Photograph by the author*)

      (c) Entrance to the enclosure of the Step Pyramid of Djoser (2780 B.C.) (*Photograph by courtesy of the Department of Antiquities, Cairo*)   65

      (d) Jewellery of Princess Sit-Hathor-Unet (12th Dynasty) found in her pyramid (*Photograph by courtesy of the Metropolitan Museum of Art, New York*)

PLATE 3 (a) Palace of Phaestos (Crete) (*Photograph by the author*)   112

      (b) Court Ladies (fresco from Palace of Knossos, Crete) (*Photograph by courtesy of the Ashmolean Museum*)

Illustrations—cont.

(c) Reconstruction of Throne Room, Palace of Knossos, Crete (*Photograph by courtesy of Macmillan and Co.*) *facing page* 113

(d) The 'boy-god'. Statuette found in Palace of Knossos, Crete (*Photograph by courtesy of the Ashmolean Museum*)

PLATE 4 (a) The Lion Gate, Mycenae (*Photograph by the author*) 128

(b) Reproductions of objects found in the shaft-graves at Mycenae (*Photograph by courtesy of the Ashmolean Museum*)

(c) Hittite city of Alaja Hüyük (*Photograph by courtesy of the Exclusive News Agency*) 129

(d) Reliefs of Hittite warriors, Yassilikaya, Boghazkeui (*Photograph by courtesy of the Exclusive News Agency*)

PLATE 5 (a) Akhnaten (*Photograph by Lehnert and Landrock, Cairo*) 160

(b) Nefretiti (*Photograph by Lehnert and Landrock, Cairo*)

(c) Tomb-fresco, banqueting scene, 18th Dynasty (*Photograph by the author*) 161

(d) Colossal statue of Ramesses II, showing his queen (*Photograph by the author*)

PLATE 6 (a) Part of processional way, Babylon, built by Nebuchadnezzar, showing wall reliefs (*Photograph by courtesy of the Hulton Press Library*) 176

(b) View of excavations, Babylon (*Photograph by courtesy of the Exclusive News Agency*)

(c) Assyrian relief showing hunting scenes (*Photograph by courtesy of the British Museum*) 177

(d) Winged bull of Assyria (*Photograph by courtesy of the British Museum*)

PLATE 7 (a) Head of the statue of Demeter from Cnidus (about 330 B.C.) (*Photograph by courtesy of the British Museum*) 224

(b) Bronze statuette of a running girl, probably Spartan (about 500 B.C.) (*Photograph by courtesy of the British Museum*)

(c) Detail from an Attic Red-Figured Amphora (about 480 B.C.) A rhapsode chanting an epic poem (*Photograph by courtesy of the British Museum*)   *facing page* 225

(d) Attic Black-Figured Amphora (about 540–530 B.C.) Achilles slaying Penthesilea (*Photograph by courtesy of the British Museum*)

PLATE 8 (a) View from the site of the Temple of Delphi, Greece (*Photograph by the author*)   240

(b) The Acropolis of Athens seen from the Theseum (*Photograph by the author*)

(c) Base of the Parthenon, showing 'entasis' (*Photograph by the author*)   241

(d) Temple of the Four Winds, Athens (*Photograph by the author*)

Acknowledgements

In addition to the authors mentioned in the Prologue, I would like to express my thanks to the author and publishers of the following works which have been of especial help to me in the preparation of this book; they are also listed in the Bibliography. *The Palace of Minos* by Sir Arthur Evans; *The Pyramids of Egypt* by I. E. S. Edwards; *The Literature of the Ancient Egyptians* by Erman (translated by Blackman); *Ancient Near Eastern Texts* edited by James Pritchard; *Foundations in the Dust* and *Early Anatolia*, both by Seton Lloyd; *Women in Antiquity* by Charles Seltman; *The Greeks* by H. D. F. Kitto; *Ur of the Chaldees* by Sir Leonard Woolley; *The Archaeology of Crete* by J. D. S. Pendlebury; *Greek poetry for Everyman* by F. L. Lucas.

May I also thank the publishers of my own books, *The Lost Pharaohs*, *Life under the Pharaohs* and *The Bull of Minos*, for kindly permitting me to reproduce extracts, and the British Broadcasting Corporation for permission to use certain material obtained when preparing documentary programmes on their behalf.

Finally, my gratitude is due to Mr. I. E. S. Edwards, Egyptian Department, British Museum, and Dr. Frank Stubbings of Emmanuel College, Cambridge, for kindly reading the script and for their suggestions and criticisms.

LEONARD COTTRELL

13

Prologue

There are a number of reasons why authors write books, apart from the obvious and by no means negligible one of earning a living. The poet and the novelist absorb experience, then weave it into new shapes on the loom of their imaginations. The biographer and the travel-writer each in his separate way, strives to express a selective view of a person or a place. The historian studies the records of Man's past achievements, choosing, rejecting, analysing, assembling and reassembling facts, imposing, if he is successful, the discipline of scholarship on to what would otherwise be an incoherent mass of material. Each seeks a pattern.

This book, which I hope will be the first of three, derives its main impetus from a search for a pattern, and is in that sense, and that sense only, a personal book. It deals with an area of the earth's surface which I have visited several times, and which I find of inexhaustible fascination and interest. In the scale of the world's great oceans and land-masses, the area is not large. From east to west it stretches roughly from Corsica in the Mediterranean, to the valleys of the Tigris and Euphrates, approximately the distance between Los Angeles and Charleston in the United States of America. From north to south it is even narrower. From the Balkans to the southern frontier of Egypt about the distance which separates Nova Scotia from the island of Jamaica. The whole area of mountain, plain, sea, and desert is less than one-sixth the size of Soviet Russia.

Yet within that limited space civilisation first arose on this planet. Here, for the first time, when the wandering tribes became Man the citizen, developed political and economic organisations favourable to art and industry, conducted the first experiments in what we have come to call civilisation. There were a number of such experiments, Egyptian, Cretan, Sumerian, Babylonian,

Prologue

There are a number of reasons why authors write books, apart from the obvious and by no means negligible one of earning a living. The poet and the novelist absorb experience, then weave it into new shapes on the loom of their imaginations. The biographer and the travel-writer, each in his separate way, strives to express a selective view of a person or a place. The historian studies the records of Man's past achievements, choosing, rejecting, analysing; assembling and reassembling facts; imposing, if he is successful, the discipline of scholarship on to what would otherwise be an incoherent mass of material. Each seeks a pattern.

This book, which I hope will be the first of three, derives its main impetus from a search for a pattern, and is in that sense, and that sense only, a personal book. It deals with an area of the earth's surface which I have visited several times, and which I find of inexhaustible fascination and interest. In the scale of the world's great oceans and land-masses, the area is not large. From east to west it stretches roughly from Corsica, in the Mediterranean, to the valleys of the Tigris and Euphrates, approximately the distance between Los Angeles and Charleston in the United States of America. From north to south it is even narrower, from the Balkans to the southern frontier of Egypt, about the distance which separates Nova Scotia from the island of Jamaica. The whole area of mountain, plain, sea, and desert is less than one-half the size of Soviet Russia.

Yet within that limited space civilisation first rose on this planet. Here, for the first time, Man the wandering hunter became Man the citizen, developed political and economic organisations favourable to art and industry, conducted his first experiments in what we have come to call civilisation. There were a number of such experiments; Egyptian, Cretan, Sumerian, Babylonian,

Assyrian, Mycenean, Phoenician, Greek, Roman. Moreover, by far the greater part of the laws, institutions, languages, arts and industries of the modern Western world were first hammered out on that anvil. Can it be wondered that the countries surrounding the Eastern Mediterranean, and in the deserts to the east and south of it, have attracted generations of historians, archaeologists, and ordinary travellers.

I must admit frankly that I fall into the third category. I am neither a professional historian nor archaeologist, though, as a writer, these subjects have absorbed me for many years. Innumerable books have been written about the eastern Mediterranean and adjoining lands, from learned monographs on specialised aspects of the ancient civilisations, to popular expositions which paint a broader picture. For two hundred years, from Gibbon onwards, writers have been filling in larger or smaller portions of that picture. One of the most remarkable was Winwood Reade who, in 1872, published his *Martyrdom of Man*, a majestic and sombre panorama. The Marxists, of course, have made their analyses, and Mr. H. G. Wells, in his *Outline of History*, galloped his political hobby-horse through the ancient world, heedless of scholarly sniping.

In more recent years, such giants as Petrie, Breasted, and Reisner have opened up fresh vistas of Egypt, Woolley of Sumer, Sayce of Assyria, Evans, Wace and others of pre-Hellenic Greece and Crete, to name only a few. Other scholars have attempted, with some success, to give more comprehensive accounts of Man's development in these areas. Such works as de Burgh's *The Legacy of the Ancient World* and Gordon Childe's *What Happened in History* combine fine scholarship with simple exposition: they have placed thousands of readers in their debt, not least the present writer.

It is doubtful if a completely comprehensive, definitive work on the growth of civilisation will ever be written. The subject is too vast, and, as new discoveries are made and fresh researches carried out, the picture constantly changes. Certainly this volume makes no such absurd pretence. It is, in essence, a quest; an attempt to clarify in my own mind some of the many impressions I have received of these ancient lands, in personal travels, in conversations with archaeologists, and in a great deal of un-organised reading. In these days of swift, easy transport, thousands of new travellers are seeing for the first time such countries as Greece, Turkey, the Lebanon, Syria, Iraq, Jordan, and Egypt. Travel stimulates curiosity, and during my own journeys I have often been asked for information by people who, knowing my interest in the ancient world, innocently expected that I could give them a precise answer to any questions.

Sometimes I could help them by recommending a book, but the yawning gaps in my own knowledge soon made themselves apparent. In Egypt I was on fairly firm ground, and, to a lesser extent, in Greece and the Holy Land. The difficulty arose in integrating one's knowledge, in recognising the chronological sequence in which the various cultures developed and decayed, where and how they touched and influenced each other. What was happening in the Hittite Empire when Ramesses III ruled in Egypt? What was happening in Greece and the islands when the Phoenician merchants were capturing the Mediterranean mercantile trade? Who was King of Egypt when Joshua stormed Jericho; or when the first Minoan palace rose at Knossos? Few of such questions can be answered precisely, and some not at all, but for my own satisfaction I decided to make an attempt, first by drawing up a chronological table of known dates, with cross references, and then endeavouring to fill in the gaps. From this a faint pattern began to emerge, and it is this pattern which forms the basis of this book. Its principal theme is the growth of civilisations in the areas bordering the eastern Mediterranean, beginning with that of Egypt, the earliest, and ending with the glory of Periclean Athens, a period of some three thousand years. During that time other civilisations rose, in Crete and the Greek mainland, in Asia Minor, and along the coast of the Levant. It was also necessary to take into account the impact of cultures lying outside the limits of the Mediterranean; e.g. the impact of Babylon and Assyria on Canaan and Judea, and to a lesser extent on Egypt; the effect of Egyptian conquest and colonisation of what is now Israel and the Lebanon, and Jordan, the influence of the Hittite Empire, which seems to have originated in the mountains of Asia Minor but which thrust

B

southward into Syria; the colonisation of parts of Asia Minor by the Myceneans, the precursors of the classical Greeks, and the impact of the latter on Egypt, Phoenicia, and other countries along the Mediterranean littoral.

Inevitably I have had to set limits to my explorations. The area I selected, and which I have called the Anvil, was chosen because the civilisations which arose within its boundaries are those which have given birth to the three principal components of our western culture; Greek thought, Roman law, and the Christian religion. But Greece was profoundly influenced by Egypt, and Egypt by Syria, and traces of even these remote cultures have affected our life and thought. Of course, other civilisations existed, for example, in the Indus Valley, and in China, but their influence on the western world has been, by comparison, negligible. Culturally the vast majority of the peoples of Europe, and of their descendants scattered throughout the world, are children of the Mediterranean Sea.

And what a sea it is, glimpsed far-off from the Eastern mountains, or from the wave-washed harbour of ancient Byblos, where the Phoenician galleys rode, or from Ida's mighty peak, birthplace of Zeus, or where the Nile rolls into its depths the rich mud of fertile Egypt; Homer's 'wine-dark sea', which bore Agamemnon's ships to Troy, Odysseus to the arms of Penelope, Saint Paul to his trial; mother of arts, beguiler of how many writers, good and bad; begetter of how many books!

Even this one, which some may regard as a doubtful progeny, the product of little learning and much art. Perhaps they are right. The best that its author can say is, that like the children of some other irregular unions, it was at least conceived in love.

LEONARD COTTRELL

Hampstead,
*London, N.W.*3.

CHAPTER I

The Beginnings

The earliest written records of mankind begin at about 3000 B.C. and are found in three places; in the Nile Valley, in Mesopotamia, and in the Indus Valley; of these three forms of writing, only the first two can be read. Before 3000 B.C. archaeologists can trace Man's story only by digging up the objects he has left behind; his tools and weapons, fragmentary remains of the houses he lived in, the vessels in which he stored his food, the bones of the animals he hunted or domesticated, his ornaments and those of his womenfolk. These can be dated only approximately from the levels at which they were found. On a site which has been more or less continuously occupied for several thousand years, the objects found at the lowest levels are obviously older than those found in the upper strata. Many such sites exist in the Middle East, especially in Mesopotamia and Syria. In some of these, occupation layers exist far below the level at which the earliest written documents have been found. Since we know that writing began at about the beginning of the Third Millennium (3000 B.C.), the lower levels clearly antedate this period.

The remote prehistory of mankind is outside the scope of this book; the earliest limit I shall set myself is 4000 B.C., a thousand years before the beginning of what Professor Childe has called 'The Urban Revolution'—the time when men first began to live in large settled communities, the period of the earliest civilisations. 'The thousand years or so immediately preceding 3000 B.C.' he writes, 'were perhaps more fertile in fruitful inventions and discoveries than any period in human history prior to the sixteenth century A.D. Its achievements made possible that economic reorganisation of society that I term the urban revolution.'[1]

[1] *What Happened in History*—Gordon Childe: Pelican Books, London, 1942.

These achievements included the making of bricks for building, the construction of the potter's wheel,[1] wheeled transport, the sailing-ship and the harnessing of domestic animals for transport and haulage. But the most important discovery was the metallurgy of copper and bronze. Before this discovery Man had had to rely for his tools and weapons mainly on stone, hence those familiar but convenient labels, Old Stone Age (*palaeolithic*) and New Stone Age (*neolithic*). In the lower levels of prehistoric sites in Hither Asia we find stone axes, flint knives, flint spear-heads, and so on. Stone weapons were used for hunting, fighting, and for cutting up the skins and flesh of animals. Stone tools were used to cultivate the land, bone sickles set with flint 'teeth' to reap the crop.

Such tools continued to be used for millennia after the properties of metals were discovered; in fact, in some parts of the world they are still used today. But at some time between 4000 and 3000 B.C. Man had learned that copper could be reduced from ores, that it could be given a cutting edge as hard as that of flint; or it could be beaten into flat sheets, bent and shaped. Furthermore, by infusing tin, an even harder metal was obtained, which we call bronze. Such tools and weapons gave the men who owned them greatly increased powers over nature, and, in warfare, superiority over peoples not so equipped.

We do not know who discovered the properties of copper or who developed the techniques of mining, smelting, casting, moulding, etc., required for the manufacture of copper tools and weapons, but we do know that, before 3000 B.C., techniques were being spread through an area which stretched from the Aegean in the west to Turkestan in the east. A thousand years later they reached Britain and China. But, save for two isolated areas in Peru and Mexico, the craft does not seem to have been practised in any other part of the world until late historical times.

The same is true of other achievements; the sailing-ship, the potter's wheel, wheeled vehicles, and the use of animals for haulage. Before 3000 B.C. all these were known within parts (not

[1] Not found in Egypt before the first Dynasty. (Lucas)

all) of the area I have called the Anvil, and east of it as far as the mountains of Turkestan; but nowhere else in the world.

Why?

By studying and comparing the findings of archaeologists who have worked independently in Egypt, Palestine, Syria, Mesopotamia and other places, it is possible to attempt a reply, though many problems still remain unsolved.

To understand why the earliest civilisations developed in these regions it is necessary to grope further back in time, to what geologists call the holocene period, after the end of the last Ice Age. As the northern ice-caps melted the steppes of Europe became temperate forests; further south, climatic changes produced by the melting of the ice transformed the prairies of the Near East, and the district south of the Mediterranean, into deserts, with occasional oases.

Up to this period, primitive Man, our ancestor, had been a hunter; while he remained so he could not form settled communities, but must have perforce remained a wanderer. These conditions continued in northern Europe, but further south, and especially in the Mediterranean area and to the east and south of it, men (or, more likely, their womenfolk) discovered that by clearing the ground of weeds and planting the seeds of certain edible grasses it was possible to obtain a food crop to supplement what could be obtained by hunting. Thus agriculture was born.

At first there would be a 'mixed economy', both hunting and agriculture being carried on at the same time. Also, crops could only be grown where there were suitable conditions—a regular supply of water, from rainfall, stream or spring, and sunshine to ripen the plants. But from very early times, probably before 5000 B.C., such conditions obtained in certain parts of the area we have described. Archaeologists have found, for example, at Mount Carmel in Israel, evidences of cave-dwellers who hunted and also cultivated crops. They were Stone Age People, who used flint knives and stone axes, but they also mounted small flints in ribbones and used them as sickles for reaping. This is proved by the 'shine' on the flints, but it is not known what kinds of cereals were grown, or whether these were cultivated or wild.

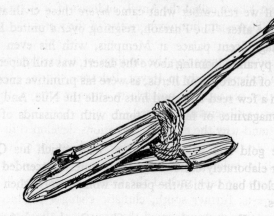

In those parts of Western Asia where the cereals, wheat and barley were cultivated by the neolithic inhabitants there were also the wild ancestors of such animals as the goat, the pig, sheep and cattle. It seems reasonable to suppose that, while the men hunted, their womenfolk tended the land and may have offered to the wild animals the grain-stubble and husks. Gradually some animals would become tame, and in time people would domesticate them, using them not only for food, but as 'living larders and walking wardrobes'. The next stage would be inducing such animals as cows, ewes, and goats to give milk, and by selective breeding, produce a type of sheep which would yield a woolly fleece.[1]

Incidentally, these facts can help us to a better understanding of the developed civilisation of Egypt, Mesopotamia and pre-Hellenic Greece when we come to them later. There we encounter civilised communities whose wealthier members enjoyed amenities equal if not superior to our own; comfortable, well-furnished houses; good communications, a wide variety of food and drink; fine clothing and adornments; sophisticated sports and pastimes; rich achievements in the fine arts. And yet these same people, Egyptians, Sumerians, Babylonians, Myceneans, counted their wealth in stores of grain, oil and wine, and in herds of cattle—a difficult conception for the heirs of an industrial civilisation where wealth consists in factories, oil-wells and mines. It is easier to

[1] *What Happened in History*—Gordon Childe: Pelican Books, London, 1942.

understand if we remember what came *before* these civilisations, not what came after. The Pharaoh, reigning over a united Egypt from his magnificent palace at Memphis, with his even more magnificent pyramid looming above the desert, was still dependent on the yield of his crops and herds, as were his primitive ancestors who lived in a few reed-and-mud huts beside the Nile. And so he stored the magazines of his great tomb with thousands of food vessels.

Even the gold and jewelled diadem with which his Queen adorned her elaborately curled wig was remotely descended from the simple cloth band which the peasant women wore when reaping the crops.

But Dynastic Egypt is a long way off yet. In the period we are considering, about 4000 B.C., there were no cities, no large groups of people living together under a common system of government. But, in the Middle East, and particularly the East Mediterranean area, there were communities living together on the same site for generations. Driving through Syria and Iraq you will often see huge mounds, called 'tells', which mark the sites of thousands of years of occupation. As the buildings, of packed clay (*pisé*) or later of mud-brick, decayed or were destroyed, new buildings were erected on top. So, generation by generation, the mound grew, so that the village which sits on top of it today is the latest of a series, the earliest of which may date from more than two thousand years before the beginning of recorded history.

Archaeologists who have dug down into these mounds have found that the so-called 'historical horizon'—i.e. the level at which they find objects datable at about 3000 B.C.—is often quite high in the mound. Objects found at a still higher level give relative dates, and thus enable the excavators to estimate the average rate of accretion over the centuries. From this they can calculate the approximate date of the lowest village on the site, which in some cases was as early as *circa* 4500 B.C.

If mankind had been forced to live perpetually in these small self-supporting communities, each producing just sufficient to feed its members, the great civilisations of the ancient world would not have arisen. They arose because, within a certain period and within a certain geographic area, a combination of circumstances enabled men to organise themselves into larger social units. By co-operating, by pooling materials, knowledge and resources, they were able to win increased mastery over nature, to obtain a surplus of wealth beyond the immediate needs of the community, protection from their enemies, and long periods of comparative peace. The fruits of this co-operation, in science and technology, art and politics, enabled Man to make more material progress in the next two millennia than he had made in the previous hundred.

Among the factors favouring this development were the inventions and discoveries described above, but these alone did not bring about the Urban Revolution. It took place because, at three places on the earth's surface, conditions occurred which encouraged Neolithic Man—already a primitive farmer and herdsman—to settle in considerable numbers within a large but clearly defined area. Two of these places, the Nile Valley and the Valleys of the Tigris and Euphrates, lie within the Anvil. The third, the Indus Valley, lies east of it.

Authorities rightly stress the importance of the geographic and climatic conditions in these areas in nurturing civilisation, but it would be wrong to think that these alone were responsible. The explanation is less simple. The valleys of the Nile and Tigris-Euphrates provided conditions favourable to permanent settlement; a great river whose annual flooding brought a gift of fertile mud on which crops grew readily; an abundance of game—mammals and wildfowl; and on each side vast, inhospitable deserts which acted as defensive barriers against invasion. Equally important, perhaps, were clear, cloudless skies, which enabled men to study the movement of the stars and so learn to measure time. Such conditions provided the soil in which to plant the seeds of technical discovery and invention from which civilisation could grow.

One story proper begins with the next chapter, but before we watch the curtain rise on those two earliest civilisations of mankind—Egyptian and Sumerian—let us try to catch a glimpse of the stage being set. It can only be a vague glimpse, because the archaeological evidence is insufficient to give a clear picture, and in any case scholars differ in their interpretation of it. The guide I have chosen is Professor Childe, whose theory seems to be logical and reasonable.

Before about 3000 B.C. we find a large number of relatively small, self-sufficient communities scattered over a large area, and in many of these the craft of the potter, the wheelwright, the smith, are known. These communites are also using pack-animals —asses and, in a few cases, possibly horses—for carriage, and oxen for drawing a primitive plough. Their women also wove and spun. After about 3000 B.C. many societies continue to live in this way, but in the two districts mentioned men are beginning to organise themselves into much larger social units which include not only farmers and pastoralists, but numbers of *specialists*, stone-masons, smiths, carpenters, shipwrights, and wheelwrights. We can also see the emergence of a new class of experts, 'who toil not, neither do they spin'. These are the scribes, the men who have learned the new and difficult art of writing, an invention of more portent for the future than any of the others.

How and why did this slow, difficult transition take place? For no one reason, thinks Childe, but many. The development of techniques during those vital thousand years before 3000 B.C. led to an increase of population, which is proved by the spread of certain 'cultures' over wide areas of Asia and Europe. But the trouble with those simple, self-sufficient neolithic communities was that they could only expand up to a certain limit. If numbers rose above a certain amount, food-supplies and raw materials were insufficient and the only solution was for the surplus population to move away, find—if it could—new and preferably unoccupied grazing and agricultural land and found a fresh settlement. But the amount of land available in which conditions were suitable— e.g. an adequate water supply—was limited, and sometimes fighting took place between the occupiers of land and those who wished to occupy it. Among the by-products of this enforced wandering, archaeologists have demonstrated two which were of great significance: (1) it caused the spreading of 'cultures'. An invading tribe would bring with it a knowledge of crafts and skills unknown to the invaded; and (2) man-killing weapons became extremely important. Childe has an interesting comment to make on this. He points out that even after the secret of producing copper had been discovered, the peoples of Mesopotamia did not use it to any extent for some time. The thing which finally drove them to it, he believes, was the fact that it was much more reliable when it came to the manufacture of weapons. He points out that in all early Mesopotamian graves *the first objects of copper to be found were not tools, as one might have expected, but weapons.*

But even if the wandering tribe found an unoccupied site suitable for settlement, or succeeded in subduing the owners of an occupied one, a time came, inevitably, when the same pattern would repeat itself. The site could only support a limited number of people; if the numbers grew too large, they had to get out, or perish. Again, the very self-sufficiency of the small unit contained the seeds of danger. Reserves of food could be stored, but only in small quantities. A prolonged drought, flooding, or other natural catastrophe could cause disaster. A famous historical example is the Bible story of Joseph's brethren, who had to go to Egypt to buy corn when famine threatened their own land. And of course, over large parts of Africa, Asia, and Latin America the same conditions apply to this day.

This terrible dependence of Man on nature has a vital bearing on the development of the religions which figure so prominently in the history of civilisation. The importance of this cannot be overstressed in any consideration of the ancient world. If we do not make an attempt to understand the religions of the early civilisations, and especially their origins, we shall never be able to understand the people. This is all the more difficult for us for two reasons: first, the fact that the gods themselves, and the worshippers' attitude to them, are so foreign to our own conception of the Deity, and second, because in our sophisticated western world, religion has become more and more divorced from everyday life, and is completely separated from technology. For instance, it is impossible to imagine the director of the Bethlehem Steel Corporation having a statue of the God of Steel erected within his factory, and making an offering to it before going to his office. But the Egyptian and Sumerian technologists, the coppersmiths and bronze-workers, would not have thought it at all strange. To them it would have been natural, and indeed essential.

Similarly, it is difficult for modern minds to understand why the ancient peoples worshipped animals, or at least Gods with animal attributes—goddesses like Sekhmet with the body of a woman and the head of a lioness, or Sobek, who has the body of a crocodile, or Amun, King of all the Gods in Egypt, who, in one of his manifestations, bore the head of a ram. If I may be permitted to quote briefly from one of my own books, the explanation may be that——'before Science showed the mechanism which animates plants and animals, before man knew that animals, reptiles and birds were of a lower but kindred species to himself, he could only judge them in relation to his own humanity; what interested and awed him was the fact that they were so different from himself, and that they possessed powers and functions which he had not. The bird with its power of flight, the lion with its immense strength, the crocodile which lurked in the river and could take off a man's leg with a snap of its jaws, the snake with its secret, silent, furtive life, and the ibis with its dignified air of wisdom; he did not catch these animals and study them in zoos; he respected and revered them because they possessed super-human powers. And therefore, in time, the high-flying falcon became one of the insignia of royalty, the crocodile the infernal monster which devoured guilty souls, the ibis became Thoth, the god of wisdom (and of writing) and the lion, as the Sphinx, symbolised kingly majesty.'[1]

I believe that religion arose partly out of magic; not merely the magic of the medieval necromancers and their modern imitators, but something much more fundamental. Like their palaeolithic ancestors, the wandering hunters of the Old Stone Age, the peoples of these neolithic Asian communities were constantly aware of forces outside themselves, forces which they could not control by any physical means; winds and tides, rainfall, floods and drought, and the fertility of the earth. In remote parts of the world there are still races who have not progressed beyond the Stone Age; e.g. the Bushmen of Africa, and the Australian aborigines. Anthropologists who have studied them have observed that such

[1] *Life under the Pharaohs*—Leonard Cottrell: Evans Bros., London.

people regard these unseen and uncontrollable forces as human and from the archaeological record there is no doubt that the peoples of 4000–3000 B.C. did the same. If you have to deal with a man much more powerful than yourself, whom you cannot hope to defeat by physical force, you *may* be able to avoid his anger by propitiating him with gifts. Much more difficult, if you have to cope with the wayward, whimsical, unpredictable ways of a woman—you may, if you are lucky, win her support by pleading (prayers), gifts (sacrifice), or flattery (worship). It is significant that the earliest deities seem to have been female. What could be more natural than to believe that the earth itself was female, since she brought forth life, as women do? Or that a male god lived within the thundercloud, or was manifest in the beneficent, but also destructive, heat of the sun? These were major deities, but other spirits lurked in every grove and stream, in every prominent rock or mighty tree. In the words of Professor Frankfort:

'There is justification for the aphorism of Crawley; "Primitive man has only one mode of thought, one mode of expression, one part of speech, the *personal*". This does not mean (as is often thought) that primitive man, in order to explain natural phenomena, imparts human characteristics to an inanimate world. Primitive man simply does not know an inanimate world.

'For this reason he does not "personify" the inanimate phenomena nor does he fill an empty world with ghosts of the dead, as "animism" would have us believe. The world appears to primitive man neither inanimate nor empty but abundant with life; and life has individuality, in man or beast or plant, and in every phenomenon which confronts man—the thunderclap, the sudden shower—the eerie unknown clearing in the wood, the stone which suddenly hurts him as he stumbles while on a hunting trip. Any phenomenon may at any time face him, *not as It, but Thou*' (*my italics*)[1].

Now there is another way of dealing with these unseen forces which we call 'natural', but which primitive man thought of as personal; by finding out 'what makes them tick'. One side of Man's nature, the intellectual, reasoning element, studies the properties of matter, experiments, observes, makes deductions, and then

[1] *Before Philosophy*—Frankfort, Wilson & Jacobsen: Penguin Books, London.

makes use of his knowledge for practical ends. It was through this process of observation and reasoning that men learned to make and use fire, to smelt copper, to invent the wheel and the sail. I say men; it may well have been women who first discovered that the fleece of certain animals could be spun into thread, and then woven into cloth; women may also have discovered how to tame the wild animals who gathered round the oases, while men only hunted them.

But there is the more powerful, emotional, irrational element in which fear and wonder predominate. This is the world of the magician, the witch-doctor, the medicine-man. Such men are not necessarily tricksters and charlatans, though many were and are. There occur, even in sophisticated societies, men and women who appear to possess paranormal powers; the nineteenth century rationalists scoffed at this, but the twentieth is less sure. Scientific experiments have proved the reality of what is called extra-sensory perception, and J. W. Dunne has led many to doubt the reality of physical time. We have reluctantly come to recognise that phenomena sometimes occur which cannot at present be explained by any natural law. It is, perhaps, easier for us to appreciate the power and influence which would be wielded in a primitive society by people who appeared to possess 'second sight' or supernatural powers over nature.

To the writer, it seems clear that in a society dominated by ignorance and fear, a society in which there were no such things as 'natural causes', men with such powers would achieve far greater importance than they enjoy today. Many of them would be men of superior intellect, men who had, in fact, acquired certain knowledge, skills and techniques which appeared magical to the masses. (One has only to observe the effect of striking a match in front of a modern savage to appreciate this.) From this it would be a short step to believing, and making others believe, that they had powers over nature (through the Gods who ruled nature) which in fact they did not possess. Power is a heady drug.

Such men would naturally become *priests*—guardians of sacred mysteries, interpreters between the Gods and mankind. There would be a shrine or home of the god to which only the priests had access, and we find, even in the lower levels of the 'tells' of Hither Asia, remains of buildings larger than the rest which seem to have served this purpose; at Gawra, in Iraq, for instance, where these shrines, as they appear to have been, were rebuilt on the same site time and time again, even when the place had passed into the hands of new settlers. Religio-magical traditions were strong; certain sites became sacred.

Such magician-priests would claim, as their modern counterparts do, power to control events by spells and ritual. If I may be permitted a personal reminiscence, I myself watched, in 1949, an African witch-doctor performing a ceremony which purported to bring together two hostile tribes in peaceful amity. It took place on the slopes of Mount Kenya. The tribes were the Kikuyu, a Negro race, and the famous warrior-tribe, the Masai, who are Hamitic, and therefore remotely related to the Ancient Egyptians. The Masai warriors with their slim, smooth-skinned bodies, as lithe as gazelles and as beautiful, stood watching, spears in hand, while the wizened old Kikuyu, who must have been nearly a hundred years old, crouched over a fire, and kept passing a rod to and fro within a wooden loop. To my white companion and myself it was a fascinating piece of Freudian symbolism; the concord of the tribes was being pre-figured by a rite symbolising the union of the sexes. But to the elegant, aristocratic Masai and the thick-lipped, flat-nosed Kikuyu, this was a sacred ceremony. They believed that in that gnarled old body there resided the power to alter their lives. I remember thinking that on such occasions one is nearer to the spirit of the ancient world than when standing in the mighty, but now derelict temple of Karnak.

So much for the priests. But there was another way of attaining power, through military prowess. In the inter-tribal struggles for land, certain men would distinguish themselves by their qualities of leadership and courage in battle. These natural leaders would become chiefs, kinglets, and in some societies their sons would inherit their power—or try to. But here we encounter a difficulty; in some societies the functions of King and High Priest were separate, in others they merged. There are numerous historical examples, for instance the evident rivalry between the kings of

Judah and their prophets which we can discern in the Old Testament. In Egypt also the Pharaoh and the priesthood were often rivals for power, and at certain periods the high priests themselves became Pharaohs. But the outlines are not clear, because kingship was closely linked with religious ritual. Anthropologists have shown that quite recently in some primitive societies, kings or chieftains were identified with the prosperity of the people they ruled, and the fertility of the soil on which they depended. There is evidence that when their health and virility began to fail they were sacrificed, and a new king appointed in their place. Such ceremonies probably took place in the prehistoric world, although as time passed the 'death' of the king became purely symbolic, and his life was ritually renewed by magic, as we shall see when we consider the 'heb-sed' ceremony in Ancient Egypt.

In any case, whether the chief-king belonged to a priestly line, or held power by virtue of his military ability (or those of his ancestors), his was a sacred office. When the Jews called for a king, David had to be anointed by Samuel, and in Egypt the Pharaoh was not only King but also Chief Priest of the god Amun. Documents prove that these facts are true of the historical epoch, long after the period we are considering, but there can be no doubt that such beliefs and customs stem from much earlier times.

To sum up: we see, towards the end of the Fourth Millennium, a very large number of independent tribal communities scattered throughout our chosen area. Some, though not all, have acquired techniques which give them potentially greater control over their environment than their ancestors of a thousand years earlier. Some, more advanced than others, have the potter's wheel, wheeled vehicles, pack animals, and the ox-drawn plough. Many have a knowledge of metallurgy and are using copper and bronze implements, made for them by a new class of specialists, craftsmen who are not themselves food-producers, but are supported by the community. These men, bound together in 'secret societies', sanctified and set apart by religious or pseudo-religious ritual,[1] jealously guard the mysteries of their craft and transmit them only to their chosen successors. Some of these men, by reason of their

[1] Cf. the modern Freemasons.

31

higher intelligence, skill and knowledge, have become what we would call priests—intermediaries between common men and the uncontrollable forces to which they are subject. Rivalling them for power is another class of men, warrior-chiefs, on whom their peoples rely in times of danger. Sometimes, though not always, priest and chieftain are one.

These societies, however, are incapable of expanding beyond a certain limit. When they reach it, small groups split off from the parent community, and establish new settlements elsewhere. Thus there is mobility, a constant spreading and admixture of cultures, but as yet no chance of large-scale co-operation.

Except in three places; along the Nile Valley, the valleys of the Tigris, Euphrates, and their tributaries, and, further east, along the valley of the Indus, where large numbers of independent tribes have been settled for generations. Here there is every inducement for them to stay; an abundant supply of water for irrigation and transport; plenty of wild game; wild plants to supplement the food supply; perennial flooding to renew the vigour of the land—so that it is unnecessary to wander in search of fresh soil and pasture—and protective deserts on each side as a deterrent to invaders.

Thus the Anvil stands ready for the first stroke.

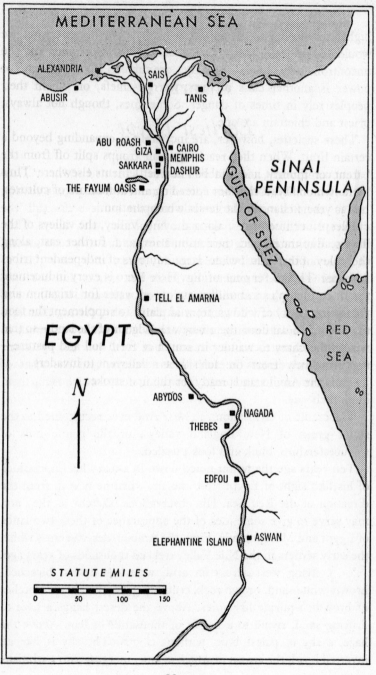

MEDITERRANEAN SEA

ALEXANDRIA
SAIS
ABUSIR
TANIS

SINAI
PENINSULA

ABU ROASH
GIZA   CAIRO
SAKKARA   MEMPHIS
            DASHUR
THE FAYUM OASIS

GULF OF SUEZ

EGYPT

N

TELL EL AMARNA

RED
SEA

ABYDOS
            NAGADA
THEBES

EDFOU

ELEPHANTINE ISLAND   ASWAN

STATUTE MILES

0   50   100   150

CHAPTER II

Earliest Egypt

'I never thought it would be like this . . . it's so *arid*. . . .' How often one hears that bewildered comment from people visiting for the first time the lands which the guide-books call 'the cradles of civilisation'. And one sympathises with them. They have read of the hanging gardens of Babylon and they see a mound of broken potsherds beside a muddy river; they have read of Imperial Thebes, capital of Egypt in her prime, and see only tombs and temples in a wilderness of rock and sand. In summer a paralysing heat beats down from an empty sky, driving men into the shade. In autumn the rivers are laden with brown mud; in winter the climate can be pleasant, but even then the eye turns apprehensively from the lush green valleys, and the glint of irrigation canals, to the sterile, forbidding desert which hems them in on each side.

The cradle of civilisation . . . *this*? And eyes accustomed to the softer green of New England valleys, or the gentle hills of Gloucestershire, blink and look puzzled.

Ten years ago the writer noted down in a diary his impressions of his first sight of Egypt from the air, when he flew in from the direction of the Red Sea. His observations, sketchy as they are, may serve to give some idea of the appearance of these two lands of Egypt and Mesopotamia. First, the Arabian desert, across which the early settlers in the Nile Valley trekked thousands of years ago.

'. . . flying west across an arid, waterless desert, bleached, brown-white sand, brown rock, crumbling, parched, with blotches of brownish-purple like sores. Above the desert hangs a haze of drifting sand, rising to a height of thousands of feet. Above the haze, a sky of palest blue, without clouds. The sky is like an inverted bowl, the crown of which is blue, merging into a whitish-

brown at the edges, from which comes a fierce glare. There is no horizon . . .'

'. . . the Red Sea falls away behind us to the east, as we fly further and further inland to meet the Nile at Luxor. Now flying over low, ribbed brown hills, a mass of peaks and sharp ridges, with the white sand, like salt, threading through the valley bottoms like rivers. Dull, parched, monotonous landscape, which seems to go on for ever. Not a tree, not a green field . . .'

'. . . At last, the Nile. It is about thirty miles away, a grey gleam against a ribbon of dark green. The brown desert laps up to it, and billows away beyond it to the west. Apart from that thin green strip, utter barrenness and emptiness . . .'

If you are flying towards Iraq from the north-west, across Israel and Jordan, again the main impression is one of utter sterility.

'Coming up now to the Dead Sea. As we approach the western shore we cross tumbled brown hills, with white patches. Ahead the long narrow sea, slate-grey, and from this height looking no bigger than Lake Windermere in Westmorland. . . . Now crossing the eastward shore. Sand, sand and more sand. Away to the north, in the plain below is a small, faint patch of green; that is Jericho. But now to the right I can see up the valley of Jordan, with its stain of green meandering through the brown desert. To the north is the greenish-blue of the salt-pans. And then the desert again.'

Beyond Jordan, as you fly south-eastward towards ancient Babylonia, you see nothing from the plane except a parched wilderness. You are flying at some three hundred miles an hour, but as the hours tick by the landscape hardly changes.

'Now the landscape is even more desolate. The golden-brown sands have gone. Now we fly over barren hills the colour of charred wood, veined with *wadis* (valleys) of a lighter brown. Dust-clouds drift above them, giving them a hazy, nebulous quality. Sometimes the desert is disfigured by black bituminous deposits, reminding one of a photographic enlargement of some horrible skin disease.'

'The endless forests of Newfoundland were a paradise compared with this desiccated horror, burned-out, blasted and scoriated by wind-blown sand.'

Then one's first sight of the Euphrates:

'Away to port, getting nearer every minute, is a black line snaking across the waste, the Euphrates. Now the desert shows patches of dusty green, mingled with the scrofulous bitumen-deposits. No mountains. No hills. Only a dead flat plain of shining yellow sand dappled with cloud shadows. Across it coils the mighty river, along the banks of which the Babylonian kings built their high-walled cities.'

Flying southward towards the Persian Gulf one crosses the land which rivals Egypt as the birthplace of civilisation; Sumer, the Biblical 'land of Shinar'.

'Babylon passed us to starboard. Could see where the river had been diverted during the siege, as described by Herodotus. Passed near Ur and Uruk, where Woolley found the self-immolated concubines of the Chaldean kings, their poison-cups beside them. The Tigris winds, doubles back on itself, a sand-coloured river bordered by green patches like verdigris. Sometimes the black tents of the Bedouin cluster in the *wadis*. And now the sand gives way to a strange grey earth, the colour of wood-ash, criss-crossed by dykes, roads and water-channels. Millions of human lives have left their faint marks on this flat plain, which is like a blackboard used again and again, a palimpsest of the centuries.'

Finally, as the aircraft begins to descend for the landing at Basra, you see the great flood-plain of the Two Rivers, an enormous expanse of black water, partly covered with what at first appears to be green fungus, but at a lower height turns out to be half-submerged trees. The efflux of the rivers looks exactly like a huge stagnant pond, scores of miles wide. Some of the green 'fungus' becomes detached from the main mass and appears to float in isolated clumps, like pieces of a jig-saw puzzle. The whole delta is flooded. Thousands of palms, in symmetrical rows, lie half-submerged, with only their tops breaking the surface. The steamy heat of the Gulf begins to seep into the cabin as you sweep low over the white roofs of Basra. Below you, under the flood, lies the legendary site of the Garden of Eden.

'Civilisation . . . is the settlement of men upon an area continuously cultivated and possessed, who live in buildings continuously inhabited, with a common rule and a common city or citadel.'[1]

Some scholars believe that the first civilisation conforming to this definition grew up beside the Nile, a little, but not long, before those of Mesopotamia. Relics of Stone Age man, in the form of flint tools and implements, are often found below the desert cliffs. It is impossible to estimate the proportions in which African, Asiatic and perhaps even European elements were mixed in those primitive inhabitants, but once settled, they continued to live along the fertile banks of the great river, where there was an abundance of game and fish, a perpetual water-supply and almost perpetual sunlight. Here they could grow all the cereals and vegetables necessary for man, and to east and west the hostile deserts acted as a protection against possible enemies. At first, of course, there would be hundreds of small, independent settlements, each with its own chief and its own gods. But, unlike the communities described in the last chapter, scattered over the steppes of western Asia, the inhabitants of the Nile Valley had the advantage of a great waterway which acted both as a fertilising agent and a road. The river linked them, though it did not at first unite them. Also the deserts, where no permanent settlement was possible (save at a few oases) forced the Nile Peoples to live *near* the river. Egypt, as Herodotus says, 'is the gift of the Nile'.

The astonishing fact about the Ancient Egyptians is that, when we first encounter them, at the beginning of the First Dynasty (which began at about 3200 B.C.), they are already enjoying a highly developed civilisation. The tombs of their kings and princes are of great size, and contain beautifully-made stone vessels, objects of copper and bronze, evidence of fine carpentry, metalwork and jewellery. Writing has been invented, and already the names of some of the gods and goddesses familiar from later Egyptian inscriptions are present. And from the design of their tombs, which imitate in mud-brick the forms of their dwellings, one can recognise a developed architecture which already foreshadows the glories to come.

[1] *The Outline of History*—H. G. Wells, London, 1931.

Professor Walter Emery, who has recently excavated some of the great tombs of the First Dynasty kings at Saqqara, told the writer that in his opinion practically all the elements of the Old Kingdom —the 'Pyramid Period'—which is generally regarded as the Golden Age of Ancient Egypt (2780–2100 B.C.), existed at the time of the First Dynasty[1] (3200 B.C.). Such achievements obviously imply a long period of development before that date; and yet, compared with our knowledge of the historical period—from Menes, the first king of the First Dynasty, to the Ptolemies (332–30 B.C.) hardly anything is known of this prehistoric or 'pre-dynastic' epoch.

Graves of these pre-dynastic ancestors of the historical 'Ancient Egyptians' have been found at several points along the desert fringes. They date from about 4000 B.C. or even earlier. There are several 'cultures'[2] (of which the principal were called by Petrie for convenience *Badarian, Amratean,* and *Gerzean,*[3] after the sites where their objects were first identified. The people of the first two cultures were mainly hunters, though they also practised agriculture and stockbreeding in a primitive fashion. They buried their dead in shallow graves in the sand, furnished with jars for food and drink, weapons and toilet articles, including slate palettes for grinding their green eye-paint.

They were acquainted with copper and gold, but at this stage seem not to have learned that these metals could be melted and cast. The bodies in these little graves are often wonderfully preserved, without the aid of embalmment. Often we find skin and hair still adhering, although the bodies were buried more than six thousand years ago. The bodies lie in a crouching position, unlike the Egyptian burials of historical times, when the corpses were buried prone.

In the later, *Gerzean,* stage of development hunting became less

[1] Manetho, an Egyptian historian writing about 305–285 B.C. divided the names of the Pharaohs which had come down to him into thirty Dynasties. His list is not accurate, and he left out a number of names, but the list is still useful as a rough guide.

[2] The word 'culture' often crops up in archaeological reports. Broadly speaking, people following the same customs and using similar objects—e.g. tools, weapons, pottery—are said to belong to the same culture, though they are not necessarily all of the same race.

[3] The two last cultures are now usually designated Nagada I and Nagada II.

important; the emphasis was on farming and fishing. By this time the Nile valley peoples, or some of them, had learned the art of smelting copper.[1] They imported foreign products, such as lapis-lazuli from Asia, and some archaeologists have suggested that the presence of these and other Asiatic products in Upper Egypt may indicate an invasion or infiltration of Semitic peoples from that area.

Relics of these three prehistoric cultures have been found in *Upper* Egypt; i.e. the southern part of the country below the Delta. The first dynastic kings also had their capital and built their tombs in Upper Egypt. We also know from the writings that the first king to bring the whole land under his dominion—Narmer, or Menes—came from this part of the country. And yet there is a puzzling cultural gap between the settlements of primitive farmers and herdsmen buried in shallow graves in the sand, and accompanied by a few pathetic little pots, and the great cemeteries of the early dynastic kings at Abydos. Their enormous tombs of mud-brick, divided up into numerous chambers or magazines, originally stocked with beautifully-fashioned vessels of alabaster, diorite and other stone, exquisite jewellery, furniture adorned with gold, could only have been produced by a large body of skilled specialist-craftsmen which a small primitive society could not have supported.

Yet there is no doubt that these primitive peoples, the Badarians, Amrateans and Gerzeans, were the cultural ancestors of the Ancient Egyptians of historic times. When Sir Flinders Petrie first discovered their graves at Nagada, in Upper Egypt, he thought that they might have been those of some semi-savage race which had invaded the Nile Valley in historical times, and had been permitted by the civilised Egyptians to settle on the outer rim of the valley. In fact he called them, in his early publications, 'the lost race'. But Petrie, one of the greatest of all archaeologists, went on excavating more and more sites, and by careful examination and comparison of pottery was able to establish a chain of development. In fact he invented the system which we call 'sequence dating' which enables archaeologists to establish the *comparative* age of a site by the type

[1] Small pins and beads of copper have been found on Badarian sites.

of pottery found on it, even when it lies below the 'historical horizon'—i.e. the period when written inscriptions are found. He was able to satisfy himself that there was a definite link between the little men crouched in their pit-graves and the builders of the pyramids. For instance, he found crudely-drawn signs, roughly painted on pottery, which occur much later in Egyptian writing. There were representations of boats made from papyrus-stems bound together, such as one finds thousands of years later in Egyptian tombs. Some of the slate palettes for grinding malachite for eye-paint bore symbols identifiable with some of the Egyptian gods of historic times. And at Hierakonpolis J. E. Quibell found a large slate palette, which bears the name of Narmer, first king of the First Dynasty, and which from its size could only have had a ceremonial or ritual function. It bore the symbol of the hawk-headed god Horus, and a carved relief of the king standing, club in hand, in the familiar attitude in which the later Pharaohs were sculptured.

Furthermore, Petrie established that the type of pottery and stone vessels found in the latest tombs of the pre-dynastic period (before 3200 B.C.) bore obvious resemblances to the type of vessels found in the royal tombs at Abydos. The chain of development was clear. Yet still there is something missing. The line of advance can be traced through gradual changes in the shapes and styles of pottery and tools. But where is the final link between the skeleton crouched in the sand and the great chambered sepulchres of Wadji, Udimu and Khasekhemui?

Perhaps the answer to that question lies buried deep beneath the mud of the Delta.

The ancient writings tell us that before Narmer brought all Egypt under his dominion the land was divided into two kingdoms —that of Lower Egypt, which stretched from the river-mouth to a point somewhere near modern Cairo, and that of Upper Egypt, which comprised the southern part of the country as far as the frontier of Nubia (modern Sudan). The vast majority of surviving Ancient Egyptian antiquities are in Upper (or southern) Egypt. Yet even down to late historical times the memory of the ancient division of the land was retained. One of the Pharaoh's titles was

'King of Upper and Lower Egypt'. He wore on his crown the twin emblems of the Two Lands, the serpent of Lower and the vulture of Upper Egypt. In very ancient times the serpent was the cult-sign or religious emblem of a tribe inhabiting a site in the Delta, the capital of which was Buto. The vulture was the cult-sign of a district in Upper Egypt, the capital of which was Nekhen. There were other twin emblems, too; a bee for Lower Egypt, a plant for Upper Egypt, and the entwined stems of the lotus and papyrus were sometimes used in art to symbolise the union of the Two Lands.

Yet we know practically nothing about this kingdom of Lower Egypt, which occupied the rich, fertile Delta, and must have been a far more attractive place for permanent settlement than the narrow valley to the south. By all the laws of reason and logic the Delta should have been the place in which the earliest Egyptian civilisation grew up; the fact that there are hardly any visible relics of such a civilisation is easily explained. If they exist they must be covered by deep deposits of alluvial mud brought down each year by the flooding river. Even so, monuments of the historical period still exist, at such places as Sais, and elsewhere, and we know from the writings that such cities were important in very remote times.

But there is other evidence which points to the Delta as being the home of the earliest civilisation in Egypt; evidence which exists not in the form of tombs and material remains, but merely as tiny signs scrawled on scraps of worthless potsherd. Yet from these miniature scrawls, and from a study of the later Egyptian writing, philologists have been able to make some fascinating deductions. In 1923 the late Professor Percy Newberry, a distinguished British Egyptologist, delivered an address to the British Association for the Advancement of Science,[1] in which he pointed out that, although many pre-dynastic cemeteries had been thoroughly explored in Upper Egypt, no grave had yielded a single fragment of hieroglyphic writing.

[1] *Egypt as a field for Anthropological Research*—Professor Percy E. Newberry, M.A., O.B.E.: 'Report of the British Association for the Advancement of Science, 1923', pp. 175-195.

'The only inference that can be drawn from this is that hiero-glyphic writing was unknown, or at all events unpractised, by the inhabitants of Upper Egypt before dynastic times. On the other hand, the discoveries at Naqada, Hierakonpolis, and Abydos (all in Upper Egypt) had shown us that all the essential features of the Egyptian system of writing were fully developed by the beginning of the First Dynasty.'

Yet obviously such a system must have taken a long period to develop before it appeared in the tombs of the early dynastic kings (*circa* 3000 B.C.). Could it, perhaps, have been developed outside Egypt, and been introduced by invaders? Newberry thought not. He happened to be a botanist, as well as an Egyptologist, and as numerous Egyptian hieroglyphs are based on forms derived from plant and animal life, he was able to bring a specialised knowledge to their study. After a minute examination, he ascertained that the flora and fauna depicted were all such as could be expected to have existed in Egypt at the time. Some, such as the papyrus plant which once grew in profusion along the Nile banks, have since disappeared from Egypt, but they are still found in the Sudan, to the south. Others still flourish in Egypt.

All this strongly suggested that if the hieroglyphs were not a foreign importation, but a native product, and if they did not originate and develop in Upper Egypt there was only one alter-native—the Delta.

This is a cogent piece of reasoning, but not enough on which to base a sound theory. But more impressive evidence was forth-coming. For instance, Newberry pointed out that, in historic times, the Egyptian hieroglyphic sign for 'East' was a drop-shaped ingot of metal upon a sacred pereh, and this was the cult-object of a clan or tribe living in pre-dynastic times in the *eastern* Delta. The sign for 'west' was an ostrich feather placed on a semi-circular stand, and this was the cult-object of a people of the *western* Delta.

Now to the Ancient Egyptians, the country lying south of the apex of the Delta (near modern Cairo) was known as *Ta Shema*—the 'Reed Land'. Newberry noted in his address that——

'The sign for "south" was a *scirpus*-reed; this was the cult-object of a clan which dwelt on the east bank of the Nile a little above the

modern village of Sharona in Middle Egypt. . . . It must therefore
have been at some point north of the apex of the Delta that the
scirpus-reed was first used to designate the south. It must also have
been somewhere in the Central Delta that the cult-objects of the
Eastern and Western Delta were first used to designate "east"
and "west".'

Even more significant, in the writer's opinion, is the fact—also
observed by Newberry—that the hieroglyphic signs for 'right'
and 'left' were the same as those for 'west' and 'east'; in other
words, whoever invented the Egyptian system of writing orientated
himself to the south, with the west on his right and the east on his
left. Again this seems to point to a Delta origin of Egyptian
writing.[1]

[1] The same idea was expressed independently by the German scholar K.
Sethe.

CHAPTER III

'Lord of the Two Lands'

There seems to be little doubt, then, that the Delta peoples were the founders of Egyptian civilisation. But who were they, and where did they come from? Some undoubtedly came from Libya, the land lying west of the Delta; even as late as the fifth century B.C. the Greek historian Herodotus states that the inhabitants of the western Delta called themselves Libyans, and did not even speak the Egyptian language. There is evidence that this Libyan element was present in prehistoric times, too. Archaeologists who have excavated pre-dynastic graves in between Giza (near Cairo) and Kostamneh in the south frequently found a certain type of decorated pottery inscribed with rough drawings of boats with cult-objects raised on poles. These signs include the 'harpoon', the 'crossed arrows', and the 'mountain'. Now in historic times the 'harpoon' was the cult-object of the Mareotis Lake region; the 'mountain' and the 'crossed arrows' belonged to peoples dwelling on the right bank of the Canopic branch of the Nile. Both are in the Delta region. Newberry states:

'Out of 300 boats figured on vases found in graves in the Lower Nile Valley south of Cairo, 222 belong to cults which can be located in the north-western corner of the Delta.'

And he adds a very significant fact:

'At the beginning of the historic period the cult-objects of the people of the north-western Delta included (1) the harpoon, (2) the figure-of-eight shield with crossed arrows, (3) the Mountain, (4) the Double Axe, and (5) a Dove or Swallow. With the exception of the harpoon all these cult-objects *are also found in Crete*' (my italics).

This is worth remembering when we come to consider the development of the early civilisation of Crete.

Beside the Libyan strain there seems also to have been a strong link with the peoples of western Asia—e.g. Syria and the Lebanon. We have already mentioned a Semitic element in the Ancient Egyptian language, which points to an Asiatic influence. But apart from the writing there are other signs of Asiatic contacts. One is connected with the very early use of *timber* in Ancient Egypt. The climate of the country does not favour the growth of large trees. Today, as in ancient times, the principal trees are the sycamore and the sunt-acacia. The former is so coarse-grained that straight planks cannot be cut from it. The latter is so hard that it can only be sawn while it is green, is irregular in texture, and has so many branches that it cannot be cut into boards of more than two feet in length. Herodotus, in his fascinating chapters on Egypt, says that the Egyptians built their river-going ships of short planks bound together by cords. Yet, on the famous pre-dynastic knife-candle found at Gebel el Araq there is a representation of what appears to be a sailing ship, with a tall mast, in port with sails lowered. Also, on the well-known slate palette of King Narmer (First Dynasty) there is a reference to the Great Port, which apparently was on the Delta. The existence of such a port, and such ships, implies trade relations with other countries. Also, where did the Egyptians get the wood to make the mast? Not in Egypt, for the reasons we have given. But in the Lebanon and in Syria pines, cypresses, and cedars grew abundantly. Everyone has heard of the 'cedars of Lebanon'—which were probably not cedars at all, but cypresses. We know that the earliest Egyptian ships were made of bundles of papyrus-stems bound together. These would be suitable for river traffic, but not for a sea crossing. If the pre-dynastic Egyptians had sea-going vessels, as seems to have been the case, they must have been built of timber, almost certainly obtained abroad. And the people nearest the source of supply would have been the Delta folk.

If space were available one could quote many other examples; for instance, there are representations on pre-dynastic pottery of what appear to be temples with tall poles in front of them from which standards were flown. You can see the sockets for such poles today in the pylons at the front of the great temple at Karnak. If such temples existed before the dawn of written history, as from the evidence of the potsherds they did, where did their builders obtain those tall masts? Not from Egypt, clearly, but most likely from the Lebanon. Then there is architecture. No dwelling-houses of pre-dynastic times have come down to us, but, most obligingly, the Ancient Egyptians reproduced in their tombs the architectural forms of their houses in mud-brick, and later in stone.

From the study of these 5,000-year-old tombs one can recognise two architectural styles. The first is based on wattle-and-daub construction, which is indigenous to Egypt. The second employs timber in lengths which could not have been obtained locally.

'As early as the reign of King Djet (First Dynasty) the palaces of this type were beginning to be built of the native wattle-and-daub in combination with wood, and by the end of the Pyramid Age the style disappears entirely, though the memory of it is preserved in the false-doors of tombs and stelæ. Brick buildings similar to those of the "palace style" in Egypt are also found from early Babylonia, and they were at one time regarded as peculiarly characteristic of Sumerian architecture. In Babylonia, as in Egypt, timber was scarce, and there are records that it was some-times obtained from the coasts of Syria. . . I may observe in passing that in this "palace" style we have the transition of form between the nomad's tent and the permanent building of a settled people.'[1]

Time has been unfair to the peoples of the Delta. The successive deposits of more than five thousand years of Nile floods have buried the remains of their cities, whereas the land of their southern conquerors has suffered far less. The modern tourist, hurrying across the Delta by train from Alexandria, looks un-interestedly at the miles of flat, fertile fields, almost devoid of historic monuments of the more spectacular kind, and waits impatiently for the pyramids, the temples of Luxor, the Valley of the Kings, and all the other glories of Middle and Upper Egypt. Yet there, in that wide-spreading, fertile plain, there is little doubt that Egyptian civilisation began. Thumbing through his

[1] 'Report of the British Association for the Advancement of Science, 1925.'— Percy E. Newberry.

guide-book, the tourist learns that the earliest relics of that civilisation were found in the far south, and date from about 3200 B.C. Yet when the southern conqueror, Menes, brought all that vast land under his heel, he took over a culture which was already well-developed long before his time. The products of that culture—the science of writing, recording and measurement; architecture, carpentry and metal-work; mathematical knowledge, astronomy, the calendar, planned agriculture—all these had begun to penetrate the more remote southerly tribes, carried to them via the great river which was the life-stream of Egypt. But the southern peoples were probably tougher. They had to scratch their living from the narrow band of fertile land between the desert cliffs. Their not-so-remote ancestors had had to trek across the barren lands to the east to find their haven beside the Nile, just as, thousands of years later, the Jewish nomads came at last to the country of Judah, and found it 'a land flowing with milk and honey'. At first there would be independent tribes scattered along the valley, each with its own chieftain and its own chief god. The memory of these ancient tribal divisions survived into historic times. Even when Egypt became a united kingdom under one monarch, the country was divided, administratively, into provinces which the Greeks called 'nomes', each with its provincial governor and his staff of officials whom we would call Civil Servants. These southerners were related, ethnically, to the ancestors of the modern Galla and Somali races of East Africa.

They and their northern neighbours lived in the valley-bottom, probably in simple dwellings of reeds plastered with Nile mud, very like the temporary shelters which the modern *fellahin* build during the time of sowing and harvesting today. Sir Flinders Petrie, whose *Social Life in Ancient Egypt* is a most valuable source of information, believed that in pre-dynastic times the early chiefs had portable timber houses which were moved down to the valley in spring, among the reed-huts of their shepherds, and then, when the inundation came, moved up to the desert plateau. He writes:

'The planks, about 12 to 14 inches wide, and 6 to 7 feet high, overlapping so as to form a panel-pattern, were set upright. Being lashed together at the edges, the overlap was kept close, and slid

47

to and fro, as the night dews or sirocco expanded or contracted the wood. The doorways were all along the sides, so as to give plenty of air when still and warm. They projected into the hall, and so left sleeping places between each, where the chief's followers could keep guard around the hall. The pattern of houses gave rise to the copying of external panelling *in brick work* (our italics) for the "eternal house" of the dead chief, a pattern which lasted down to the Eighteenth Dynasty (1555–1350 B.C.).'[1]

However, some archaeologists have contested Petrie's theory. Dr. Frankfort, for example, states that similar structures of brick existed in Jemdet Nasr, in Mesopotamia, that the Egyptian buildings were also derived from the same Mesopotamian tradition, and that there is no conclusive evidence of their having originated in wooden structures.[2]

The roofs of such houses would be supported by columns made of reeds bound together, or in some cases by the thick stems of wild plants, such as the *heracleum gigantium* which has a fluted stem (important when we come to study the development of the first stone buildings in Egypt). In more substantial buildings there were ceilings of palm-logs, which were also reproduced in stone during the historical period. Eventually hinged doors were introduced, though, as in some Oriental countries today, some doorways were closed merely by a hanging mat of plaited reeds, which could be rolled up when not in use. All these perishable materials have, of course, disappeared; we can only conjecture their existence from the imitation in stone and glazed tiles which the later Egyptians incorporated in their tombs.

To the north, beyond the point where the swelling Nile broadened into the Delta, lived other more highly-developed peoples. The southerners were in contact with these Delta people; they saw their ships passing or stopping to trade. Even in the early pre-dynastic tombs of Upper Egypt archaeologists found pottery roughly inscribed with pictures of ships flying the flags of the Delta provinces, the crossed arrows of Sais, the harpoon of Lake

---

[1] *Social Life in Ancient Egypt*—Sir W. Flinders Petrie: Constable, London.
[2] See Frankfort's 'Monumental Architecture in Egypt' in Vol. 58 of the *American Journal of Semitic Languages*.

1(b) King Djoser (2800 B.C.) in running posture

1(a) Narmer (Menes), Founder of the 1st Dynasty (3200 B.C.) with a kneeling captive. Slate palette commemorating his victories

1(c) Ancient Egyptian quarry showing method of quarrying stone

1(d) Egyptian writing tablet used by schoolboys, showing 'hieratic' script

Mareotis, and others. Over a long period of years the culture of the northern peoples interfused with that of the south. Techniques would be learned and ideas exchanged.

For some seven hundred miles from the sea the Nile was navigable even by the largest ships. But just beyond the island of Elephantine (near modern Assuan) the First Cataract bars the way; the river races between high cliffs and is broken by boulder-strewn rapids, a natural frontier between Egypt and Nubia (the Sudan). Nubia was a land of negroid peoples with whom the Egyptians were frequently at war throughout their long history. It was a mysterious land, an invitation to bold adventurers, as the Atlantic was to the sea-rovers of Europe in the sixteenth century A.D. The parallel is a close one. Beyond the Atlantic lay the end of the world, for all the early navigators knew. Beyond the frontiers of Egypt lay the same hazards, for who knew where the great river had its infernal source? But if the risks were great, the rewards were greater. The Elizabethan admirals brought back the gold of America; Senusret and Tuthmosis returned with ivory, giraffes, ostriches and slaves. One Pharaonic general even brought back a pigmy for the amusement of his royal master.

There is plenty of evidence that even the prehistoric Egyptians were in contact with Nubia. They traded there for ivory, and the cult-sign for Elephantine occurs on the rocks below Assuan, with other pre-dynastic signs, covered with the brown patina of some five thousand years.

Both in the Delta area and in the southern provinces there would be inter-tribal wars. Sometimes one chief, more powerful and astute than the others, would manage to secure the co-operation of his neighbours in overcoming an enemy. Coalitions would be formed, originally for military offence or defence, but there would also be peaceful by-products in the form of trade, or the pooling of resources.

There was one constant factor in the lives of these peoples which favoured such co-operation—the Nile, on which they all depended for their existence. It was their main means of transport, and its annual flooding refertilised their soil, enabling them to sow and reap their crops year after year without having to move to fresh

D

ground. Among them a class of men arose who were freed from the burden of manual toil, supported by the surplus crop which the fertility of the land made possible. These were the priests, the wise men, who were the scientists and technicians of the ancient world. Of course, it was always necessary to propitiate the Gods who ruled men's lives, and upon whose will depended whether there was a 'good Nile' bringing full harvests, or a 'bad Nile' bringing famine, or disastrous floods. Worship, sacrifice, propitiation were always necessary.

It was not the 'gift of the Nile' which made the Egyptians into a civilised community, but the fact that sometimes the gift was withheld. Rainfall would be insufficient to drag enough fertilising mud from the far-off mountains of Abyssinia, or it would be too heavy, causing floods which made the river rise too high, sweeping away villages and drowning men and cattle.

'The Nile's annual flood,' wrote the late Professor Glanville, 'is the key to success or failure of agriculture. Most that is significant in Ancient Egyptian civilisation derives from this fact—from the central control of government to the conservative temper of the peasant.'

Very gradually, over the years, the wise men learned to predict the movements of the river. They observed, for instance, that the rising of the water coincided with certain aspects of the stars. Whereas in more northerly countries sun, moon and stars are often veiled, in Egypt they are nearly always visible; the eternal, unvarying movement of planets and stars could be observed and studied.

It was this which led to perhaps the greatest achievement of Egyptian science—the invention of the solar calendar. This Ancient Egyptian calendar was introduced into Rome by Julius Caesar, who rightly considered it the most practical and convenient in use. From the Romans it has come down to us.

The ability of the priest-technicians to predict the time of the Nile's rising, to calculate the amount of its flooding, and therefore of the eventual harvest, must have raised them high in the estimation of the people, and as no doubt they guarded their secrets jealously, their power would be great. The growth of this intellectual class, relieved of the burdens of labour, may have been parasitic in certain ways, but it helped to bring about the great advances in engineering, mathematics, political and social organisation on which the civilisation of the Old Kingdom was founded. It must have been such men who taught the Egyptians how to conserve their water supply by dams and irrigation canals, to adopt a standard system of weights and measures—a decimal system was in existence in 3200 B.C.—so that they could calculate accurately the yield of their crops and herds, and re-parcel out their land after the floods had washed away visible landmarks. Thus the science of geometry, which eventually made possible the planning and building of pyramids, temples and tombs, was ultimately a product of those two constant factors—the cloudless sky of Egypt, and the annual flooding of the Nile.

All these arts and sciences had a strictly practical purpose, and so had the greatest of all Egyptian inventions—*writing*. When men first acquired the power to communicate information, and later, ideas, without personal contact, a new chapter opened in the history of the human race. It was not a step, but a leap, onward, with which there is no comparable example save the invention of wireless telegraphy. Today, after five thousand years of literacy, it is almost impossible to imagine a world in which the only means of intelligent communication was the human voice. Yet such was Man's condition for hundreds of thousands of years. This afternoon (if I may be forgiven a short personal illustration) I walked on Hampstead Heath, London, trying to sort out in my mind the ideas I wished to communicate in this chapter. Six thousand years ago I could have passed them on to a group of friends, or, at most, to a gathering of a few hundred people. Those people could in turn have transmitted them to others, and they to still more, but in a short time my original conceptions would have been distorted out of all recognition. Yet merely by writing twenty-six little signs on a piece of paper, I can enable other human minds, separated from me by vast distances of space, or time, to get into direct contact with mine (an unimportant fact in my case, but of considerable consequence if one happens to be a Galileo or a Newton).

We owe those twenty-six symbols to the Romans. But they

adapted them from the Greeks, who in turn borrowed their writing-system from the Phoenicians, a mercantile people. They, according to some scholars, may have 'streamlined' the more elaborate Egyptian writing into a simple alphabet to facilitate their commercial transactions. Thus the signs we read every day in our books and newspapers are remotely descended from the primitive pictographs used by the inhabitants of the Nile Delta about six thousand years ago.

Some authorities suggest, however, that the alphabet may have been a Palestinian invention derived from the hieroglyphs.

To explain how and why the hieroglyphs were invented would require several books of this size. Like other systems, it began as a form of 'picture-writing' which served well enough to recall something to the writer's mind, but from which a reader would have difficulty in discovering the desired idea. Erman, in his excellent book, *The Literature of the Ancient Egyptians*, gives this simple illustration:

'If two people agree that one is to supply an ox in three months' time, in return for which the other will pay five jars of honey, pictures of the moon, the ox, the bee, and the jar, in addition to small strokes indicating the numbers, suffice as tokens for them both, but a third person would never be able to explain these signs with certainty. This preliminary structure must therefore undergo considerable development. Individual peoples arrived at all sorts of writing of words and syllables. The Egyptians alone were destined to adopt a remarkable method, following which they attained to the highest form of writing, the alphabet.'[1]

Picture-writing was practicable so long as the Egyptian wanted only to represent concrete things—the sun, a bird, a beetle, a house. The difficulty arose when he wanted to write words which it would be impossible to draw, because of the complexity of the symbols. He solved the problem by substituting for such words other words, *which had a similar sound*, but which were easier to draw. Take for example the hieroglyphic sign for the swallow, which has the sound *wr*. In the Ancient Egyptian language the sound *wr* also meant 'great', and by looking at the context the

[1] *The Literature of the Ancient Egyptians*—Erman and Blackman: Methuen.

reader could easily find out which meaning was intended. Then there is the well-known scarab-sign, representing a beetle, which was pronounced *khpr*. This same sound also meant 'to become'.

In the Ancient Egyptian and related languages it is the consonant which determines the meaning of a word, while the vowel determines its grammatical form. Therefore, in deciding the meaning of a word, an Egyptian reader would consider only the consonants, disregarding the vowels. To take an English example, the words 'heed' and 'head' have the same consonants 'h' and 'd'. To an Ancient Egyptian it would be easier to represent an actual head to stand for either 'head' or 'heed'. The reader could easily decide which word was meant by the place in the text. He would know immediately if the word was pronounced with long or a short 'e'. We would not, which is the reason that it is so difficult to decide how Ancient Egyptian words were pronounced, and why it took so long for philologists to understand the grammatical system, which was tied up with the missing vowel-sounds. It was only the fact that elements of the ancient tongue survived in Coptic church ritual that enabled Champollion and other great scholars to find a partial solution.

It is now generally accepted that the Ancient Egyptians adapted the Sumerian writing system to their own language. Many Sumerian words are identical with Egyptian words. In pre-dynastic times there seems to have been a migration from southern Mesopotamia to Egypt by an unknown route.

Gradually, over what must have been a long period of time, the Egyptians' writing-system became more flexible. It began, as did other systems, purely as a working tool, a means of *recording*. The earliest examples of writing are inventories, lists of objects; so many hundred jars of oil, so many thousand head of cattle, so many captives. We shall find the same situation when we come to consider the Mycenean writing of pre-Hellenic Greece. In the writer's opinion it was this need to keep permanent records which gave birth to writing. Much later, as the system developed, the scribes were able not merely to represent concrete things, but ideas. A time came when they were able to represent, on papyrus or potsherds, the actual sounds and rhythms of speech. Even as early as 3200 B.C., the approximate date of the earliest written documents in Ancient Egypt, the Egyptians had developed, in addition to the formal *hieroglyphs* (a Greek word meaning 'sacred signs') a more flowing, cursive form of writing called *hieratic*.

Such then was the situation near the beginning of the Third Millennium B.C. After centuries of inter-tribal warfare the peoples of the Nile Valley had coalesced into two kingdoms; those of the North and the South. Both these kingdoms, thanks partly to their intellectual class, had learned the value of co-operation. But probably neither would have united of its own accord; this was brought about by the rival class of leader—the tough, the strong-arm man. The use of these terms may shock some orthodox scholars, but I use them without apology. We are dealing with a period before the beginnings of recorded history. In the absence of written documents, surely the only way in which we can hope to understand how Egypt developed from the anarchy of independent tribes to a unified state is by thinking of the situation in contemporary terms. Are there any modern parallels? I think there are—but not within the official pattern of the twentieth century state.

Nowadays, when warfare has become respectable, when generals are socially acceptable figures with orders and medals, we shall look in vain for any parallels with the warrior-chiefs who unified Ancient Egypt. To find them we have to explore the anarchic substratum of modern society, the world of the gangster. The little kings of Soho and Chicago, who carve out personal Empires with razor or tommy-gun, are the spiritual heirs of the tribal chiefs of the Nile Valley. The gangster uses the resources of modern science in the struggle with his rivals; firearms, high-explosive, the hypodermic needle. If he is successful in attaining supreme power, as Hitler did, the highest achievements of applied science are his to command. Similarly, the warrior-lords of the Nile Valley must have made full use of the technical inventions of their wise men. The modern thug and his henchmen over-awe a whole district, extracting 'protection-money' from timid tradesmen who wish to go peacefully about their business. The Egyptians, having conquered a neighbouring tribe, extracted tribute in the form of cattle and grain, in return for freedom from molestation. Rival gangsters fight it out for the control of territory. Similarly, rival Egyptian chiefs struggled with each other for the control of wealth.

Inevitably such men would gather around them subordinates capable of carrying out their orders, and in the conflict of tribe against tribe would develop techniques of warfare, superior weapons, more skilful tactics. In the Old Kingdom (2780–2100 B.C.) armies are already using standardised weapons and marching in step. Savages do not fight in such fashion—therefore there must have been a long period during which the art of war was developed.

Eventually two chieftains rose to pre-eminence, the lords of the north and south, each controlling a large number of subordinate tribal governors who were allowed to rule their separate provinces in return for military allegiance to the king. But inevitably a time would arise when the two kingdoms clashed. Probably there were a number of such wars before the king of the south finally triumphed. The fact that victory came to the southerners is significant. We know that the civilisation of the north developed earlier than that of the south. From later examples we know that over-civilised people usually fall victim to their hardier neighbours. This may well have happened in the Delta, with its wide-spreading fertile lands, nourishing vast herds of cattle, and rich crops.

To the peoples of Upper Egypt, hemmed in a narrow valley, and with a constantly growing population, such a land would be a constant temptation. When the curtain goes up on recorded history we see the chief of the south, Narmer (or Menes, as the later Greeks named him) moving northward in a triumphal campaign which carried him eventually to Sais, the capital of the Delta kingdom. At Hierakonpolis, J. E. Quibell discovered the great ceremonial palette in which this triumph is celebrated. It is one of the most important documents in the history of mankind. On it we see the victorious king, smiting the chieftain of the north, while on the reverse side of the palette is a scene of a festival at the Great Port, which was perhaps situated near the Canopic branch of the Nile.

Another precious relic of this conquest is the famous ceremonial mace-head of Menes, now preserved in the Ashmolean Museum in Oxford. The carvings on this ivory object tell us practically all we know of a military leader whose achievements can be equated with those of Charlemagne. Of his physical appearance, his personality, his history, we know nothing. The priestly records from which, three thousand years later, Manetho compiled his king-list, merely state that he was the first king to rule a united Egypt, and the founder of the First Dynasty. A ruined tomb, which may be his, was excavated by Amélineau, and later by Petrie, at Abydos. For the rest, there is only the ceremonial palette and the mace-head, on which we see Menes wearing the Red Crown of Sais (symbol of dominion over conquered Lower Egypt) and an inscription recording that he had captured 120,000 prisoners, 400,000 oxen, and 1,422 goats.

'This immense number of oxen and goats is clear evidence,' writes Newberry, 'that the north-western Delta and the region to the west of it (Tehenu-land) must have included within its boundaries extensive grass-lands.'

A slate palette, now in the Cairo Museum, records that Menes conquered the people of Tehenu-land. The name means 'olive-land', and on an earlier, pre-dynastic palette, there is a picture of olive trees with the name written beside them.

Other carvings on the mace-head show the conqueror clad in a long, close-fitting garment, and holding in one hand the so-called 'flail' which in historical times was one of the symbols of kingly power.[1]

A group of officials stands behind him, and he is flanked by two fan-bearers. Before him, in a palanquin, sits a princess of the land he has conquered, and behind her are figures of running men. This is the earliest known representation of the Egyptian *sed-festival*, which was probably of Libyan origin, and which figures on royal inscriptions throughout Egyptian history. In it the vigour of the

[1] Newberry once told the writer that he believed that the so-called 'flail' was actually a 'ladanisterion'—a rod with pendent cords used by some Mediterranean goatherds to gather gum from certain gum-bearing shrubs. He had also observed that goats grazing in such areas tend to get their beards matted with this gum. He suggested that one of the tribes inhabiting the eastern Delta were goatherds. Their god, Anzety, wears a head-dress of bi-cornute shape, like the vulva of the female goat. The ceremonial 'false beard' of the Pharaohs suggests a similar connection.

king was ceremonially renewed; originally this ceremony took place every thirty years, but in later times at more frequent intervals.

The figure of the princess may indicate a marriage festival. We know that in later times the Pharaoh could only rule by right of marriage to the heiress, and this may have been true even at that early period. Probably the conqueror married the daughter of his defeated rival in order to establish his right to the throne.

There sits Menes, on the throne of the Two Lands, ruler of a united kingdom, forerunner of a long line of kings. Henceforth the royal titulary will always include the phrase 'Lord of the Two Lands'. Now let us leave Egypt, and consider what has been happening during the same period along the banks of the Lower Euphrates.

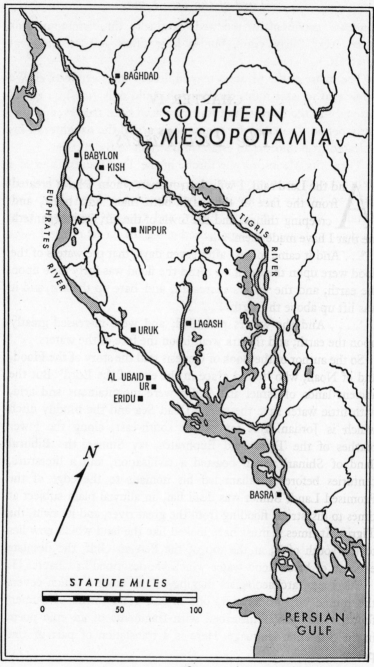

SOUTHERN
MESOPOTAMIA

BAGHDAD

BABYLON
KISH

NIPPUR

LAGASH

URUK

AL UBAID
UR
ERIDU

BASRA

EUPHRATES RIVER

TIGRIS RIVER

PERSIAN
GULF

N

STATUTE MILES

0   50   100

CHAPTER IV

The Two Rivers

'And the Lord said, I will destroy man whom I have created from the face of the earth; both man, and beast, and creeping things, and the fowls of the air; for it repenteth me that I have made them. . . .

'. . . And it came to pass after seven days, that the waters of the flood were upon the earth. . . . And the flood was forty days upon the earth; and the waters increased, and bare up the ark, and it was lift up above the earth. . . .'

'. . . . And the waters prevailed, and were increased greatly upon the earth; and the ark went upon the face of the waters. . . .'

So the author of the Book of Genesis told the story of the Flood, and of Noah, who 'found grace in the eyes of the Lord'. But the ancient lands of Israel and Judea were mountainous and arid, with little water save the sterile Dead Sea and the muddy ditch which is Jordan. But far to the south-east, along the lower reaches of the Tigris and Euphrates, lay Sumer, the Biblical 'land of Shinar' which boasted a civilisation, and a literature, centuries before Abraham led his nomads to the edge of the Promised Land. Sumer was dead flat, an alluvial plain subject at times to disastrous flooding from the great river, and its twin, the Tigris. At times it must have looked like the land which now lies to the south of it, at the top of the Persian Gulf; the desolate expanse of black flood water which we described in Chapter II.

Years ago, archaeologists digging in the mound which covers the buried city of Nippur, one of the great towns of Sumer, found a clay tablet inscribed with fragments of an epic poem in the Sumerian language. Here is a translation of part of this poem:

59

> *By our* (decree) *a flood* (will sweep) *over the cult-centres*
> *To destroy the seed of mankind* . . .
> *Is the decision, the word of the assembly* (of the gods)
> *By the word commanded by Anu and Enlil*
> *Its kingship, its rule* (will be put to an end) . . .
>
> . . . *All the windstorms, exceedingly powerful, attack as one,*
> *At the same time, the flood sweeps over the cult-centres.*
> *After, for seven days* (and) *seven nights*
> *The flood had swept over the land*
> (And) *the huge boat had been tossed about by*
>   *the windstorms of the great waters*
> *Utu came forth, who sends light on heaven and earth.*
> *Ziusudra opened a* window of *the huge boat.*
> *The hero Utu* brought his rays *into the giant boat.*
> *Ziusudra, the king*
> *Prostrated himself before Utu.* . . .[1]

The annual flooding of southern Mesopotamia by the Tigris and Euphrates was far more violent and less predictable than the flooding of Egypt by the Nile. When the floods came there were no cliffs to hem them in; instead, the waters could spread for miles across the plain. Also they came at less regular intervals than the Nile inundation. All the same, the conditions in these two widely-separated lands were broadly similar. In each case there was perennial water-supply and an annual bestowal of fertilising mud. There was game and there were fish. And there was almost perpetual sunshine by day, and cloudless skies by day and night. More elaborate irrigation was perhaps necessary, but, given that, it was possible for large numbers of people to settle permanently along the river banks, to grow crops and breed cattle, while the easy communication afforded by the river would tend to break down the isolation of independent groups. It is not surprising, therefore, that Sumer and Akkad, its northern neighbour, are Egypt's closest rivals as the birthplace of civilisation.

[1] Translated by S. N. Kramer, in *Ancient Near Eastern Texts*, edited by James B. Pritchard. Princeton University Press.

There were, however, disadvantages. The 'Land of the Two Rivers' is less shut off from the surrounding world than the Nile Valley. It was always open to invasion, either by the highland peoples from Armenia, in the north, or from the nomads of the surrounding steppes. It may be for this reason that the civilisation of Sumer and Akkad developed somewhat later than that of Egypt. However, archaeologists have proved that during the thousands of years in which the Nile Peoples were moving towards the unification of the Two Lands, before 3000 B.C. the riverine peoples of southern Mesopotamia had also made great progress.

In Chapter I we described how the self-supporting Neolithic communities of Iraq and Syria learned the use of the wheeled cart, the pack-animal, the ox-drawn plough, the potter's wheel, and the art of spinning and weaving, and of casting bronze tools and weapons. These techniques also reached the peoples living along the banks of the Lower Euphrates and Tigris, and, as in Egypt, these people could communicate freely, could co-operate with each other and interchange ideas. More important still, the richness of the soil, perpetually fertilised by the great rivers, enabled the settlers to produce a surplus of food more than sufficient to support an intellectual class of specialist-technicians, astronomer-mathematicians, scientist-priests. These men were given time to think, contrive, originate, and plan. It was they, and not the labouring masses, who laid the foundations of the civilisations of Sumer and Akkad: they, and the warrior-lords who eventually forced the independent clans to coalesce.

Who were the Sumerians and the Akkadians? The names are merely convenient philological labels.

The Akkadians, who inhabited the northern part of the district, were a Semitic race, speaking a language remotely related to that of the Hebrews and the Arabs. They seem to have been connected also with the swarthy, crinkly-bearded Assyrians of the north— later to become renowned for their ruthless cruelty.

The Sumerians, to judge from the innumerable statues and figurines whose pop-eyes stare at us in our national museums, were a very different race of people; some look like jolly little aldermen, with rotund bellies, long, straight noses, domed foreheads, and thin lips. The priests shave both their chins and their heads; they have a smooth aldermanic look—the kind of men with whom one could have discussed business but not art. No one knows where they came from; they appear to be related to no race known on earth.

These two races, Akkadian and Sumerian, speaking different languages—unlike the Nile Valley peoples who were united by a common tongue—made great progress during the thousand years before 3000 B.C. At Erech, one of their greatest cities, one can trace a continuous record of development, from a Copper Age village to a Bronze Age city. The 'tell' is sixty feet high. At the bottom are cult-shrines consecrated to some deity, but no larger than a village church. At the top is a huge temple measuring 245 by 100 feet, made of mud and sun-dried bricks, with a tower 35 feet high containing narrow chambers, a cult-room, and doors of imported pine.

Obviously there must have been priests to serve such temples, and Professor Childe has suggested that these priesthoods may have originated in the secret societies such as one finds among modern barbarian tribes. By the time historical records begin, the Sumerian priests were bound together in societies or corporations of a permanent character, so that if an individual priest died, his office continued and was filled by another. The land belonged to the gods, and the priests were their officers—a not unprofitable occupation. They would direct the work on which the surplus wealth of the gods' estates was spent.

Although the peoples were distinct, they knew each other. For instance, the gods of Sumeria were also those of Akkad; in fact, the gods have Semitic features. The Sumerian city of Nippur is the dwelling of a god, Ellil, who is sacred to Sumerians and Akkadians alike. Other cities, such as Lagash, Uruk, Ur, Eridu, and Larsa, were later sacred to both communities. Each had its gods and attendant priesthoods.

But the old Babylonians have also learned from the Sumerians; for instance, the art of writing. Just as the Egyptians had invented their hieroglyphic picture-writing, the peoples—or rather their priests—of the lower reaches of the Tigris and Euphrates had learned to make written records. But stone was scarce in the area and the convenient papyrus-plant suitable for paper-making does not grow there. Therefore the Sumerians learned to write in tiny wedge-shaped characters on cylinders and tablets of baked clay, the local material. We call it 'cuneiform', and it remained the standard form of writing in Mesopotamia and further north for thousands of years. The Babylonians and the Assyrians also used it, and the peoples further west.

These documents—which begin at about 3300 B.C.—comprise receipts and bills, religious texts, epic poems describing primeval gods and god-like men, secular literature, legal documents and medical and scientific texts. One of the most splendid poems of the ancient world, the *Story of Gilgamesh,* comes near to the heroic spirit of Homer. The story of the Deluge, quoted above, is another. There are also more practical documents, such as cures for impotence, spells and charms to ward off disease, besides legal documents and plain records of commercial transactions.

Thousands of such written records have been dug from city-sites in Mesopotamia, and doubtless many more will be found. They provide most of the evidence we have of the religious, social, and political organisation of Sumer and Akkad. But, as in Egypt and Mycenae, the earliest examples of writing are accounts and inventories.

How are we to imagine their cities? It is more difficult to re-create them than the settlements along the Nile Valley, where conditions have changed less. The elaborate system of canals and waterways which the Sumerians and Akkadians built have long since been destroyed, although one can still trace their outline from an aeroplane. But from the material remains, from documents, and the records of travellers who visited Babylonia in historical times—e.g. Herodotus—it is possible to imagine them.

First, one sees the dusty, wide-spreading plain, stretching without interruption on either side of the rivers until it merges with the sky. On each side of the broad, muddy rivers are green fields of wheat, barley, and other cereals, divided by canals and ditches. There are olive-groves and plantations of figs and vines. Some land is given over to pasture, grazed by sheep, goats, and cattle in large numbers. It is an orderly landscape, in which the land is carefully divided and apportioned; much is owned by the god, and the priesthoods who serve him; other land is the property of the king or his officers. The workers who till the soil and watch over the herds do not own them; they are allowed to consume sufficient for their sustenance; much of the rest goes to Church and State, although some land is in private hands. An army of scribes and officials keeps accurate records of the yield of each plot. Surplus grain is collected and stored. There is an elaborate system of taxation, and officials to enforce it, backed by the ultimate sanction of force. The bulk of the peoples are probably less free and independent than their ancestors, but the community as a whole is richer. This is known as civilisation.

The rewards? To find them one must look towards the nearby city rising above the plain. There, piercing the sky, is the temple-tower of the god or goddess, served by attendant priests. A great, tiered tower climbs into the blue sky; a tower made of mud-brick reinforced with thousands of fragments of potsherd. Flights of steps lead to the top, where there is an asphalt platform (there are many bitumen deposits in the desert) topped by a temple with whitewashed walls, and containing many dark, narrow chambers. In one of these is the cult-statue of the deity, in gold, silver or bronze, never seen except by the High Priest and his closest followers. But the men and women bending over the fields know that on the will of the Being who inhabits that temple rests the prosperity of the land, the fertility of the soil, protection against the evils of flood and drought and all the misfortunes which we would call 'natural adversities'. So the people are content that a tithe of their produce should pass regularly through the gates of the temple as an offering to the god, though they may grumble occasionally about extortion, and perhaps look with envy at the legions of priestly officials whose hands never have to grip a hoe or drive a plough.

Not far away rises another great building, the Palace of the King and his family. The King wears a crown of gold adorned with semi-precious stones imported from far-off lands. His Queen and his concubines wear costly ornaments of gold and silver, and

2(a) *left:* Impressions from Sumerian cylinder seals

2(b) *right:* The Egyptian Goddess Sekhmet

2(c) Entrance to the enclosure of the Step Pyramid of Djoser (2780 B.C.)

2(d) Jewellery of Princess Sit-Hathor-Unet (12th Dynasty)
found in her pyramid

their rooms are decorated with rare objects—goblets and fine ornamented pottery, furniture made of imported wood embellished with precious metal. They wear fine garments of woven cloth, musicians play for them at banquets in chambers fragrant with flowers, and poets delight them with stories of the gods, or the achievements of their royal ancestors. However, the King was not aloof but mixed freely with his people. He was chief judge and priest.

All around the Palace and Temples, in scores of crowded high-walled streets, hundreds of tradesmen work; carpenters, coppersmiths, goldsmiths, sculptors and painters. Along the dusty, narrow streets pass carts and war-chariots, and trains of pack-asses bringing the produce of foreign lands. Ships glide swiftly between city and city. The young and vigorous ride out to hunt wild game in the steppes; the old and the idle lounge in bird-haunted gardens, talking, or listening to music, or making love, undisturbed by the clamour of the workaday world, shut off behind high walls.

If this picture seems fanciful, read Woolley's *Ur of the Chaldees*, in which he describes the objects found in the tombs of the Chaldean kings—including not only the furniture they sat on, the clothes and ornaments they wore, but even the instruments which the musicians played for their amusement some four thousand five hundred years ago.

Admittedly, the royal graves at Ur date from a period some five hundred years later than 3000 B.C., but it is certain that cities and temples of this type, though smaller in scale, existed at the beginning of the Third Millennium. They were, however, independent and self-sufficient; unity did not come to the lands of the Two Rivers until the twenty-fourth century B.C.—eight hundred years after Menes united the two lands of Egypt.

The material remains of Sumer and Akkad are far less spectacular than those of Dynastic Egypt, where there was an abundance of building stone for monuments. Whereas in Egypt palaces and private dwellings were built of mud-brick, by the beginning of the Third Millennium the Egyptians had begun to build their temples, pyramids and tombs of stone, and many of these monuments have survived. In Sumer and Akkad stone was a rarity; it had to be brought from afar, and was sparingly used. Their monuments—temples, palaces, and houses alike—were built either of beaten mud (in the early stages) or of sun-dried brick, of which usually only the foundations remain, buried under later accretions. Where timber was used, it has usually perished, though the outlines remain imprinted in the mud, enabling archaeologists to make reconstructions.

It is, however, much more difficult for archaeologists to establish what the Sumerian and Akkadian buildings were like, though, by meticulous excavation and measurement, remarkable feats of reconstruction have been achieved.

To sum up, round about 3000 B.C. we see, for the first time on earth, two large groups of human beings among whom we can detect the lineaments of civilisation. Both are living in broadly similar conditions; both live on the banks of rivers subject to annual flooding which refertilises their land. Both possess certain knowledges and techniques which give them increased control over their environment, although in this they differ—e.g. the wheeled vehicle will not reach Egypt for another 1,500 years, and in Sumer the art of writing has only just begun, whereas in Egypt it is already well developed.

Egypt is more advanced than Lower Mesopotamia. The country enjoys a common rule, and speaks a common language, whereas the land of the Two Rivers is occupied by two races speaking different languages, although they have a common language for literacy. Sumer and Akkad are far from being unified; their peoples live in independent city-states such as Ur, Uruk, Eridu, Larsa, each with its local deities and kings. In Egypt also the old tribal divisions still exist. Each has its tribal god and tribal overlord, though the latter owe allegiance to one king, successor to the southern conqueror Menes, who united the Two Lands.

Both groups of peoples have progressed beyond the boundaries of self-sufficiency. They have become *traders*. Sumer is beginning to exchange her textiles, jewellery, and weapons for imports of metal, wood, lapis-lazuli and other stones. The Egyptians trade with their southern neighbour, Nubia, for ivory and gold; they mine copper and malachite in the deserts of Sinai; they are in contact with their Libyan neighbours of the Western Desert.

Both groups of peoples—Egyptian and Sumerian-Akkadian—produce a surplus of food and other essential requirements sufficient to support a class of priest-technicians, who, because of their superior knowledge, are increasing their power and influence, and are accepted as the mediators between the gods and men. Their chief rivals are the war-lords, who use the technological inventions of the intellectual class to further their own power and ambition. But here the picture is confused, because sometimes king and priest are one, or at least, the king derives his power in part from priestly sanction; may even be god-descended.

In both areas the mass of the people till and sow the fields, keep watch over the herds; the women-folk help to reap the crops, spin and weave the cloth; they accept with little protest the power of their masters—the priests who guard the secret mysteries of knowledge, and the kings and princes 'strong in battle'.

CHAPTER V

Egyptian Religion

To use a mundane simile, all the earlier part of this book has been like the effort of a motorist to break clear of the confines of a modern big city; traffic lights halt him; one-way streets turn him from his intended path; there are frustrating delays; sometimes he loses his way. If the last four chapters sometimes give this impression, my sympathies are with the reader. But groping in pre-history is like that. Now, however, he has reached a point where the bewildering obstructions fall away, and the broad highway opens out, clear and inviting; he can put his foot down on the accelerator. The sign-board marking the city limits bears the words *The Invention of Writing*. From now on, although there are occasional un-signposted sections of the road, the reader (and, happily, the writer) is moving through the epoch of *written records*.

We are back in Egypt. Menes, or Narmer,[1] the southern conqueror, rules the Two Lands, round about 3200 B.C. His home-town was This (or Thinis) near Abydos in Upper Egypt, but, presumably because it was so far away from his newly-won dominions in the north, he shifted the capital of Egypt to Memphis, which lay at a point just before the Nile broadens out into the Delta. Throughout the period which archaeologists call the Old Kingdom (2780–2100 B.C.), Memphis remained the capital of a united Egypt. It was on the west bank of the Nile. On the same bank lay the great cemetery of Sakkara, site of the first pyramid to

[1] When the Greeks and Romans occupied Egypt during the last 300 years of her history, they gave new names to the kings and cities of Ancient Egypt. No-Amun, capital of Egypt in the Eighteenth Dynasty, became *Thebes*. Senusret became *Sesostris*. Manetho, though an Egyptian, wrote his history in Greek; so King Narmer became *Menes*. But the two names probably represent the same king.

be built in Egypt, and burial place of generations of Ancient Egyptians—kings, princes, and officials.

Narmer was followed by seven other powerful kings; Aha, Djer, Djet, Den, Adjib, Semerkhet, and Qu'. Amélineau and later Petrie, excavated mud-brick tombs at Abydos bearing the names of these kings, but since the Abydos tombs were discovered other great monuments have been unearthed at Sakkara itself, some of which also bear the names of these kings. Professor Emery, for example, is at the time of writing examining a tomb at Sakkara which he attributes to Djet. It is not yet established whether the Sakkara monument was the actual tomb of this king, or merely a cenotaph; though Emery (and he has supporters) believes that these kings of the First Dynasty were buried at Sakkara, and that the 'tombs' at Abydos did not contain their bodies, but had some ritual significance.

To explain why these, and later, Egyptian kings may have been furnished with two tombs, it is necessary to examine briefly the foundation of Egyptian religious belief. Egypt is a very dry country, with hardly any rainfall. Even the un-embalmed bodies of the pre-dynastic peoples have been preserved for more than six thousand years—in some cases with the hair and skin still adhering to the skeleton. From very early times the Ancient Egyptians believed that the preservation of the body was connected with the survival of the spirit, or *ka*, in the after-life. Even the pit-graves of the pre-dynastic Egyptians are furnished with vessels containing food-offerings for the deceased, and such simple tools, weapons and implements which they would be expected to use in their future existence. Over the centuries this developed into an elaborate system of mortuary customs; kings and high officials were furnished with magnificent, cunningly-contrived tombs which were, in effect, their dwelling-places after death (the Egyptian name for them was 'House of Eternity') and were designed (a) to protect the body against the effects of time, (b) to prevent violation by robbers, and (c) to furnish the spirit of the dead man or woman with a sufficiency of food, drink, and other material needs to ensure its survival.

Because life is short and death is long, the Ancient Egyptians devoted far more attention and care to the building of their tombs than to their dwellings. The tombs had to last for ever; palaces and houses were occupied only for a relatively short space of time. The result has been that whereas the daily habitations of the Ancient Egyptians have perished, thousands of their tombs have survived; so have their temples and religious monuments. This fact often misleads visitors to Egypt into imagining the Egyptians as a gloomy, mystical people, obsessed by death. The reverse is more likely to be true. From the innumerable paintings, sculptured scenes, and objects which they left in their tombs, it would seem that the Egyptians were a happy, life-loving people, who could imagine no better fate in the next world than a continuation of the pleasures they had enjoyed in this one.

Also, they were essentially materialistic; there was nothing mystical about their approach to life. At parties they loved getting drunk—in fact it was essential to do so for maximum enjoyment. So, side by side with religio-magical inscriptions, we see in some tombs pictures of a gay party with the slave-girls serving wine, and a woman guest, who has imbibed a little too freely, being quietly sick in a bowl held by a slave.

'I wish to drink until I am drunk,' cries one high-born lady. 'My inside is like a straw!' The inscription, in well-drawn hieroglyphs, is there for all to see, above a picture of the lady holding out her wine-cup.

In other tombs we see the great landowner surveying with pride and pleasure his herds of cattle, while a scribe keeps a record; rows of serving-men march in line, bringing offerings of meat, fish, fowl, beer and wine. The soldier has his troops, the sailor his ships. Rank is carefully delineated. The owner of the tomb wants you to be quite sure that he held high office under the king; he was 'fan-bearer on the right hand of His Majesty', or 'Chief of the Scribes'.

'It was a great work which I did there,' boasts Ineni, chief architect under Tuthmosis I, who supervised the building of that king's tomb. 'No one seeing, no one knowing. I shall be praised for my wisdom in after years . . . I was foreman of the foremen . . . and I never blasphemed against holy things.' Rex Engelbach, the hard-bitten British archaeologist, who for many years held high office in the Department of Antiquities, commented on this inscription:

'If he handled Oriental labour for forty years without blaspheming, that was not the least of his achievements. . . .'

There is so much lovable, fallible humanity in Ancient Egyptian writings that it is difficult to avoid digressions, but we must return to the subject of Egyptian religion.

The pre-dynastic Egyptians worshipped innumerable gods. Every local tribe living along the 750-mile length of the river had its quota. Some were deified chieftains; some were deified animals. Some were totems, such as trees, rocks or pillars. To quote just a handful, there was Ape't the hippopotamus-goddess, Ubaste, the cat-goddess of Bubastis, Bes the fat little god of music and dancing, Sekhmet the lioness-headed goddess of Memphis. Over *two thousand* of these primitive gods have been recorded, and no doubt there were more.

But certain gods and goddesses became supremely important, such as Re the sun-god, whose worship was centred on Heliopolis, Horus the falcon-headed god, Amun, principal god of Thebes (later integrated with Re under the name Amun-Re) and, above all, Osiris, god of the dead, and his sister-wife Isis. Then there was Seth, the wicked god, whose original home seems to have been in the Delta. Why and how these deities achieved dominion over the others is interesting. If, again, I may be allowed a personal illustration, I can cite a fairly recent incident which throws light on the workings of the Egyptian mind.

About ten years ago an Egyptian archaeologist told me about a village called Tanta, in the Delta. It was originally quite a small community, and like nearly all Egyptian villages had its local Moslem saint or Holy Man, who had died some 400 years ago and whose tomb-shrine was the principal object of worship. His name was Sa'id. Some years ago the authorities decided to make Tanta the site of an important railway junction, and the village grew into a large town. When this happened, said my Egyptian friend, 'the peoples of Tanta made the propaganda. They said that it was all due to Sa'id, and he became very important, *much* more important than the saints of the other villages.'

There is little doubt that this was the way in which such gods as Horus and Osiris, Amun and Re, rose to an eminence over-shadowing the other gods. Take Menes, for example. The emblem of his southern *nome*, or district, was the falcon, the sign of the god Horus. When his conquest of the south raised him to supreme power, the power of his god rose also, and throughout Egyptian history Horus was one of the most powerful of Egyptian deities. Horus did not eliminate the worship of the other gods. They retained their place, but under his authority, just as Menes himself allowed the local chieftains to retain their power, while owning allegiance to him. We shall see similar examples later—such as Re, the sun-god of Heliopolis, who became the chief god when the kings of Egypt reigned from Memphis, nearby. Then there is Amun, ram-headed god of Thebes, originally a mere provincial deity, but raised to supreme power when the Theban princes gained control of Egypt; then he had to be integrated with his chief rival, Re, under the title Amun-Re.

But we have not yet explained why the kings of the Old Kingdom had two tombs, one in Upper and one in Lower Egypt. The origin of this may rest with the worship of yet another powerful Egyptian god, Osiris. Of all the gods and goddesses of this strange land, Osiris, his wife Isis, and their son, Horus, retained the most powerful hold on the imagination of the people. It is not certain where Osiris came from, but we have noticed, in Chapter IV, that there was a Delta god named Anzety, a male human figure wearing a head-dress in the shape of the vulva of a female goat, and carrying a rod with pendent strings, which is usually described as a flail, though Newberry believed it to have been a *ladanisterion* (see footnote on p. 56). Now Osiris is always represented as a mummified figure carrying this emblem, and sometimes both emblems of Egyptian royalty, the crook and the 'flail'. In origin he was almost certainly the Libyan deity, Anzety. But by the time of the Middle Kingdom (2100–1700 B.C.) he had become Osiris, god of the dead and judge of the souls, the central figure within a religious myth, the cult-centre of which was Abydos in Upper Egypt. According to this myth, Osiris was one of four children born to the gods Geb and Nut. Geb was the earth, Nut the sky. The other three children were Isis (who became the wife of Osiris), Nephthys, another goddess, and Seth.

'Osiris succeeded to the throne of his father and governed the world wisely and justly, aided by his sister-wife Isis. Seth, jealous of his brother's power, plotted to destroy him and eventually succeeded, afterwards cutting up the body of Osiris into pieces which he buried in various parts of Egypt. The head he buried at Abydos, in Upper Egypt. The faithful Isis recovered the scattered fragments of her husband's corpse, and with the aid of the jackal-god Anubis, who subsequently became the god of embalmment, re-animated it. Though unable to return to his life on earth, Osiris passed to the Underworld, where he became the god of the dead and later judge of souls. Isis bore a son, Horus, who took revenge on his uncle Seth, defeating the usurper in battle and winning back his father's throne.'[1]

This legend in its full maturity, belongs to a period some thousand years after the time we are considering, but it must have been of great age. Certainly Abydos itself was a holy place of immense antiquity. As we have seen, the kings of the First and Second Dynasties had their tombs (or cenotaphs) there, even when their capital was at Memphis, some four hundred miles away, in the north. Menes' ancestors came from Upper Egypt, and their original capital was near Abydos. There are also references in Old Kingdom texts, to a pilgrimage to Abydos, to the shrine of the god Osiris, the place at which his head was buried. This may have been the reason why the kings, and in some cases their nobles, sought burial at Abydos. It would also explain why the kings needed *two* tombs, one near Memphis, their capital, and one in the land of their ancestors, near the shrine of the god-king through whose mediation it was possible for the dead to enter the land of the blessed spirits. Some archaeologists have suggested that one of the boats buried beside the pyramid-tombs of the Old Kingdom kings was intended for the daily journey across the sky

[1] *The Lost Pharaohs*—Leonard Cottrell: Evans Brothers, London, 1949.

with the sun-god Re. But this is mere conjecture, and cannot be proved.

Two tombs would present no problem to the Ancient Egyptians. The spirit of the dead king could inhabit either at will, just as in life he would journey between one palace and another.

No attempt will be made in this book to unravel the complexities of Egyptian religion, which, in the writer's view, must have been as bewildering to the mass of the Ancient Egyptians as it is to us. It is not difficult to understand the origins and development of such religions as those of Christ and Mahomet. Each is mono-theistic, with one Founder and one faith. Ancient Egyptian religion can be compared with the store-room of a house of which the owners cannot bring themselves to throw anything away. The innumerable gods of the Ancient Egyptian pantheon, which originated among the primitive inhabitants of the Nile Valley, savage conceptions which a less conservative people would have discarded, were retained to the end. History became mingled with myth—e.g. the prototypes of Horus and Seth may well have been the rival chieftains of the north and south (Seth was a god of the Delta; Horus of Southern Egypt). Osiris himself may have been originally an earthly king. The conception of the good son who avenges his father is not unknown in the myths of other ancient peoples—e.g. Orestes and Agamemnon, heroes of Greek legend. But whereas other peoples eventually discarded their ancient beliefs, or accepted them merely as fairy-tales, the Egyptians clung to theirs to the end.

The local gods of the *nomes* never lost their appeal, even when the state religion prescribed the worship of Re, Amun and Osiris. From time to time the priesthood tried to organise these many gods into a single theological system, but the task was beyond them. It is, I suggest, also beyond us.

CHAPTER VI

Egypt to the Middle Kingdom

The period between Menes, the first king of the First Dynasty, and Cheops (Khufu), greatest king of the Fourth Dynasty, covers approximately 500 years. In the field of technological progress, there is only one comparable period in the entire history of the human race—and that is the history of the past two hundred years. Even that is hardly a fair comparison, for whereas by A.D. 1750 we had begun to invent machines which could do the work of many men, the Ancient Egyptians, throughout their long history, commanded only a few simple metal tools. The rest they achieved by mental ability and the superb organisation of muscle-power.

At the beginning of this period neither the Egyptians nor any other peoples on earth could build in stone. At the end of it the Egyptians had erected the Great Pyramid, composed of nearly *two and a half million blocks of stone*, each weighing about two and a half tons, cut and laid to an accuracy of a fraction of a degree, orientated with such precision that compass errors could be checked against it. For 4,500 years it was the highest building on earth—i.e. down to the early part of the nineteenth century A.D.

It was built in about twenty years, with no mechanical appliances apart from the lever, the roller, and the inclined plane. No cranes, no pulley-blocks, not even the simplest machinery. At this period they did not even possess the wheel.

Two questions immediately spring to mind. *How* did they do it? And *why* did they do it? The answer to the first can be summed up in one phrase—centralised control of power. Before Menes unified the Two Lands, most—though not all—of the technical resources were available, but unorganised and undisciplined. But once one man had supreme control and could exercise it through a highly-organised system of government—the officials of which were drawn from the literate, intellectual class—the rest followed naturally. Another important factor was the system of agriculture, dictated by the annual flooding of the Nile. There was already a surplus of food sufficient to maintain an army of technicians and craftsmen. But these alone would be insufficient to produce the labour needed to build a pyramid. However, for three months of the year, during the annual inundation, the field-labourers were idle. Organised into gangs, they could provide the man-power needed for hauling the stones from the quarries to the site of the building, and for moving the great blocks into position. The skilled work of quarrying the stone and of shaping it accurately into building blocks would, of course, be done by a smaller group of specialist-craftsmen.

The answer to the second question—*why* did they do it?—may be found in the Egyptian religious beliefs outlined in the last chapter. By the time of Menes these beliefs had been formulated into a system. At this remote period there seems to have been a close connection between the welfare of the king and that of the people over whom he ruled. We have already noted the 'heb-sed' ceremony commemorated on the mace-head of Narmer. The spirit of the king may also have been expected to watch over his people in the life beyond the grave; therefore the preservation of his body, on which the survival of the spirit depended, was important, not only to him, but to his people. Menes and his successors—Djer, Djet, Semerkhet, etc.—were buried in large, elaborate tombs of mud-brick of rectangular shape, containing a central chamber for the royal body, and numerous subsidiary rooms which originally contained furniture, clothing, weapons and tools, and a large store of beautifully-carved stone vessels for grain, oil, wine, beer, etc. These vases, bowls, cups of alabaster, diorite, and other stones reveal a quite astonishing standard of craftsmanship. Nothing more beautiful has ever been produced in Egypt than these products of the early dynastic or 'Archaic' period. The suavity of line, the graceful, unornamented shapes, the skilful exploitation of material—all indicate a long experience of working in stone. And yet, at this period, stone was not used for *building* purposes. One tomb—that of Khasekhemui, last king of the Second Dynasty— has a stone-lined burial chamber, but the rest of the tomb, like its predecessors, is of mud-brick.

Similar tombs, called *mastabas*,[1] exist at Sakkara, opposite the ancient capital of Memphis to which Menes and his successors moved after the conquest of Lower Egypt. These, too, are of mud-brick.

Then, quite suddenly, and apparently without previous prepara-tion, the Egyptians began to build monumentally in hewn stone. The transformation is astonishing. Khasekhemui built his tomb of mud-brick just like his predecessors. But his successor, Djoser or Neter-khet, first king of the Third Dynasty (2780–2720 B.C.), was buried under an enormous pyramid of masonry, nearly four hun-dred feet square and over two hundred and fifty feet high. Under it Djoser's builders excavated a shaft eighty feet deep, with a granite-lined burial chamber at the bottom (the granite was brought by river from Assuan, nearly seven hundred miles away). Around this stone mountain was a complex of buildings, also of stone, surrounded by a high stone wall, faced originally (as was the pyramid) with fine white limestone, and enclosing an area one hundred times bigger than the area of the great brick tomb at Nagada, attributed to Menes.

For many years Egyptologists assumed that this pyramid, which is built in steps (hence its name 'the Step Pyramid') must be of later date than the more famous straight-sided Great Pyramid built by Cheops at Giza. They were misled by the fact that addi-tions had been made to it by the Saite kings of the seventh century B.C. But we now know that Djoser's monument was built more than seventy years before Cheops; it is, in fact, the *first* pyramid, and the oldest large stone building in the world.

How was this miracle achieved? The answer, probably, is that

---

[1] After the Arabic name for the rectangular mud-brick benches found outside the houses of the modern *fellahin*.

as at other crises in human history, the hour brought forth the man. From the mists of legend and fragmentary history which surround this remote epoch, one figure looms up; we know his name— Imhotep. We know that he was the architect of King Djoser. Twenty-five centuries after Imhotep's death, the historian, Manetho, poring over the priestly chronicles, extracted and transmitted to us one tantalising scrap of information:

'In his reign'—i.e. that of Djoser—'lived Imouthes (Imhotep) who because of his medical skill had the reputation of Aesculapius, *and was the inventor of the art of building in hewn stone.*[1] He also paid attention to writing.'

That is all; four or five lines of history, a few later legends (in which Imhotep has become a god and magician), a few inscriptions and *graffiti*, are the only literary evidence we have of the existence of this great man. For great he must have been; a genius who can stand beside the intellectual giants of later history. Yet even he could not have created the Step Pyramid had not the conditions favoured him. First, the successors of Menes had finally consolidated the conquest and unification of Egypt. The resources of the entire kingdom, in wealth and manpower, were now at the disposal of the king and his ministers.

But why, it may be asked, did the Egyptians suddenly begin using stone after building for so long in mud-brick and timber? Dr. George Reisner, the distinguished American archaeologist, suggested an answer.

The reason for this change, he believed, was that near the new capital of Memphis there was an abundant supply of good-quality limestone, easily worked, and lying close to hand. Limestone cliffs exist on both sides of the river and have been quarried for thousands of years. There was already a long-established tradition of craftsmanship in the making of stone vessels; now the Egyptians learned to cut and shape blocks of limestone and use them for building *exactly as they had used mud-bricks*. A time came when, says Reisner:

'. . . the Egyptian craftsman had mastered the cutting of blocks of limestone to such an extent that they were able to quarry lime-

[1] My italics.

78

stone blocks of almost any size and on royal demand excavate large pits and trenches (or stairways) in the rock.'[1]

Sakkara, where the Step Pyramid still stands, is one of the most stirring archaeological sites in the world. For here one may study the very beginnings of stone architecture. In an earlier chapter we observed that the kings and nobles of the Early Dynastic period modelled their tombs on their dwelling-houses, which were of mud-brick and timber. In the Step Pyramid and its surrounding buildings we can see this carried a step further. The earlier forms are still preserved, but *in stone*. Thus the courtyard of Djoser's pyramid is approached by an entrance colonnade, at each end of which stands a stone door, exactly imitating the wooden doors which, no doubt, were used in his long-vanished palace. The hinges are there, and the recess for the draw-bolt. But the doors are immovable; they are dummies. Similarly, the enclosure wall itself is built in a series of bastions with recessed panels, copying timber-work. The columns of the colonnade are fluted, in imitation of the bundles of reeds with which the primitive Egyptians supported the roofs of their mud-brick dwellings. These columns support a roof consisting of semi-circular blocks of stone— representing palm-logs.

Even more fascinating is the complex of small chambers cut out of the rock eighty feet beneath the pyramid enclosure. There are two such sets of chambers, one beneath the pyramid itself, and another, better preserved, at the southern end of the enclosure. Monsieur Jean-Philippe Lauer, who has devoted most of his life to preserving and restoring Imhotep's monument, happily described these chambers as 'le petit apartement du *ka*.'[2]

There is no doubt that these rooms are representations of part of the royal palace in which Djoser lived, five thousand years ago. The walls are adorned with a pattern of green-blue tiles of faience, in imitation of the reed mats which the pre-dynastic and early dynastic peoples used in their homes. Even the rolled-up mats which hung above the doorways are carefully reproduced in the

[1] *The Development of the Egyptian Tomb down to the time of Cheops*—George Reisner: Harvard University Press, 1936. Oxford University Press, London.
[2] i.e. of the King's spirit—the *ka*.

same tiles. A stone-cut corridor represents the road outside the palace; one wall is plain; the other represents the palace façade with its doorways. One of these doorways is open, admitting to chambers within; the others are sealed by stone *stelæ* beautifully carved with sculptured reliefs of Djoser himself, with his name in hieroglyphs above. In one relief he is shown wearing the crown of Lower Egypt, in the other that of Upper Egypt. A particularly delightful touch—some of the hieroglyphs have been given tiny human hands holding ostrich-feather fans, inclined respectfully towards the King.

Beyond the open door is a suite of rooms, one of which was probably the bed-chamber; others would be rooms of state, and beyond were the royal granaries. Perhaps when the tomb was first made the rooms were furnished—we do not know. But when the builders sealed them beneath eighty feet of rubble masonry, no other human beings—save the ancient tomb-robbers—ever saw them again, until they were re-opened by the nineteenth century archaeologists. The king's *ka* could, if it wished, move from the body in its granite burial chamber and occupy the rooms; or, if it tired of them, could move across the courtyard to the other royal apartments under the pyramid itself. Some scholars have suggested that these two tombs within the same enclosure—one on the north and the other on the south—may have symbolised the two sepulchres which earlier kings were obliged to have in Upper and Lower Egypt.

We have dwelt at some length on the Step Pyramid of King Djoser, first king of the Third Dynasty, because it marks an epoch in human history—the beginnings of stone architecture; and also because it may be said to typify Egyptian religious beliefs. With its burial chamber deep beneath the rock, its suites of rooms for the royal *ka*, its maze of underground store-rooms stacked to the ceiling with stone vessels, the pyramid tomb of Djoser represents Egyptian funerary customs at their most elaborate.

Manetho gives the names of other kings of the Third Dynasty, successors to Djoser; but they remain merely names—Sa-nakht, Khaba, Nefer-ka, Anu (or Huni). Recently, however, the Egyptian

archaeologist, Zakaria Goneim, discovered the lower courses of a hitherto unknown pyramid of the Third Dynasty a little to the south-west of Djoser's monument. Like the latter, the rock beneath was riddled with a warren of galleries and store-chambers, most of them empty, though large numbers of stone vessels have been found, and an interesting set of Third Dynasty jewellery, golden bracelets which probably belonged to a princess. On some of the jar-sealings Goneim found the royal name of a king—*Sekhem-khet*, which means 'powerful of body'. One of Djoser's names (the Pharaohs bore several names) was *Neter-khet*; the similarity might suggest that Sekhem-khet may have belonged to the same family as Djoser, although his name does not appear in Manetho's king-list. But in 1955 Goneim found an inscribed ivory tablet with another royal name, *Djeserti-ankh* (Djeser and Djoser

81   F

are the same), and this name does appear in Manetho's list of Third Dynasty kings, in which he is stated to have been Djoser's successor. From the architecture of this newly-discovered pyramid, which also had a large enclosing wall of similar pattern to Djoser's, it seems reasonably certain that Sekhem-khet was indeed the next king after Djoser.

When the writer was last at Sakkara, Goneim pointed out to him a faded inscription in red ochre painted on the white limestone wall, newly revealed for the first time in 5,000 years. The inscription read 'Imhotep', together with other barely legible signs which might be read as 'every day'. Nearby, on the same wall, as fresh as when it left the builders' hands, was a thin red line made by flicking a cord tipped in red paint against the surface to establish the horizontals: '*Imhotep* . . . (inspected this monument?) . . . *every* day . . .' Did the great architect work on the pyramid of his master's successor—perhaps the king's son? That red line dissolved fifty centuries. If Imhotep himself had appeared round the corner, a commanding deep-browed figure in a white robe, accompanied by his assistants, it would hardly have seemed strange.[1]

'Look out . . . *he*'s here again . . .'—the word would be passed along the line, and a hundred brown-skinned workmen would suddenly become very busy indeed.

Imhotep was a supreme product of the intellectual class of priest-technicians thrown up by the Urban Revolution. One imagines him to have been one of those universal geniuses, like Leonardo da Vinci, master of many skills. Manetho says that 'because of his medical skill he had the reputation of Aesculapius' (the Greek god of Medicine) and that 'he also paid attention to writing'. For all we know, the last cryptic phrase may mean that he re-drafted and improved the whole system of Egyptian writing, which at this period, says Sir Alan Gardiner, 'can be seen developing almost before our eyes'. His reputation was such that two thousand years after his death, Egyptian scribes used to pour out libations to him before beginning their work.

[1] Jean-Philippe Lauer, architect to the Department of Antiquities, and responsible for the restoration of Djoser's pyramid, calls himself 'le dernier assistant du Vizier Imhotep'.

His tomb has never been found.

The Step Pyramid was not planned as such from the start. It began as a simple stone-built *mastaba*, which was progressively increased in size until someone—probably Imhotep—had the idea of building a succession of smaller *mastabas* on top, thus producing the stepped form. Later kings abandoned the steps and built straight-sided pyramids of even greater size. Huni, one of the last kings of the Third Dynasty, began an enormous one at Meydum, which was completed by his successor Snofru. His son, Cheops, founder of the Fourth Dynasty (2720–2560 B.C.) built the largest pyramid of all, the famous Great Pyramid of Giza, about twelve miles from Sakkara. It is the sole survivor of the Seven Wonders of the World, 755 feet square, 481 feet high, and, apart from its internal chambers, a solid mass of monumental masonry comprising two and a half million blocks of limestone. Even more remarkable than its bulk is the precision with which it was built. Petrie, who spent two years surveying and measuring it, gives figures, of which the following are a few samples:

'. . . the mean thickness of the eastern joint of the northern casing-stones is 0.02' (1/50th of an inch).

The mean variation of the cutting of the stone from a straight line is only one-hundredth part of one inch.

'. . . these joints, with an area of 35 square feet each, were not only worked as finely as this, but cemented throughout. Though the stones were brought as close as 1/500th of an inch, or, in fact, into contact, the mean opening of the join was 1/50th of an inch, yet the builders managed to fill the joint with cement, despite the great area of it, and the weight of the stone, some 16 tons . . .'

The internal core of masonry was quarried locally. The fine limestone blocks of the outer casing (which has since disappeared) were quarried from the cliffs on the opposite bank of the Nile and floated across the river in barges, presumably during the inundation season, when the river reached its widest extent. Some of these barges could carry one thousand tons. The feat of manœuvring them across the fast-flowing current was in itself no mean achievement. The blocks were cut out of the virgin rock with copper tools, aided by wedges driven into slots to break off the blocks after three sides had been cut. They were hauled up to the pyramid plateau by men dragging sledges (the wheel was unknown to the Egyptians at this period) and moved into position by manpower alone. There were no cranes or lifting-tackle.

As stated earlier in this chapter, the Great Pyramid remained, for nearly five thousand years, the highest building in the world. And yet, only *one hundred years* before the Great Pyramid was built, there were no stone buildings anywhere in the world. The Egyptians, the most advanced peoples, were still building in mud-brick.

Sometimes mankind can move fast, a fact which may offer us some consolation in our present emergency.

But though the technical achievements of the Ancient Egyptians are perhaps those which impress most deeply our mechanical age, it would be a gross error to imagine them merely as engineers with a death-wish. Their funerary monuments remain. Their palaces, mansions, and humbler dwellings; their shops and offices, warehouses, roads, and forts have disappeared. The reason is simple enough; these buildings were of perishable materials—mud-brick, timber, wattle-and-daub. Yet in its prime the capital of Memphis stretched for some ten miles along the western bank of the Nile, opposite the barren desert plateau where the eternal homes of their god-kings still pierce the empty sky. But Memphis has gone. The pyramids and their attendant *mastabas*—the tombs of the nobles and high officials—remain. Therefore, to gain some knowledge of the kind of life which these people lived, how they looked, the clothes they wore, the furniture they used, their occupations, sports and amusements, we have to penetrate their tomb-chambers, on the walls of which they have left permanent records in sculptured stone. It is these which enable us to know more about the daily lives of the men and women of the Old Kingdom, who lived five thousand years ago, than we can learn of our own Anglo-Saxon ancestors who are so much nearer to us in time.

By the time of Khufu (Cheops), builder of the Great Pyramid, royal power was absolute. The reins of government were in the hands of the king, and his officials seem to have been drawn to a large extent from members of the royal family. He ruled the entire land through provincial governors, who were often members of his family, and through a host of minor officials, members of the priestly class, who were literate, and who administered the highly elaborate system of taxation, which was in kind. The Egyptians had no system of coinage until very late in their history. The king had an army, and sometimes conducted campaigns against the Nubians of the south, the Asiatics of the north-east, and the Libyans of the west. Scenes representing his triumphs over these peoples (in which the Asiatics are shown as bearded and the Nubians as negroes) occur in monuments of this and later Egyptian periods. But at the time of the Old Kingdom Egypt had no Empire. That came much later.

The kings of the First to the Fourth Dynasties sent expeditions into the peninsula of Sinai to mine copper and malachite, and to Nubia for gold and slaves. Slavery was a new conception in human development; instead of killing a captured enemy, you made him work for you; men could be domesticated as well as animals.

The multitudinous gods of the provinces had begun to be absorbed into a system; Anubis, the jackal-god, guardian of the cemeteries—Thoueris, the crocodile-god—Hat-hor, goddess of love—Thoth, god of writing, with his ibis-head (incidentally, he came from the Delta, which may be significant)—Isis—Osiris—and Horus. But the dominant god is *Re*, the sun-god of Heliopolis, near Memphis. There are some archaeologists who believe that the pyramid-shape itself may be a representation in stone of the descending rays of the sun breaking through cloud. Others suggest that the origin of the step-pyramid may be, not an evolution from the simple *mastaba*, but a representation in stone of the heavenly stairs by which the dead king ascended to the sky. [1]

In a country such as Egypt, with its almost perpetual sunshine, the conception of a deity residing in the life-giving sun was bound to become prominent. Re was observed to rise each day in the east, to cross the heavens, and set in the west. But the Egyptians, always a practical people, could not imagine that he achieved this feat without some means of transport; and as the most common

[1] *The Pyramids of Egypt*—I. E. S. Edwards: Penguin Books, London, 1947.

form of transport was a boat, they gave him a heavenly barque in which to make the journey. The king, who at this period was regarded as the god's descendant, the 'Son of Re', believed that in the after-life he would accompany the sun-god in his boat, which may explain why such boats were frequently buried beside the pyramids.

The priests of Re must have become extremely powerful. At one period—that of the Fifth Dynasty (2560–2420 B.C.)—the kings incorporated the god's name in their own, e.g. Sahu*re*, Neferirka*re*, Niuser*re*. These kings also built 'sun-temples' to the god, at Abusir, between Sakkara and Giza; the central feature of these temples was an obelisk. It may well be that the pyramid-shape had some religious significance.

Only a king could be buried in a large pyramid; his queens sometimes were buried in smaller pyramids nearby. But the nobles, however exalted, had to be content with *mastabas*, either of mud-brick or stone. Hundreds of these rectangular buildings were arranged in streets under the shadow of the royal tomb, so that their owners could attend the king in death as they had done in life. It is from the sculptures and inscriptions on the inner walls of these monuments that we derive most of our knowledge of the Old Kingdom. The pyramids themselves were uninscribed until the end of the Fifth Dynasty, when the so-called 'pyramid texts' appear—but these were simply columns of religious texts, many of which appear to date from a period long before that of the pyramids. The pyramids contain no sculptured scenes of everyday life such as adorn the walls of the *mastabas* of the officials.

These beautifully-sculptured scenes impress every visitor to Egypt. Weary with walking over sand and rock in the hot sun, he enters the cool depths of a tomb, and there, on the walls, the ancient peoples come suddenly and startlingly to life. Here is the official himself, the 'Chief Scribe to His Majesty' or the 'Vizier' (prime minister of the king), wearing a white kilt of linen and seated on a chair of office, watching ranks of his servants bringing offerings of meat, bread, beer and wine. Here men are spearing fish, or plucking fowl. Women-servants are reaping the crops, or grinding corn in stone querns. Butchers are carving up the carcasses of cattle, while others carry the severed haunches to their master. Nearby a man drives a group of asses bearing loads. But the sculptor, tiring of the conventional scenes which he has to depict in every tomb, has introduced, as artists will, a note of variety. One of the asses is giving trouble; and two men are wrestling with the stubborn little beast, in whose eyes is a devilish glint. One grasps his foreleg; the other hauls at his bridle. For one moment the humorous observations of an individual who died fifty centuries ago reach us, and we smile with him.

We look upwards, and there is yet another scene; the elegant wife of the official, her slender body clothed in a close-fitting robe of fine, transparent linen, and wearing rich jewellery on her arms and neck, presides with her husband over a party; her guests sit on chairs or recline on cushions, served with wine and delicacies by naked slave-girls. A group of musicians plays for the guests, and a girl dancer sways her hips to the rhythmic clapping of hands, the tapping of tambourines and the strumming of lutes. In one corner a rank of chorus-girls is executing a concerted high-kick of which the Tiller Girls would not be ashamed. One can see such a scene in the tomb of Mahu at Sakkara, and at other places.

Let your eye wander further along the wall, and you are enjoying a day's sport in the marshes, with the official, his wife and daughter. A light skiff made of bound papyrus-stems glides beside the reeds. Beaters have roused the wildfowl, which circle over our heads; the official, owner of the tomb, sends his throwing-stick whirling among them, while his daughter clings on to his leg to prevent him falling into the water. His wife holds a duck in her hand, while the servants go to gather the fallen birds. All these scenes are carefully described in hieroglyphic texts above or below the sculptured reliefs.

Here, before our eyes, is a sophisticated people who enjoyed sport, who understood the art of dress, music, and civilised entertainment, who valued fine cooking and good wines, who, without doubt, also had a literature. For by this time the art of writing had developed far beyond mere recording. Although we do not possess any papyri of the Old Kingdom *written at the time*, scribes of later periods wrote down on papyrus stories whose origins go back to this first flowering of Egyptian civilisation.

They are mainly fairy-tales, stories of magical adventures. King Snofru, father of Khufu (Cheops), builder of the Great Pyramid, is bored, and asks a magician, one Zazamonkh, to devise some entertainment for him. The magician replies:

'If Thy Majesty would but betake thee to the lake of the Great House' (i.e. the Palace), 'man thee a boat with all fair damsels of the inner apartments of thy palace. Then will the heart of Thy Majesty be diverted, when thou shall see how they row to and fro.'

The King decides to improve on this idea. He orders that twenty maidens shall be brought to him:

'... "of those with the fairest limbs, and with beauteous breasts and braided tresses, such as have not given birth, and moreover have brought me twenty nets, and to give these nets to these women instead of clothes." And it was done according to all that His Majesty commanded, and the heart of His Majesty was glad when he beheld how they rowed.'

But then an accident occurs. One of the maidens, getting her paddle entangled with her 'braided tresses', loses her 'fish-pendent' of malachite (a hair ornament) in the water.

'Then she became silent and ceased rowing, and her side (the girls on her side of the boat) became silent and ceased rowing.'

The King offers to give the girl a new pendent, but she replies not unnaturally:

' "I want my pot down to its bottom",' meaning that she wants her right in full. Doubtless the phrase was a proverb. So magic has to be called in, and the magician performs, in miniature, the feat which Moses achieved when he held back the waters of the Dead Sea. Zazamonkh folds back the waters of the lake, like a cloth, revealing the bottom, and so enables the aggrieved lady to recover her ornament. Whereupon, presumably, the King's entertainment is resumed.

When we study the reliefs, inscriptions, and literature of the Old Kingdom, the picture which emerges is of an Oriental despotism, probably fairly mild, with a small sophisticated, aristocratic society at the top, enjoying a high standard of material life, supported by the labours of millions of peasants. These anonymous masses tilled and reaped the fields, served in Pharaoh's armies, grumbled at the tax-gatherers, and produced the fine objects of skill and craftsmanship which are now their only memorial. They lived in simple mud-brick dwellings beside the Nile, very like those of their modern descendants. There were no elaborate tombs for them; only nameless graves in the sand. But we need not feel too sorry for them. They were certainly not unwilling slaves, driven to their tasks by brutal taskmasters.

Religion, the mysteries of which were guarded by the literate, permeated their lives to an extent which is hard for us to realise. To them the Pharaoh was truly a god, guardian and protector of their destinies, on whose prosperity depended the welfare of the whole kingdom—the yield of the crops and cattle, the flooding of the great river on which they depended. A few of the more intelligent could enter the priestly colleges, learn the sacred art of writing, and themselves become priests, with the opportunity of rising to high rank. But for the vast majority their needs were simple; bread, beer, and occasionally meat; a roof over their heads in the mild winter; fuel for their fires; wives as bedfellows and workmates; children to support them in their old age. And there was always the ever-present sun, which shone on rich and poor alike.

After about five hundred years the highly-centralised autocracy of the Old Kingdom finally collapsed in anarchy. After the time of Khufu, the kings never had such absolute power. The pyramids of his successors—Chephren (Khafre), Mycerinus (Menkaure)—were smaller; those of the Fifth and Sixth Dynasties at Sakkara are relatively modest structures which Khufu would have despised. As in Europe during the Middle Ages, the power of the king was challenged by the provincial lords, the *nomarchs*, as they were called. Eventually a time came when centralised control was no longer possible, and there was an interregnum of some one hundred and seventy years when Egypt was ruled by weak kings of the Seventh to the Tenth Dynasties. Archaeologists call this, for convenience, the First Intermediate Period.

After about 2100 B.C. powerful new dynasties arise, the Eleventh, Twelfth, and Thirteenth, which comprise the so-called Middle Kingdom (2100–1700 B.C.). The founders of the Twelfth Dynasty were provincial nobles from the then obscure town of No-Amun, or Thebes, in Upper Egypt. Later it was to become the capital of Egypt under the New Kingdom.

'The Middle Kingdom has been called Egypt's Feudal Age. The Pharaohs of this period, men such as Amenemhet, Senusret II, Senusret III, though they eventually secured control of the country, never wielded the absolute power commanded by the Memphite kings. The king had to rule through the nomarchs, keeping constant watch lest they should become too powerful. He now employed professional soldiers called "Followers of His Majesty" though he was able to call on his feudatories to supply men and arms for foreign expeditions. Of these there were many. The Pharaohs of the Middle Kingdom pushed the frontier southward into Nubia. Senusret I, Amenemhet's successor, carried the war above the Second Cataract. Amenemhet II reopened the gold-mines of Sinai in the north-east, and Senusret III caused his engineers to cut a channel 260 feet long and 34 feet wide through the granite of the First Cataract to enable his war-galleys to sail farther up the river. He also invaded Syria for the first time. This was a period of foreign conquest and trade expansion.'[1]

But perhaps the greatest achievement of the Middle Kingdom was the creation of the artificial lake of Moeris, in the Fayum, an area of low-lying land west of the desert cliffs south of Dashur. The Egyptian engineers drove a great canal through the cliffs, thus letting in the Nile to flood and fertilise a great expanse of land. Herodotus, who saw this lake in the fifth century B.C. (some sixteen hundred years after Amenemhet), attributed it to Amenemhet III.

'Since the Nile kept no definite bounds in its rising and the fruitfulness of the country depended on the river's regularity, the king dug the lake to accommodate the superfluous water, so that the river should neither by its strong current flood the land unreasonably and form swamps and fens, nor, by rising less than

[1] *The Lost Pharaohs*—Leonard Cottrell: Evans Brothers, London, 1949.

was advantageous, damage the crops by lack of water. Between the river and the lake he constructed a canal, 80 stades in length and 300 feet in breadth. Through this canal, at times, he admitted the water from the river, at other times he excluded it, thus providing the farmers with water at fitting times by opening the inlet and closing it scientifically and at great expense.'[1]

However, it is not certain that Herodotus was correct in his facts. According to Mr. I. E. S. Edwards, one of the leading authorities on Ancient Egypt, the lake was almost certainly in existence before the time of Amenemhet III, 'though he may well have undertaken some irrigation or land reclamation schemes in the neighbourhood of the lake.'[2]

Whoever was responsible, it was one of the greatest achievements of the Ancient Egyptians, whose skill in hydraulic engineering exceeded that of any other peoples of the ancient world.

In religion, Re, the sun-god, remained supreme, but the Old Kingdom saw the rise of the Osiris-cult mentioned in the last chapter. This legend became the most popular of all Egyptian folk-myths, probably because of its basic humanity, Osiris becoming the type of devoted father, Isis that of the faithful wife, and Horus that of the loyal son who avenges his father.

But the other gods and goddesses were there, too. Hat-hor, goddess of love, was a particular favourite. Usually she is represented in the form of a cow, but she appears in slightly more attractive guise as an ornament on the mirrors before which the Twelfth Dynasty ladies primped themselves. In these she has the face of a woman, but her bovine origin is indicated by cow's ears.

Sculpture, in the round and in relief, reached a standard exceeded only slightly by that of the Old Kingdom. In the writer's opinion, no artists of whom we have records—not even the Greeks —succeeded as did the sculptors of the Old and Middle Kingdoms in suggesting the essential nobility inherent in a fine human body. The figures of these men and women, whose calm faces seem already to be contemplating a state of being beyond earthly things,

---

[1] Herodotus: *The Histories*. Translated Rawlinson. J. M. Dent & Sons Ltd., London.

[2] *The Pyramids of Egypt*—I. E. S. Edwards: Penguin Books, London, 1947.

are truly god-like. By fining down the human frame to its essential proportions, eliminating superfluous detail, these wonderful artists seem to release the spirit of man from its imprisoning flesh. There is the strength and vigour of the male without his animal brutality. The women could not be more feminine, but in their gentle eyes, serene profiles, and slender limbs, there is a suggestion of beauty which goes beyond the physical—the vision which has haunted poets and artists for generations, and will no doubt go on haunting them to the end of time.

The Jews, whose genius was poetic and prophetic, were uninterested in visual creation. Their stern prophets execrated 'graven images' and called upon their peoples to destroy them. Yet it was a Jewish writer who said that 'God created Man in His own image'. In the writer's view, the Egyptian artists understood this instinctively, and it is in their work, and not in the gibberish of their priests that we come nearest to the spirit of Egyptian religion.

During the whole of this period, from 3200 to 1700 B.C., the peoples of Lower Mesopotamia were developing their own distinctive civilisations. There, too, great cities were built, kings rose and fell from power, art and science flourished. Yet there was no martial conflict between the two peoples; trade contacts were few; perhaps a small number of travellers brought back stories of another great kingdom far off across the desert wastes—and would not be believed. The Egyptians, however, were in remote contact with another civilisation—that of Crete, far out in the Mediterranean Sea. We shall hear more of this island kingdom later. Meanwhile, let us return to the flat alluvial plain near the mouths of the Two Rivers—the land of Sumer—and see what its people achieved during the period when Khufu was building the Great Pyramid, and Amenemhet III his great lake of Moeris.

CHAPTER VII
Sumer and Babylon

At the time when Cheops was building his Great Pyramid (2720 B.C.), a powerful dynasty ruled at Ur on the Euphrates, near the point where that river is joined by the Shatt Charraf. It was then a harbour town, covering about four square miles of mud-brick buildings, with quays for shipping running far into the city. It was one of a number of independent, self-governing city-states, such as Lagash, Umma, Eshnunna, Kish, Uruk (the Biblical Erech), and Nippur. Excavations at these sites have revealed that the cities followed a broadly similar plan. Each had at its centre a walled enclosure of mud-brick, dominated by one or more huge temples, of which the most prominent feature was a high, tiered tower. This Sumerian fondness for towers, which reached its ultimate development in the fabled Tower of Babylon, was probably due to boredom with the monotonous plain on which the inhabitants had to live. They were artificial mountains, and some had quite large trees growing on them.

None of these cities exists today, but, by a minute examination of the ruined remains, archaeologists have been able to reconstruct their original appearance with a high degree of accuracy. If you were approaching such a town in 2700 B.C. you would see first the small, flat fields threaded by irrigation channels, then a high wall pierced by gateways; within this would be streets of low, mainly flat-roofed, mud-brick dwellings. Higher still rose another great wall, roughly oval in plan, enclosing the outer precincts of the temple. Within that, at a still higher level, would be a second oval wall, and if you managed to penetrate beyond that you would find yourself in the central courtyard of the temple. You might see a file of naked priests moving towards the sanctuary of the god—a rectangular building, like a medieval keep—standing on a high, raised platform at the far end.

As in Egypt, there were many gods, though a few were predominant over the rest. Of these the three greatest were nature-gods—Anu, god of the sky, Enlil (Ki) of the earth, and Ea, of the deep.

But there were many other deities, each of whom had his or her special rites and festivals. For instance, there was the young god of vegetation, Dumuzi, who every year died and descended to the Underworld. Each spring he was resurrected by the goddess Inanna, to whom he was then ritually married. Such ceremonies, with their obvious nature-symbolism, have their parallels among other ancient peoples such as the Egyptians (Osiris and Isis), the Greeks (Persephone), and the Syrians (Thammuz, later Adonis). Each symbolises the cycle of life and death in the vegetable world.

Men have investigated Mesopotamian sites since the early part of the nineteenth century; such men as Claudius Rich, James Silk Buckingham, H. C. Rawlinson, Grotefend, Austen Henry Layard, George Smith, and Hormuzd Rassam were among the pioneers of Mesopotamian excavation and research. With the turn of the century the great German archaeologists entered the field, notably Dr. Koldewey, whose work at Babylon from 1899 to 1914 was one of the most remarkable archaeological achievements of all time. The Americans at Bismayeh, the French at Kish, the British at Nimrud,[1] carried a stage further the painstaking methods which the German scholars had developed, but, says Seton Lloyd, 'all this work was secondary in importance compared with the strong line of scientific development apparent in the activities of the Deutsch-Orient Gesellschaft.'[2]

During the twentieth century efforts were made to establish the successive stages of development of Sumerian-Akkadian culture. Three phases were eventually recognised, identifiable by characteristic pottery. Phase One, the 'Al Ubaid' style, was discovered by Sir Leonard Woolley, Phase Two, the so-called 'Uruk' period, by the Germans at Warka, and S. Langdon of Oxford found Phase Three at Jamdat Nasr, which name is now applied to the characteristic painted jars of this period.

[1] Important excavations have been carried out at Nimrud in recent years by the British School of Archaeology in Iraq.
[2] *Foundations in the Dust*—Seton Lloyd: Penguin Books. London, 1947.

Sumer and Babylon

But perhaps the most fascinating prehistoric site excavated in Mesopotamia was Hassuna, near Nineveh, by the Iraqui Government's Department of Antiquities. This discovery was made quite recently, in 1947. To quote again from Mr. Seton Lloyd's absorbing book:

'During the months that the mound was under excavation the horizon of pre-history once more receded several centuries. Revealed in the simplest terms of archaeological evidence was a new and earlier chapter in what may reasonably be called civilised man. As a nomad he had first ventured out of the mountains on to these grassy uplands above the Tigris. Here at the junction of two streams he had first camped and remained long enough to reap a store of wild barley. In the lowest stratum at Hassuna were the ashes of his camp-fires, and grouped around them the simple paraphernalia of his household—flint weapons, bone implements, and the first crude pottery vessels. At the next stage he had learnt to sow as well as reap, and his nomad habits were forgotten. Primitive adobe houses began to appear, and the improved pottery was ornamented with painted designs. Near the surface was a well-built village with the practical economy of an agricultural community almost completely developed. Seventy centuries later the modern village of Hassuna is run on much the same lines.'

It was from these primitive beginnings that the great city-states of Sumer evolved over a period of some two thousand years.

Unlike their confrères in Egypt the archaeologists in Mesopotamia had to work, not among enduring monuments of stone, but in mounds of crumbling mud-brick, sinking their shafts into ancient rubbish-pits, painfully tracing the outlines of walls of which only the faintest evidence remained. Yet from their work, and from the study of the thousands of 'cuneiform' tablets, scholars have been able to bring before our eyes a vivid picture of the Sumerian, Babylonian and Assyrian civilisations, so that we know almost as much about the political history of these peoples, their religious and social customs, as we do of the Egyptians.

In 1927 the British archaeologist, Sir Leonard Woolley, made a discovery which excited not only archaeologists, but all men and women whose imaginations respond to the appeal of the remote past. Perhaps part of the appeal was in the name—Ur of the Chaldees—the city from which Abraham came. Some of it was due to the fact that Woolley found, deep beneath the debris of a long-dead city, intact graves of important—probably royal—personages, who died five thousand years ago.

And these were not mere crumbling skeletons surrounded by a handful of barbaric ornaments, but the richly-clothed bodies of kings, queens, and their attendants; there were helmets and crowns of gold, golden drinking-cups, statues ornamented with gold and lapis-lazuli, gold daggers, ornaments of silver, a harp of gold and mosaic, an inlaid gaming-board, and other objects. But there was something else. As these fragile things were gradually brought to light by the patient hands of the archaeologists, they told a story which was both horrible and magnificent. It revealed, among these ancient people, a depth of faith—or of credulity—which to us is inconceivable; and also, perhaps, a degree of courage which few of us can even imagine, let alone attain. For a brief moment human beings of the twentieth century A.D. came into contact with those of the twenty-seventh century B.C. and found that, contrary to sentimental assumptions, they were *not* 'just like us'.

Woolley uncovered a number of graves, deep beneath the earth, and consisting of chambers of *stone*—which must have been brought from thirty miles away. These stone-built tombs lay at the foot of deep pits, which had been approached by steep ramps; the whole being subsequently filled in with earth. Some of the tombs were intact, though the bodies and their equipment were decayed and damaged by falling earth; others had been partially robbed. But all revealed a common system of burial and a similarity of funerary ritual. Inside each stone chamber was the body of the king or queen in full regalia of gold, silver and semi-precious stones, with their golden drinking-cups held to their lips. In the same chamber would usually be found two or three skeletons of lesser men. Outside, in the great pit, and sometimes even in the ramp leading to it, lay the bodies of men, women, and animals. In one pit the archaeologist found the remains of two wagons, with their oxen, and the bodies of grooms and riders lying beside them. In another he found sixty-eight women, all of whom had originally been buried wearing red woollen robes, and head-dresses of gold or silver.

In another pit lay the corpses of soldiers in helmets of copper, their copper spears beside them. Beside some of the women musical instruments had been laid; lyres and harps made of wood (which had decayed, but the impression remained on the soil) ornamented with gold, silver, horn, and shell. They may have been court musicians. All these people, men and women, lay in orderly rows. There was no sign of violence or disturbance, such as would have been evident if they had been clubbed or stabbed. The ladies' elaborate and delicate golden head-dresses were in place, even though the skulls were crushed by the weight of earth. In one pit a harp had been placed *on top* of the bodies, evidently by someone who had entered the death-pit after the bodies were inert.

Beside some of the skeletons were small cups.

Woolley concluded that these men and women—who from their dress and ornaments were not mere slaves—had walked down the ramp into the pit, lain down, and taken poison or perhaps a drug such as opium or hashish, which would have rendered them unconscious. The wagons would have to be backed down the ramp, the animals slain, after which the grooms and riders also took poison. One can imagine the solemn rites which would accompany such a burial, the chanting, the prayers and offerings. For a brief time the rows of bodies, in their bright costume, the gold and silver of their ornaments gleaming in the sun, would lie open to the sky. Then at last the earth thudded down on them, sealing them from sight for five thousand years.

In his book describing these discoveries, Woolley gives one of those little human details which strike the imagination more vividly than all the sombre funeral splendours of the Kings of Ur. Of the sixty-eight female bodies found in one death-pit, twenty wore gold head-bands, which of course were perfect. From the presence of certain oxides in the soil, the archaeologist suspected that the other ladies of lesser rank had worn silver head-bands, but he could not prove it. Until one day, when examining one of the decayed skeletons, he came upon a little blackened metal object, which on being cleaned proved to be of silver. Suddenly Woolley realised what it was. It was a silver head-band, *which had been rolled up*. Perhaps its owner had been late dressing for the ceremony and had put it in her pocket, intending to unwind it and put it on before she lay down with her companions. But she forgot. The cloth of her robe protected it from corrosion, and this, and the fact that it was rolled into a tight spool, preserved it when the others had perished.

The other cities of the Mesopotamian plain, Uruk, Lagash, Nippur, Kish, and others, enjoyed a similar standard of culture to that of Ur, but until about 2400 B.C. they remained independent. Sometimes they made war on each other—the famous 'standard of Ur', discovered by Woolley, shows well-armed infantry soldiers and war-chariots—and there would no doubt be diplomatic exchanges and alliances. But in the twenty-fourth century B.C. there arose one of those dynamic leaders of men who occur from time to time throughout history. This great leader, Sargon, achieved in Sumer what Menes had accomplished in Egypt eight centuries earlier—he brought the land under one rule. He was a northerner from Kish and founded a new city, Agade, which became the capital of Akkad.

One by one he subdued the Sumerian cities, until he commanded the entire land down to the Persian Gulf. But, unlike the Egyptian king, he was not content to stay within his own boundaries—probably because his land had no natural frontiers, as Egypt had, but was surrounded by envious kingdoms. These, if not brought under his control, could soon become a menace. So he pushed eastward into Elam, and westward across Syria and the mountains of the Lebanon until he reached the sea. Thus the two earliest civilisations—Egyptian and Sumerian-Akkadian—now fronted on to the ocean which was to be the common meeting-ground of many peoples. There is a possibility that Sargon may even have invaded Cyprus, and he certainly penetrated into Asia Minor. His successors repeated these exploits, notably Naram-Sin, who penetrated as far as Diyarbekir in Northern Assyria, and deep into the Zagros mountains of Persia. His memorial stele is in the Louvre, Paris. But within a couple of centuries this first Empire of the ancient world, founded by Sargon, collapsed under the impact of barbarian pressure from the east.

In about 2125 B.C. the city of Ur, already a powerful kingdom six centuries before, rose to pre-eminence under its king Ur-nammu, who proclaimed himself 'King of Sumer and Akkad'. He reunified the kingdom and founded a dynasty which lasted about one hundred years. The cities of Larsa, Umma, Nippur, Eridu, Lagash, flourished under his rule, and it is to his reign, of some eighteen years, that we can date some of the greatest architectural achievements of the Sumerians. In his own city of Ur he built the huge temple to the moon-goddess Inanna, with an 80-foot high tower, rising in stages from a base of 200 feet by 140 feet—with a base 77 feet thick.

'He seemed,' writes Woolley, 'to build for all time and shrank from no amount of labour to that end, and it is no wonder that his reign of eighteen years did not suffice for the completion of all that he planned.'

But long before Woolley's time a previous, less scientific archaeologist, J. E. Taylor, had ruthlessly dug into the great *Ziggurat* (tiered tower) of the temple of the moon-goddess. He found, hidden in the brickwork near the top of the tower, baked clay cylinders with long inscriptions giving the history of the temple. Though the inscriptions date from only 550 B.C., during the reign of the last king of Babylon, they state that the temple was founded by Ur-nammu and Dungi, his son. It was these clay cylinders, found more than eighty years ago, which first identified the city as that of 'Ur of the Chaldees', the home of Abraham, from whom the Jews were proud to trace their descent.

Ur-nammu's achievements were many. He was more than a great builder. During his reign literature flourished, weights and measures were standardised, and text-books of the Sumerian language were employed in the schools. Like Imhotep, architect to King Djoser of Egypt, he was probably an intellectual leader, who gathered round him men of many talents. Unfortunately few written records of his reign have ever been found. We know of him only through later writings, and through the great buildings of which ruined fragments still survive. His ruling line lasted until about 2025 B.C., when again disaster struck Sumer. Once more invading hordes poured in from east and west, among whom were the Amorites and the Elamites mentioned in the Old Testament. There are divided views on what happened. Some say that Sumerian civilisation never recovered from this joint attack. Others believe that the Amorite powers took over peacefully, and that there were always two ethnic cults in Sumer. But Ur was certainly destroyed. There survives, however, one of those great laments which occur so frequently in later Semitic literature—e.g. in the Old Testament—the elegy of a Sumerian poet wandering among the ruins of Ur.

> *O thou city of high walls, thy land has perished.*
> *O my city, like an innocent ewe thy lamb has been torn away from*
> *thee;*
> *O Ur, like an innocent goat thy kid has perished . . .*
> *Thy lament which is bitter—how long will it grieve thy weeping*
> *lord?*
>
> *Its walls were breached; the people mourn . . .*
> *In its lofty gates, where they were wont to promenade, dead bodies*
> *lay about.*
> *In its spacious streets, where feasts were celebrated, scattered they*
> *lay . . .*
> *Its corpses, like fat placed in the sun, melted away . . .*
> *The old men and women who could not leave their homes were*
> *overcome by fire.*
> *The babes lying on their mothers' laps like fish were carried off by*
> *the waters . . .*
> *The judgement of the land perished. The people mourn . . .*[1]

In Egypt, when that poem was written, the peoples of the Nile Valley had begun to recover from the anarchy which followed the

[1] Translated by S. N. Kramer, in *Sumerian Mythology*. American Philosophical Society, Philadelphia, 1944.

collapse of the Old Kingdom. The strong kings of the Twelfth Dynasty had reunified the shattered State; the Middle Kingdom had begun. For several centuries after the sack of Ur, while the Senusrets and the Amenemhets ruled a united Egypt, the peoples of Mesopotamia were a prey to barbarian conquerors, though here and there minor kinglets achieved brief local power. But in about 1792 B.C. a new sun arose in the north, in a city which up to that time had been of no great importance. Its name was Babylon.

Although much of the material wealth of ancient Sumer was destroyed, the immaterial elements of the old culture tended to survive, and chief of these was the precious art of writing by which knowledge could be recorded and transmitted. From these records we know that, very early in of the Second Millennium, a young man named Hammurabi became king of Babylon, and such was his energy and military ability that he managed to secure control of the entire country. Like Sargon long before him, he then advanced westward as far as the Mediterranean, and eastward into Elam. He also conquered Assyria, in the north, a kingdom which was later to develop into an Empire even mightier than that of the Sumerians. But there is no record of his having been in contact with the Egyptians.

Hammurabi's greatest achievements were in the field of law and administration. Numerous documents of his time have survived, including part of the royal correspondence, but the chief monument of his reign is the famous Code of Laws, in which he incorporated laws and usages of business and social life which went back far into Sumerian times. Hammurabi was not the inventor of these many laws; he codified them.

In the early years of our century French archaeologists digging at Susa found a shaft of black diorite engraved with a long inscription in cuneiform.[1] It was the Code of Hammurabi, one of the most important documents in the history of the human race. Here we find the first written statement of the primal law of revenge—'an eye for an eye, a tooth for a tooth'. None the less, it represents an extraordinary advance on the legal customs of

[1] It was carried to Susa, the Elamite capital, by an Elamite king to celebrate his victory over the Chaldeans in the twelfth century B.C.

primitive societies. For instance, the *lex talionis* can only be applied through established courts; a man may not take the law into his own hands.

The Code of Hammurabi is worth studying by anyone interested in the evolution of law. There are regulations governing such matters as liability for military service (and exemption), control of trade in alcoholic drinks, fixity of tenure, banking and usury, the responsibility of a man towards his wife and children, including the liability of a husband for the payment of his wife's debts.

Hammurabi's Code was harsher on the upper-class offenders than on a poor man committing the same offence. Death was the penalty not only for homicide, but for theft, adultery and bearing false witness in cases involving the accused's life. But the graded penalties show a great advance on primitive laws, and contemporary legal texts show that the harsher penalties were rarely exacted.

Women's rights were safeguarded. A neglected wife could obtain a divorce 'on condition that she had always led a blameless life'. Even a concubine who had become a mother was entitled to the restitution of whatever she had brought with her, or a pecuniary indemnity appropriate to her social position. Professional men such as doctors and architects were kept on their toes. If a house fell on its owner, or a doctor injured his patient, the man who built the house, or treated the patient, might suffer death, mutilation, or at least a heavy fine—an idea which has much to commend it.

During the long reign of Hammurabi Babylon was the capital of an Empire, governed under the king, by officials whom the monarch appointed and dismissed. It was their responsibility to implement the legal code which he had drawn up, and which was applied throughout the land. Military power also increased, thanks to improvements in the Old Sumerian war-chariot; spoked wheels took the place of solid wheels, and instead of asses, horses were used. Improved communications made possible tighter administrative control, and the rapid despatch of troops when necessary.

The horse seems to have been introduced from the steppes of Turkestan. Before about 2000 B.C. the chief pack animal was the ass, a native of East Africa. But neither the horse nor the wheeled vehicle was known in Egypt until about 1600 B.C. when the conservative Egyptians had to adopt them in order to resist their better-equipped enemies.

After Hammurabi's long reign his kingdom survived for only a few decades. Gradually it became weaker, and once again invaders from the north and east began to make inroads, plundering the rich cities, burning crops, carrying away captives. Towards the latter end of the Second Millennium a new power began to rise in the north; the dreaded Assyrians, the 'children of Ashur', 'a nation delighting in war', were on the march. When Babylon emerges into history again, round about 1300 B.C., it is as a dependency of the Assyrian Empire.

There remains the question: 'What did the Sumerians look like?' As a general rule, archaeologists tend to develop a personal affection for the ancient peoples whom their labours have brought to life. Egyptologists generally admire the Ancient Egyptians; Hellenists love the Ancient Greeks, which is understandable; one even meets Assyriologists who claim to like the Assyrians—an almost incredible feat.

But the amateur of archaeology can afford to take a less partial view, and, to the writer, the Sumerians, with all their virtues, rank far below the Egyptians in charm and humanity. Unlike the Nile Valley peoples who, to judge from their portraits, were a slender, elegant race, the peoples of the Tigris-Euphrates Valleys were a singularly unattractive lot. From their paintings and sculpture there emerges a picture of a short, swarthy, bearded people, with a strongly Semitic cast of feature, inclined to run to fat in middle age, with thin lips, prominent noses and protuberant eyes. Their pop-eyed gods, presumably modelled on themselves, are as repellent to the eye as their names are to the ear. Compare 'Amun-Re' with 'Marduk', or 'Osiris' with 'Dumuzi'. It is the same with the names of their kings. 'Ramesses' has a noble ring, but it is difficult to feel awe for a king called 'Dungi'. . . .

If the reader who is inclined to dismiss this as frivolous prejudice visits a Museum which exhibits both Sumerian and Egyptian sculpture, the comparison may convince him.

But now it is time to pause and retrace our steps. We have watched Egyptian civilisation develop from a group of scattered independent communities into a unified kingdom. We have seen how, between 2800 B.C. and 2270 B.C., a succession of powerful kings—the first pyramid-builders—ruled a prosperous Egypt, and that after a 200-year interregnum, another dynasty rose and re-united the kingdom, reigning over it, though with lessened control, throughout the Middle Kingdom (2100–1700 B.C.). Meanwhile, in Mesopotamia, another civilisation grew up, at first consisting of independent city-states, united at first by Sargon of Akkad for two hundred years, then torn apart by invasion, reunified by Ur-nammu, King of Ur, in 2125 B.C., only to be dismembered again a century later. Finally, we have seen the young king of Babylon, Hammurabi (*circa* 1792 B.C.), reviving the glories of the Sumerian civilisation, and pushing the frontiers of his empire into Elam on the east, Assyria on the north, and the Mediterranean in the west. After less than a century this empire, too, succumbs to the in-evitable pressure of new peoples and, at the time when Egypt's Middle Kingdom ended, with the invasion of the Asiatic 'hyksos' or 'shepherd kings' (1700 B.C.), there is no strong centralised government either in Egypt or Mesopotamia.

Now, for a time we will leave Asia and travel westward, across the deserts of Iraq and Syria, breasting the high barrier of the Lebanese mountains, thickly forested, and so to the sea. We have left the barren deserts and parched steppes behind. Ahead of us, for five hundred miles, glitters the sea—less than two hours' flight in a modern aeroplane, but in the days of Sumer and Akkad, and of early Egypt, an ocean as vast and little-known as the Atlantic and Pacific were to our Elizabethan ancestors. And as we travel westwards in space we move backwards again in time, to 2700 B.C. when Cheops is building the Great Pyramid, and the officers and concubines of the kings of Ur march down the ramp to be buried in their masters' tombs.

South of us, on our left, lies Egypt; north, on our right, are the mountains of Anatolia, inhabited only by wandering herdsmen and pastoralists who are still living in the Stone Age. North-west of us lies Europe; the countries which we now know as the Balkan block—Bulgaria, Roumania, Greece, Yugoslavia—and beyond lies the Italian Peninsula, France and Spain. But in none of these lands, in 2700 B.C. is there anything approaching a civilisation. There are only forests and mountains and plains, with groups of wandering hunters, and here and there small neolithic settlements gathered along the banks of a river, or on the shores of a lake.

Now, at last, an island looms up out of the 'wine-dark sea'; a long, narrow island, only 35 miles wide at its broadest point, and ribbed with high mountains, some of them snow-capped. This is Crete. Here there are no alluvial valleys and no life-bearing rivers. Yet here, too, a civilisation is beginning; the first civilisation in Europe; the third oldest in the world.

CHAPTER VIII

The Island Kings

To tell the story of the rise of the Cretan civilisation requires the vision of a poet. Philologists, studying the Egyptian hieroglyphs or the Sumerian cuneiform, can piece together the recorded history of these two great civilisations. But as soon as we reach Crete a different atmosphere surrounds us—that of legend and myth. Here are no written documents—save a few dull inventories of tradesmen and officials. The archaeologists, admittedly, can show us splendid many-storied palaces of stone, fine roads, houses, and some delicate frescoes and exquisite miniature sculpture. But the mysterious Minoans, the slim-waisted men with grave, enigmatic faces and dark curling side-locks, the fashionable ladies with their elaborate coiffures, jewelled snoods, and flounced skirts, cannot speak to us. We can only wonder at their coloured frescoes, at the processions of young men carrying long, tapering *rhytons* or offering-cups, at the wasp-waisted women with ringleted hair, naked breasts and elegant gowns, sitting with all the insouciance of court beauties at some boring ceremonial function; and *chattering*, chattering, always chattering . . . about what?

We shall never know, for the Cretans have left us no chronicles, stories, or written poems, unlike the obliging Egyptians (who knew the Cretans and could have told us), and the podgy trading Sumerians, who didn't know them and wouldn't have approved of them if they had. But, when the archaeologists and historians fail, a poet sings to us, a Greek who lived long after the last Cretan palace had crumbled into ruin, who never knew the original island people, but who set down in immortal verse the legends which have descended to him through more than six centuries.

The Island Kings

Out in the deep, dark sea there lies a land called Crete,
A rich and lovely land, washed by the waves on every side
And boasting ninety cities.
One of these cities King Minos ruled
And enjoyed the friendship of almighty Zeus.

As Homer speaks, we see again the blue, sun-sparkled sea, and the mountains rising almost sheer from it, their peaks adrift in cloud. Our sails, filled by the warm Mediterranean wind, draw us across the dancing waves to a sun-bright harbour of white stone. Spray bursts against the jetty; the brown-skinned harbourmen come running; and high above them, companioned by clouds, rises Mount Ida, birthplace of the King of Gods.

But King Minos—does not that strike a chord somewhere? Minos, the tyrant, who commanded that each year seven youths and maidens should be brought from Athens and sacrificed, for his pleasure, to the Minotaur, a monster half-bull and half-man, who dwelt in a labyrinth beneath his palace. And there was the Greek hero, Theseus, with whom the King's daughter fell in love. Another writer, Apollodorus, tells how she enlisted the aid of Daedalus, the cunning smith, and:

'at his suggestion she gave Theseus a thread when he went in. Theseus fastened it to the door, and, drawing it after him, entered in. And after having found the Minotaur he killed him by smiting him with his fists; and drawing the thread after him made his way out again . . .'

But this is all legend, surely? But wait, Apollodorus has more to tell about Daedalus. Minos discovers his daughter's perfidy, and suspects the smith. Daedalus and his son decide to fly from Crete:

'Daedalus constructed wings for himself and his son, and enjoined his son, when he took flight, neither to fly too high, lest the glue should melt in the sun and the wings should drop off, nor to fly too near the sea, lest the pinions be detached by the damp. But the infatuated Icarus, disregarding his father's instructions, soared ever higher, till, the glue melting, he fell into the sea called after him Icarian, and perished.'

The furious Minos follows Daedalus to Sicily, where the craftsman had taken refuge with the king of that island, Cocalus.

'Minos pursued Daedalus, and in every country he searched he carried a spiral shell and promised to give a great reward to him who should pass a thread through the shell, believing that by that means he should discover Daedalus.'

Minos knew human nature. He also knew the vanity of the scientific mind. The specialist-craftsman, 'the cunning worker in bronze', was no longer a mere humble worker for his lord, useful as a maker of weapons. He had become a technician, an engineer, an indispensable adjunct of power. But, like some modern technocrats, he had his Achilles heel—vanity. Cunningly Minos baited his hook:

'Having come to Camicus in Sicily to the court of Cocalus, with whom Daedalus was concealed, he showed the spiral shell. Cocalus (lord of Sicily), took it, and promised to thread it, and gave it to Daedalus.'

Such a challenge was irresistible to Daedalus. He knew well that Cocalus, his new lord, was incapable of working out mathematically the convolutions of the shell, just as Ariadne's lover could not hope to memorise the twists and turns of the Labyrinth. So:

'Daedalus fastened the thread to an ant, and, having bored a hole in the spiral shell, allowed the ant to pass through it. But when Minos found the thread passed through the shell, he perceived that Daedalus was with Cocalus, and at once demanded his surrender.'[1]

The first great archaeologist to explore Crete, Heinrich Schliemann, was guided there by such legends. He was a German business man whose belief in the literal truth of Homer had already led him to make great discoveries at Mycenae, on the Greek mainland. Schliemann paid one visit to Crete, acquired land for excavation, but died before he could begin the work. The torch was handed on to an Englishman, Sir Arthur Evans, who went to

[1] Apollodorus. Library. William Heinemann Ltd., Harvard University Press. Loeb Classical Library 1921.

the island in search of a writing system. Once he had settled there, Crete took hold of him.

Evans, son of a distinguished archaeologist, had received the conventional education of the British upper middle-class. After Harrow and Oxford, he had become, successively, an energetic traveller in Europe, a war correspondent in the Balkans, and Curator of the Ashmolean Museum, Oxford. But academic life in a university city bored him, and his methods in reorganising and modernising the Ashmolean, a venerable institution which some University authorities would have preferred to remain venerable (and useless), so distressed them that they were relieved when in 1899 he turned his attention to Crete.

Unlike Schliemann, who had been attracted by the Homeric legends surrounding the island, Evans's motives were much more practical. He was looking for a system of writing. Some years earlier, with John (later Sir John) Myres, he had been intrigued at finding, in the antique shops of Athens, numerous small engraved stones which seemed to him to be inscribed with some kind of pictographs (picture-writing). He was told that they came from Crete, where the peasant women wore them around their necks as charms.

Up to this time it had been assumed that, unlike the Egyptians, the Sumerians and the Babylonians, Europe was illiterate until the Greeks borrowed the Phoenician alphabet. Evans was not so sure. He began to dig at Knossos, an ancient site mentioned by Homer, in a valley a few miles south of the modern port of Heraklion, in northern Crete. Within a short time he found a large number of clay tablets inscribed with pictographs similar to those he had identified on the 'bead-seals'. But he found much more. He found the remains of an enormous stone-built palace, or rather a series of palaces, the lowest foundations of which could be dated from the beginnings of recorded history. He noted in his diary:

'The extraordinary phenomenon—*nothing Greek, nothing Roman* . . . Even Geometrical (seventh century B.C.) pottery fails us— though as *tholoi* (tombs) show, a flourishing Knossos existed lower down. . . . Nay, *its great period goes at least well back to the pre-Mycenean period.*'

Evans had come in search of a system of writing, but in a few weeks he realised that he had discovered a hitherto unknown civilisation. To the interpretation of that civilisation, which he called Minoan (after King Minos), he devoted a large part of his wealth, and the rest of his long life.

Evans was a meticulous scholar, though he had a powerful but disciplined imagination. As more and more of the Palace of Knossos came to light, with its brilliantly coloured frescoes depicting the ancient people who lived in it four thousand years ago, its storage magazines, broad stairways of fine white gypsum, courtyards and rooms of state, that romantic, sensitive imagination had to be kept firmly in check—because, willy-nilly, these discoveries seemed to confirm in a most uncanny way the essential truth of later Greek legends which had been regarded as myths and nothing more. The little clay tablets, inscribed with unknown picture-writing, defied his efforts at interpretation, although he wrestled with them for more than forty years. But, on the other hand, there *was* a Bull. In the North Entrance Passage of the Palace he found fragmented remains of a great coloured fresco depicting the animal charging. In another part of the Palace he discovered something even more fantastic; a spirited fresco showing, without a shadow of doubt, a young man in the act of somersaulting over the back of a charging bull, while a young girl in 'toreador's' costume waits behind to catch him. Had there been, perhaps, some ritual sacrifice? Were these the young men and women of Athenian legend who were sent every year as a sacrifice to the Minotaur—the bull-monster?

But there was the Labyrinth. Where was that? Once again the scholar and the poet in Evans struggled for mastery. For, although there was no sinister underground cave below the palace, there was a complicated drainage system with shafts and tunnels broad and high enough to accommodate a man—a construction which would have seemed supernatural to the primitive Greeks who visited Crete long after the glories of Minoan civilisation were merely a folk-memory. Again, the complex plan of the Palace, with its innumerable corridors and courts, was itself a labyrinth.

And what a Palace it was! Built of finely-masoned stone, it had originally risen to a height of several stories. Corridors and stair-cases were supported by tapering timber columns, of which the charred remains survived. The drainage system revealed a knowledge of hydraulic engineering hardly exceeded in the twentieth century. One suite of rooms, which Evans called 'The Queen's Megaron' (or Hall), had a private bathroom (with a hip-bath) and even a w.c. with a flushing system. Who was the architect who achieved such technical mastery some two thousand years before the birth of Christ, in a tiny island lost in the Mediter-ranean, far away from Egypt, Sumer and the Indus valley, the only other countries in all the world which could boast a civilisa-tion? Was there a Cretan Imhotep? And once more Evans the archaeologist was forced to reconsider the ancient Greek legends. 'One of these ninety cities King Minos ruled. . . .' and had not Minos employed a cunning artificer named Daedalus?

For more than forty years Evans worked in Crete. He built a comfortable rest-house beside the Knossian Palace, calling it appropriately 'The Villa Ariadne'. He devoted a large part of his considerable fortune to excavating and carefully preserving the remains, so that later generations would see, not merely a tumbled heap of ruins, but an accurately-planned reconstruction of its principal elements. The Great Staircase of three flights (originally four) was unearthed, and its original timber pillars (long since decayed) replaced by facsimiles of brick and ferro-concrete. He employed skilful architects to assist him. A Swiss artist, Gilliéron, was engaged to restore the fragmented frescoes, the only remaining evidence of the physical appearance of the peoples who ruled over Crete four thousand years ago. This prodigious work of restora-tion, the product of more than thirty years of devoted work by many men, was eventually handed over to the Greek Govern-ment.

Though Evans was the pioneer of Cretan archaeology and during his lifetime its acknowledged leader, others worked devotedly in that fertile field, and, from 1908 onwards, excavated other sites in the island. Frederico Halbherr, the Italian scholar, a friend of Evans, dug out another Minoan palace at Phaestos, on the south coast. East of it, at Gournia, two Americans, Miss Boyd and Mr. R. B. Seager, laid bare a Minoan town. French scholarship made its contribution by excavating yet another palace at Mallia, and Halbherr turned from Phaestos to unearth the beautiful 'Royal Villa' at Hagia Triadha. A young Englishman, John Pendlebury, who became Evans's principal assistant and 'Curator of the Knossian Palace', did valuable research into the origins of Cretan civilisation. A career which promised to be brilliant was tragically ended when Pendlebury was killed fighting beside the Cretan Resistance. His book *The Archaeology of Crete* remains one of the most readable and authoritative works on the subject.

From the work of these and other scholars a pattern began to emerge. The men and women who excavated in Crete had no dated 'king-lists' to help them. The only way in which they could date approximately an 'occupation-layer' was by finding in it a dateable object from a known civilisation. Fortunately this happened from time to time. Egyptian and other objects began to turn up in the Cretan palaces, and as these could be dated fairly precisely, it was possible to date Cretan objects—e.g. pottery—found in the same context. For instance, if Cretan vases of a certain type were found in association with an Egyptian statuette dating from 1800 B.C., it was fairly certain that the pottery also dated from or near that period. Then, if similar Cretan pottery turned up on another site, even though no dateable objects were found, it was probable that it too dated from near the beginning of the Second Millennium. This, of course, is an over-simplification, because obviously a single Egyptian object might conceivably be considerably older than the layer in which it was found. But by studying comparative data from several sites, a broad system of chronology could be established.

The imposing palaces which showed evidence of having been rebuilt several times were the product of the middle and later stages of Cretan civilisation. But deep beneath these buildings, as Evans and his colleagues sunk their trial pits, lay deposits left by earlier generations of Minoans who were not palace dwellers. Near the bottom were flint tools and weapons, testifying to an

3(a) Palace of Phaestos (Crete)

3(b) Court Ladies (fresco from Palace of Knossos, Crete)

3(c) Reconstruction of Throne Room, Palace of Knossos, Crete

3(d) The 'boy-god'. Statuette found in Palace of Knossos,

almost continuous occupation of the same site from the New Stone Age onwards. These early deposits were, in fact, roughly contemporary with the pre-dynastic period in Egypt—i.e. before 3200 B.C. when Menes united the Two Lands.

Thus, over thirty years, from the study and classification of an incoherent mass of pottery, faience, fragmented frescoes and cult-objects, Evans was able to trace the development of Cretan civilisation from its beginnings down to the fall of Knossos in about 1400 B.C. Much is necessarily vague and sometimes conjectural compared with Sumerian and Egyptian chronology, but an outline can be observed.

Evans believed that the ancestors of the Minoans came to the island between 4000 and 3000 B.C. They had reached a neolithic stage of development, using well-shaped stone implements, and must have been seafarers. At first they were cave-dwellers, but later they built primitive shelters. As for their origins, no one can be sure. Evans suggested that they were Asiatic, and Pendlebury pointed out that their nearest cultural connection, judging from the type of artefacts, was with Anatolia and Syria.

But the Minoans of the civilised epochs were a Bronze Age people, like the Dynastic Egyptians. How did the original Asiatic settlers, cut off from the rest of the world by a great expanse of ocean, learn how to work in bronze? Without superior techniques they could never have achieved such a mastery of stone-cutting and building. People from the outer world must have taught them, but who were these skilled craftsmen?

The reader may recollect that at the beginning of Chapter III we referred to the discovery by Professor Percy Newberry that cult-signs of the peoples of the Egyptian Delta in pre-dynastic times (before 3200 B.C.) included the 'crossed spears' of Sais, the 'figure-of-eight' shield, the 'Harpoon', the 'Mountain', the 'Double-Axe' and the 'Dove' (or Swallow). It is a curious fact that *all* these symbols, with the possible exception of the Harpoon, are also found in Crete. But one of the most important symbols of the later Minoan period was the Trident, which later became the symbol of Poseidon, god of the Sea (Neptune). May not this, too, have evolved from the Harpoon-symbol? As for the Double-Axe,

H

that became in time the emblem of Zeus himself, King of the gods; one finds it carved on sacred pillars in Crete, and it was used in Minoan religious ritual. The Figure-of-Eight shield was another characteristic Cretan object; one finds it painted on frescoed walls; and on the tiny 'bead-seals' warriors are depicted carrying it; and when the Minoan culture spread to the mainland of Greece, the Mycenean Warrior-lords had it engraved, in lion-hunting scenes, on their beautiful bronze daggers which Schliemann found at Mycenae.

Of course, it is true that the Egyptians of historical times had cultural relations with the Minoans, but their influence is slight; in any case, such symbols as the Double-Axe, the Figure-of-Eight Shield, and the Trident, which figure prominently in Minoan buildings of the Middle Minoan period (*circa* 1800–1550 B.C.) were of very slight importance to the Egyptians of this period; they never appear on temple or tomb inscriptions. But to the Minoans they were sacred, and since, among all peoples, religious symbols are usually the oldest and most revered, it seems more than possible that these signs were brought to Crete by Egyptian settlers from the Delta who arrived round about 3200 B.C.— possibly refugees driven out of Egypt when Menes invaded the Delta lands. If this is true—and of course there are no written records to confirm it—it would explain how the crafts of bronze working, the manufacture of faience (famous in the Delta, as in Crete), and other arts were first brought to the island. (On the other hand the art of bronze-working may have been introduced from Asia Minor.)

But the Delta cult-signs are not the only evidence pointing to this conclusion. We have also noted in Chapter III that there was a strong *Libyan* element in the early civilisation of the Egyptian Delta. The Libyans came from the western desert; they had their own language, which was still spoken in the area as late as the time of Herodotus. They had characteristic clothing and a special method of wearing their hair. Their goddess was Neith, whose capital was at Sais, and whose emblem was the 'Crossed-Spears'—also one of the cult-signs of Crete.

Now one of the features of male dress at this remote period—

that of the pre-dynastic Delta culture—was the so-called 'Libyan sheath', which, like the medieval 'codpiece', protected the genital organs. The Minoans wore the same sheath. Young Libyan men are shown in primitive statuettes wearing their hair with a long, curling side-lock falling over the shoulder. So did the Minoans of historical times—e.g. the famous fresco of the 'Cup-Bearer', which Evans found at Knossos. These are not the only examples. Pendlebury noted that in very early tombs excavated at Messara, in southern Crete, 'idols or human figurines were found entirely divergent in type from the old Neolithic class, but identical with those found at Nagada' (a pre-dynastic site in Egypt).

It is possible, therefore, that the rich Cretan culture owed its origin in part to those mysterious, almost unknown Delta people who founded the first civilisation of Egypt.

'During the thousand years which archaeologists call for convenience the Early Minoan Period (*circa* 2800–1800 B.C.), the population of the island increased rapidly. Important towns grew up on the coast. . . . The most prosperous settlements were in the east, although in the south the Messara plain became well populated. With the concentration of population in towns and villages arose a class of professional craftsmen; art, especially that of the potter, flourished. Life became easier; communications were improved. Foreign relations—especially with Asia, Egypt, and Libya—became easier. But in metal work the Minoans were still backward. Sculpture is in its infancy and the seal-stones were of poor design and quality.'[1]

During this period there were no palaces.

The epoch which Evans called the Middle Minoan Period (*circa* 1800–1560 B.C.) coincided with the space of time which, in Egypt, separates the end of the Middle Kingdom, through the troubled 'Hyksos period' (when Asiatic invaders occupied northern Egypt), to the rise of the Eighteenth Dynasty (approximately 1555 B.C.), which marked the beginning of Egypt's imperial age. In Sumer it ran parallel with the period beginning with the rise of Hammurabi (1792 B.C.) down to the collapse of the Sumerian civilisation and the rise of the first Assyrian Empire.

[1] *The Bull of Minos*—Leonard Cottrell: Evans Brothers, London, 1953.

From 1800 to about 1550 B.C. (these dates are necessarily approximate), while Egypt was plunged in anarchy and Sumer decayed, the peoples of Crete, isolated and protected by their encircling ocean, were free to develop in peace. The advances which they made are astonishing. The three separate divisions into which the island had been divided began to coalesce. The population, ever-growing, began to spread west of Mount Ida. And Knossos, in the north, gained ascendancy over the rest of the island, becoming the chief centre of political power. Phaestos, in the south, may possibly have remained independent. Again, one can see the pattern of development in Egypt and Sumer repeating itself in Crete: centralised power; unified control; organised exploitation of natural and technical resources. And the results were similar.

Instead of living only in scattered settlements, the Minoans began to build palaces at the centres of power; though the word 'palace' is misleading. These magnificent many-storied stone buildings were not mere royal dwellings—they were a combination of royal residence, religious shrine, factory, and administrative centre. There is no modern parallel in the western world; in Great Britain the nearest would be a big medieval or Tudor country house or a big land-owning abbey like Bury St. Edmunds. At Knossos lived the king (who was probably also the Chief Priest), his family and court, and in a separate part of the huge many-chambered building hundreds of 'civil servants', record and filing clerks, store-keepers, revenue officials, naval and perhaps military officers, and, of course, the priests had their offices and dwellings—though the more important would probably have houses of their own outside the palace precincts. There were also workshops for the legions of craftsmen—potters, workers in stone, copper-smiths, bronze-workers, etc.

From this nerve-centre at Knossos—and possibly also from Phaestos—well-made roads radiated over the island, linking up the towns and villages into one integrated system. Written records were kept of food, oil, slaves, vehicles, weapons, tools. Although Evans never succeeded in deciphering these documents (apart from recognising that they were inventories), a young British scholar, the late Michael Ventris, managed to read them within the last five years—a brilliant feat of scholarship.

During this period Minoan culture became a unity. Bronze tools were developed, making it possible to cut fine masonry; buildings were carefully planned; hydraulic engineering reached a high pitch of development—for Crete, unlike Egypt and Sumer, is subject to heavy rainfall in the winter; the waters had to be mastered. So, over the years, the Minoans learned to plan and build elaborate drainage systems, and to store water. Also, as the palaces were high, it became necessary to find some means of lighting the inner apartments; the answer was found in the 'light-well', exactly as used in modern office blocks in London and elsewhere. But this was more than three thousand years ago.

A question which will arise in most people's minds is: 'where did the wealth come from?' Crete was quite rich as a food producer, though it is a relatively small, rocky island, with no fertile valleys and few plains. But there were other sources of wealth. A later Greek historian, Thucydides, repeats an ancient legend concerning King Minos, who, he states:

'is the earliest ruler we know who possessed a fleet, and controlled most of what are now Greek waters. He ruled the Cyclades, and was the first coloniser of most of them, installing his own sons as governors. In all probability he cleared the sea of pirates, so far as he could, *to secure his own revenues*' (my italics).

Thucydides, of course, was only repeating a tradition, but he was a great historian; he was two thousand three hundred years nearer Minos than we are; and he would not have repeated this story unless he had faith in its truth. And all the archaeological evidence indicates that it is true. Following up Evans's discovery, other archaeologists began to find examples of characteristic Minoan pottery on the mainland of Greece, in the Aegean islands in Cyprus—even as far away as Syria and Egypt. Moreover, Evans and others noted that again and again nautical symbols appear on Minoan pottery; the dolphin, the sea-urchin, and the octopus.

This, then, was the source of Crete's wealth, and the civilisation it made possible—extensive maritime trade, protected by a powerful fleet, with a little discreet colonisation where practicable.

The parallel with more recent colonial empires is too obvious to need stressing.

Now, for the time being, we leave Crete at the peak of her power, and return to Egypt as she gathers strength for her first bid for empire.

CHAPTER IX

Clash of Empires (1)

We are approaching one of the most absorbing, complex, and bewildering epochs in human history. Up to now it has been possible to study the developments of Egyptian, Mesopotamian and Cretan civilisation in isolation. But during the first half of the Second Millennium (between 2000 and 1500 B.C.), they begin to meet at the fringes. At first these contacts are like the delicate, probing antennae of mutually suspicious insects; later they are locked in combat, and, in some cases a struggle ensues which ends in the defeat of one or the other. Moreover, other cultures come into view—the Myceneans in Greece, the Hittites in Asia Minor, the Mittani on the 'great bend' of the Euphrates, and the Phoenicians (or Canaanites), who had long been established on the mountainous coast of the eastern Mediterranean. It is no longer practicable in a book of this length to look at each civilisation independently. Somehow one must strive for a 'bird's-eye view', but this, inevitably, means that some details will be lost. Only the broad outlines, the most prominent features of the historical landscape, will be seen. Readers requiring a more detailed study of the various civilisations which now come into our range are advised to consult the bibliography at the end of this volume.

At the beginning, our best focal point is that area of land stretching between the east coast of the Mediterranean, northwards to Asia Minor, southwards as far as Arabia, and eastwards as far as the Syrian desert. This territory, part mountainous, part desert, is now divided between the independent states of Israel, the Lebanon, Syria, Jordan, and Iraq. During the 2,000 years preceding the beginning of the Christian era it bore several names, and was the meeting-place and battle-ground of many peoples,

including the Phoenicians and large numbers of Semitic peoples—
Amorites, Edomites, Moabites, etc., and the Hebrew tribes with
whom they warred, and who eventually established the kingdoms
of Israel and Judah.

For simplicity we shall call this district Syria-Palestine.

The ancestors of the Jews seem to have come from Lower
Mesopotamia, the land of the Sumerians. Abraham himself came
from Ur of the Chaldees. The date at which he left the Sumerian
city by the Euphrates and led his tribe into the deserts to the
north-west is not known with certainty, but it was probably about
1800 B.C. It must always be remembered, when reading the Old
Testament, that in its present form it is the work of fairly late
writers, working from documents and oral traditions of a much
earlier age. Therefore, although modern archaeology confirms to
an amazing degree the comparative accuracy of Biblical history,
there are anomalies and discrepancies due to this later editing by
writers whose main purpose was didactic. They were concerned
more with religion than history.

Many of the Old Testament stories were undoubtedly brought
by the Jews from their original home in southern Mesopotamia;
e.g. the account of the Deluge, which occurs in the Sumerian
epic of Gilgamesh. At first such tales were handed down orally
from generation to generation, and to them were added, later, the
history, achievements and sayings of the Patriarchs. Then came
the Exodus from Egypt, the wanderings which followed, and the
founding of the Mosaic Law. In time these traditional accounts
were gathered together and written down, until at last they were
compiled and edited in a collection which, in its present form,
dates from about the sixth century before Christ.

Writing, which originated as a mere technical convenience,
became in the hands of the gifted peoples of Mesopotamia and
Egypt, a mighty power, able not only to transmit knowledge, but
to influence men's minds, stir their emotions, and exalt their
spirits. The man in a reed hut beside the Nile who first scrawled a
few crude signs on a potsherd, or his cousin in Mesopotamia, who
made little wedge-shaped marks on a piece of damp clay, was
forging a tool more powerful than the swords of all the conquerors

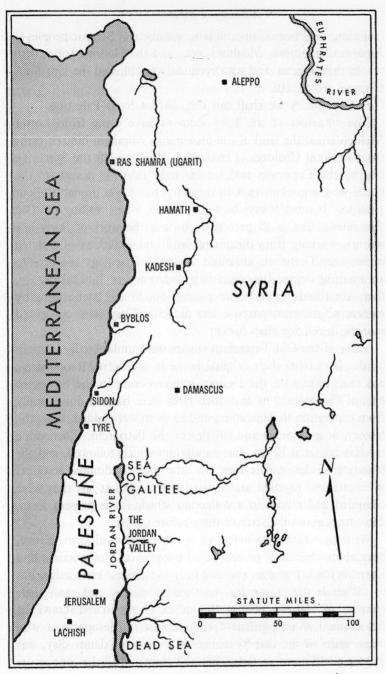

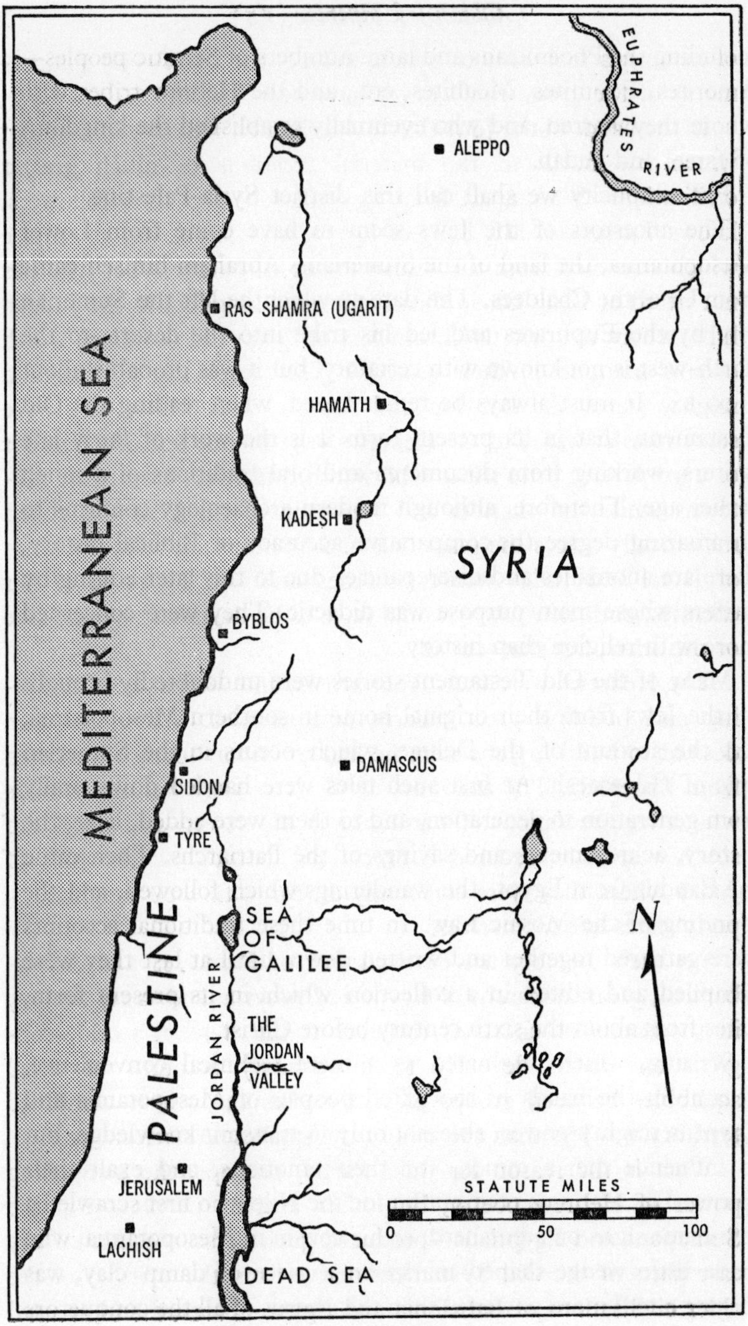
EUPHRATES
RIVER
ALEPPO
RAS SHAMRA (UGARIT)
MEDITERRANEAN SEA
HAMATH
KADESH
SYRIA
BYBLOS
DAMASCUS
SIDON
TYRE
N
SEA OF GALILEE
PALESTINE
JORDAN RIVER
THE JORDAN VALLEY
STATUTE MILES
0
50
100
JERUSALEM
LACHISH
DEAD SEA

of history; a tool without which, indeed, the names and achievements of the great would never have been known.

In the hands of the Jews that tool fashioned a literary monument which has outlasted the material creations of much greater civilisations. Who, apart from Egyptologists and their followers, knows Tuthmosis III, King of Egypt, who carved out an empire which stretched from the Sudan to the Euphrates? Yet who has not heard of King David, head of a petty kingdom in the Judean hills, whom the priestly chroniclers of Egypt did not deem worth even a mention in their records? They knew the Hittites and mighty states like Babylon and Assyria, with which they were sometimes at war. But the Hebrews were merely one of a number of unimportant little tribes who watched fearfully from their hill-towns while the chariots and war-train of the Pharaohs rolled majestically across the plain below. Sometimes, indeed, the kings of Israel and Judea would become vassals of Egypt or of her enemies, and their towns would have to be destroyed by one side or the other; but that was all.

The Hebrews were indifferent artists, and incapable of designing and building great palaces and temples. When Solomon desired to build in Jerusalem he had to import foreign workmen from Phoenicia. The ancestors of the Jews were Beduin nomads who, after generations of wandering in the deserts and steppes of south-west Asia, secured a precarious foothold in the hills of Judea where they were constantly at war with their neighbours, petty states like themselves.

Yet their memory has outlived that of Ramesses and Ashurbanipal, great monarchs of Egypt and Assyria, and every Sunday in thousands of churches throughout the western world, congregations listen devoutly to bloodthirsty accounts of tribal squabbles between groups of semi-barbarians, whose combined territory was less than the area of the smallest American state.

What is the reason for this? Partly, perhaps, the compelling power of Hebrew poetry; but other ancient peoples—e.g. the Sumerians and Egyptians—produced great verse, too, and in any case parts of the Old Testament derive from the writings of the older civilisations of Babylonia and Egypt, absorbed and re-used by the Jewish scribes. For instance, one of the Psalms can be parallelled, almost word for word, in an Egyptian hymn of the fourteenth century B.C. Many of the Proverbs come from Egypt and Sumer. The story of the Flood, in Genesis, probably derives from a Sumerian epic dating from long before the time of Abraham. The traditional site of the Garden of Eden was in Sumer.

But the fact remains that the Hebrews produced a religious literature which, translated into Greek and carried to Europe by Christian missionaries, has influenced our moral values as profoundly as Roman law has affected our system of government and Greek philosophy our thought. The answer to the question lies in the intense religious and prophetic genius of the Hebrew race. How and why this developed it is difficult to understand. The facile explanation, which has its adherents, is that the Hebrews were a race of wanderers, like the Beduin Arabs, accustomed to the barren deserts and wide skies, an atmosphere which did not encourage belief in the anthropomorphic gods of the settled peoples; hence the Jewish hatred of 'idolatry' and 'graven images', and their obsession with the 'One God', Jaweh, creator of all. But Akhnaten, the 'heretic king' of Egypt in the fourteenth century B.C., had the same idea, and his people had been settled in the Nile Valley for at least two thousand years. In any case, both the Egyptians and the Mesopotamian river-dwellers originally came from the desert.

The writer's opinion, for what it is worth, is that Hebrew religious thought originated in the minds of a few mystics who were temperamentally in revolt against the hedonism and luxury of the older civilisations. Originally, perhaps by sheer force of economic circumstance—the pressure of population—men such as Abraham were forced to lead their kinsmen away from the settled valleys and find a new home beyond the hostile deserts in which they wandered for so many years.

The wilderness was the proving-ground for their dogmas, and by sheer force of personality they imposed these beliefs on their followers who, not unnaturally, frequently fell below the standards of their leaders and 'went a-whoring after false gods'. The austerity of desert life, the recurrent disasters and misfortunes—famine, drought, defeat by enemies—would naturally encourage, in a people of such a temperament, belief in the 'wrath of Jaweh' (Jehovah), in a 'jealous god' who exacted penalties for disobedience to His will (as interpreted by the prophets) and who insisted on ceremonial observances, abstinence, sexual 'purity', and the like. The Ten Commandments and the Mosaic Law in general are just such a code of ethics as would be necessary among a wandering tribe whose very survival depended on strict discipline. They would have been laughed at in the comfortable, settled cities of Egypt and Babylonia. Unfortunately (or fortunately, according to one's point of view), they have been carried, via Christianity, to our modern world; and from Calvin, through Cromwell, down to the bigots of the present day, puritanism of one form or another continues to influence men's lives. In thousands of conventicles, from Salem to Stockholm, the older, fiercer code of the desert nomads is still preached, and reverently accepted by those to whom sensual pleasure is synonymous with 'impurity'.

In 1550 B.C. however, the Jews had not settled in Palestine, and five hundred years were to pass before King David ruled from Jerusalem. Egypt was just emerging from one of her periodic lapses into anarchy. Some century and a half earlier, the Middle Kingdom had collapsed and, following an interval during which rival princes fought with each other, Asiatic invaders entered the Delta, bringing with them an invention which was new to the Nile—the horse-drawn chariot. These invaders, called the 'Hyksos' by Manetho, came from Syria-Palestine, and appear to have been bands of (possibly) Semitic wanderers of the kind which for centuries had been pushing westward from the deserts of western Asia towards the sea. Taking advantage of the unsettled state of Egypt, they swarmed into the Delta, bringing with them their flocks and herds (hence their name—the 'Shepherd Kings'). Although semi-barbaric, they appear to have assimilated, at least superficially, the culture and language of the Nile Valley, and several Hyksos 'kings' appear on the Turin papyrus king-list. Among these is a certain *Jacob-her*. The name has tempted some historians to suggest that among these Asiatic wanderers there may have been ancestors of the Hebrews. Jacob, son of Isaac, could have lived at this period.

At this time there existed along the coast of Palestine and Syria a string of powerful city-states whose inhabitants were seamen and traders, although they also occupied much of the mountainous hinterland. These were the 'sons of Canaan', called by the Greeks and Romans the Phoenicians. At Arvad, Tyre and Sidon, Byblos and other places along the coast they had built strong cities, each ruled by its local king; these monarchs, to judge from the contents of their rock-cut tombs, had been considerably Egyptianised. Their weapons, dress and furniture show obvious Egyptian influence, but they themselves were Semitic. In 1550 B.C. they were already an old-established people, grown rich by trade. Their land was fertile, growing olives, figs, and wheat, while the mountains of the Lebanon were thickly covered with timber—the famous 'cedars of Lebanon' so much in demand in the ancient world. Hemmed in between the mountains and the sea, they were always subject to the pressure of land-hungry peoples pressing in from the deserts to the east, so from an early period they developed a maritime trade, and in later years became the principal carriers of the Mediterranean.

They were also skilful miners, and in later years exploited the gold and silver deposits of the Yemen, in Arabia, the coast of Ethiopia (Somaliland, in East Africa), and even got as far as Spain, where they founded a colony called Tarshish (modern Cadiz). At this time, however, it is doubtful if they had penetrated so far.

Round about 1550 B.C. a family of Theban princes from Upper Egypt managed to unite the peoples of Egypt and attack the invaders. One of these men was Sekenre, who became Pharaoh. In later years he became the hero of a folk-tale which is probably based on historical fact, in which he is depicted as the saviour of his country. When, in the 'eighties of the last century, Emil Brugsch found a secret tomb containing the bodies of a large number of Pharaohs from the Seventeenth to the Twenty-first Dynasties, he discovered the body of Sekenre, whose name was inscribed on the mummy-wrappings. When these wrappings were removed from the head, the archaeologists found grim confirmation of the truth of the ancient tale. The king's skull was hideously mutilated. A great hole had been smashed through it by some weapon, and the lower part of the face was also damaged. Almost certainly Sekenre met his death in battle, fighting the Hyksos.

An even greater king was Kamose, who pursued the invaders into Syria, and after him a succession of warrior-kings consolidated and extended the Egyptian dominions. For by this time the Egyptians, who for more than fifteen hundred years had been protected from invasion by their very isolation, found that they could no longer protect themselves by guarding the frontiers of Egypt. In the new age, Semitic peoples were constantly moving into Syria, and behind them a new and powerful Empire—that of the Hittites—had arisen in Asia Minor, and was steadily moving down into Syria, intimidating the smaller states. The Pharaohs of the Eighteenth Dynasty (1555–1350 B.C.) realised that the only way by which they could protect their country and ensure its survival was to gain control of the country from which their old enemies, the Hyksos, had come. They were forced to push the frontiers into Syria and beyond, and to compel the obedience of the petty kingdoms of Canaan and of Palestine, from which they could also exact tribute, and thus to create a buffer between themselves and the Hittites.

Thus began Egypt's Imperial Age, and her emergence as a world power—in the sense that the Egyptian 'world' was bounded by the Euphrates in the north-east and the lower reaches of the Nile in the south. The Nubians of the south were old enemies. Semibarbarians, they could be dealt with. But the peoples of Asia presented a much greater problem.

The Hittites (or the 'Kheta', as the Egyptians called them) are a mysterious people. Archaeologists who first discovered their great walled capital at Boghaz-Keui, in Turkey, wrote enthusiastically of the 'Hittite Empire', but no one has any clear idea as to how far it actually extended. The Hittites are mentioned in the Old Testament. In Genesis xxiii, 10, they are called 'the children of Heth', dwelling at Hebron in Palestine, to which Abraham went to buy 'the cave of Machpelah' as a burial-place for his wife. The vendor was 'Ephron the Hittite'. But at this period, about 1800

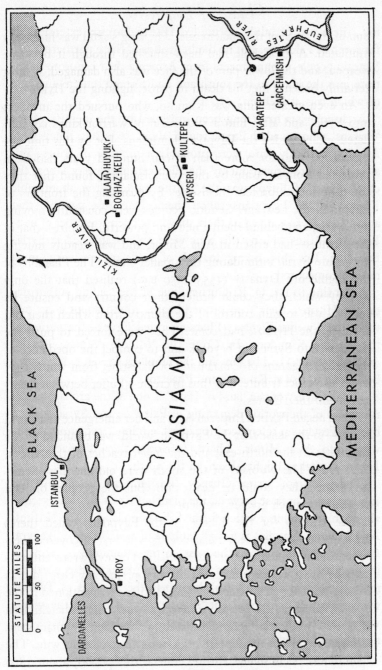

EUPHRATES RIVER

CARCEMISH

KARATEPE

ALAJA-HUYUK
BOGHAZ-KEUI

KULTEPE

KAYSERI

KIZIL RIVER

N

ASIA MINOR

BLACK SEA

MEDITERRANEAN SEA

ISTANBUL

TROY

DARDANELLES

STATUTE MILES

0   50   100

B.C., there was certainly no unified Hittite Empire, extending as far south as Palestine. But no doubt groups of these northern, non-Semitic people, mountaineers from Armenia, had begun to penetrate into the lands to the south and had formed settlements, one of which was at Hebron.

Archaeologists have long been intrigued by the identity of the 'Hyksos' who invaded Egypt round about 1670 B.C. They were Asiatics, certainly, and were probably a mixture of tribes. But after they were driven out by the Eighteenth Dynasty kings, the chief object of Egypt was the Hittite nation—'the abominable Kheta', as the Egyptians called them. It is just possible that among the Hyksos invaders there may have been a number of non-Semitic Hittites who by this time were well-established in Syria-Palestine. But this, owing to lack of sufficient evidence, must remain conjectural.

According to Dr. O. R. Gurney, one of the leading authorities on the Hittites, their true history begins round about 1900 B.C. when the Twelfth Dynasty Pharaohs ruled Egypt—the period of the Middle Kingdom. In Crete the 'Middle Minoan Period' (1800–1550 B.C.) had begun, and the fabulous Cretan palaces were beginning to rise at Knossos and Phaestos.

The discovery of the 'land of Hatti' is one of the archaeological romances of the world. Beginning in Palestine and Syria (guided by Old Testament references) the quest led the investigators northward into Asia Minor. There, in 1907, they discovered the Hittite capital at Boghaz-Keui, in the north.

'The last step,' writes Gurney, 'is significant because of the fundamental contrast between the plains of Syria and the essentially highland country which formed the homeland of the Hittites. Asia Minor (Anatolia) is a high table-land which rises in general from the Aegean coast to the west, to the mountains of Armenia in the east . . . Seen from the Syrian plains, these northern mountains form a mighty wall known to the Romans as Taurus, which seemed to the ancient geographers to divide the whole world east of the Mediterranean into "inner" and "outer" (i.e. northern and southern) halves.'[1]

The Hittites—O. R. Gurney: Penguin Books, London, 1952.

4(a) The Lion Gate, Mycenae

4(b) Reproductions of objects found in the shaft-graves at Mycenae

4(c) Hittite city of Alaja Hüyük

4(d) Reliefs of Hittite warriors, Yassilikaya, Boghazkeui

From these mountains, completely contrasted with the fertile valleys of Egypt and Mesopotamia, came the third most ancient civilisation in western Asia—that of the Hittites. Their settlements in Syria-Palestine were merely advanced outposts. Their home was far to the north, shut off behind the high mountain-wall of the Taurus.

They were quite unlike the Egyptians or the Sumerians. Their sculptured reliefs depict them as short, heavily-built, with markedly non-Semitic faces; prominent bones, sloping foreheads, long noses and short chins. 'Parrot-faced', Sir Harold Nicolson unflatteringly calls them; it is not a bad description. Their dress reveals their mountain origin. No diaphanous garments of fine linen for the Hittites, but long robes of wool, worn over a tunic, high conical caps, and long 'Russian' boots turned up at the toes. Their women, equally unattractive, wore a long veil or shawl covering their heads and falling to the feet.

Their gods were borrowed from Babylonia, as was their writing-system. They readapted the cult of the Babylonian goddess Ishtar (Ashtoreth) and in turn may have introduced her worship to Lydia, in Asia Minor, where the Greek colonists of later years worshipped her as Cybele, 'the great mother of the Gods'.

In these early years, at the beginning of the Second Millennium, the Hittites were split up into separate independent cantons ruled by local kings, but in time the country was united under one king, and this unification led gradually to the same centralisation of power which had occurred in Egypt and Sumer. The later Hittite kings traced their descent back to a certain King Labarnas. The writings tell us that:

'Formerly Labarnas was king; and then his sons, his brothers, his connections by marriage and his blood relations were united. And the land was small; but wherever he marched to battle, he subdued the lands of his enemies with might. He destroyed the lands and made them powerless and he made the seas his frontiers. And when he returned from battle, his sons went each to every part of the land, to Hupsina, to Tuwunauwa, to Nessa, to Landa, to Parsujanda and to Lusna, and governed the land, and the great cities of the land were assigned to them.'[1]

[1] O. R. Gurney, *op. cit.*

I

By 1550 B.C., when the Eighteenth Dynasty began in Egypt, the Hittites had moved out of their mountain stronghold and were thrusting southward into Syria and beyond. And as they advanced they overawed and made vassals the petty kings of Syria, and Palestine, who by themselves counted for little in the balance of power, but under Hittite domination could become a menace to the Egyptians. There was also another kingdom, that of the Mittani, an Aryan people who had settled in the 'great bend' of the Euphrates. More powerful and highly organised than the Semitic kingdoms, the Mittani were a more serious threat to the Egyptians, particularly if they allied themselves with the Hittites.

And now we see one of the most extraordinary and heroic episodes in the history of the world. The Egyptians who, for more than two thousand years, had been living a settled existence in their protected valley, free from the danger of invasion, roused themselves to the danger and, for the first and only time in their long history, became a military people. Since Menes first unified the Two Lands, seventeen centuries before, they had already known two rich blossomings of civilisation; the Old and the Middle Kingdoms. They had also seen their land torn apart by civil war and then watched helplessly as swarms of Asiatics, primitive herdsmen whom they despised, squatted on their rich land, aping in their crude way the material forms of the ancient culture of Egypt. The Egyptians, led by such warriors as Sekenre and Ahmosis, threw the intruders out. But they did not stop there. They adopted the new-fangled device of the invaders—the horse-drawn chariot—and moulded it into a deadly weapon. Their young men learned the art of war; leaving their pleasant valley, they penetrated into the mountains of Palestine and Syria, and beat the mountain-dwellers at their own game. To realise what an achievement this was one must recognise that few Egyptians had ever seen a mountain, or felt rain and snow on their faces. To them water came, not from the sky, but from the Nile. So when they entered Syria and encountered rainstorms they could only account for them by imagining a 'heavenly Nile'. In the Pharaoh Akhnaten's hymn to the sun, which dates from about 1370 B.C. occur the lines:

All the distant lands, thou makest their life.
Thou settest a Nile in heaven that it may descend for them.
And make floods on the mountain like the sea,
In order to water their fields in their towns. . . .

What this warfare was like we can learn from Egyptian literature of this period. There is, for instance, this sardonic account by an old campaigner in Syria, reproving one of his subordinates, the 'scribe of the army', Amenemope, who had boasted to his superior that he was now a *mahir* (hero). The old veteran was a little irritated by the youngster's presumption, so he wrote:

' "I am a scribe, a *mahir*" you say again. There is truth in your words, we say. Come forth so that you may be tested . . .'

'A horse is harnessed for you, swift as a jackal . . . and it is like a storm of wind, when it goes forth. You loosen the reins and seize the bow. Now we shall see what you can do. I will tell you the nature of a *mahir*, and show you what he does.'

'Have you gone to the land of Khatti' (e.g. the land of the Hittites) 'and have you seen the land of Upe?'[1]

'Khedem—do you know the nature of it, and Igedii too; what is it like? Sumur of Sesse—on which side of it lies the town of Kher . . . What is its stream like? Have you marched to Kadesh and Tubikhi? Have you gone into the region of the Beduins with the auxiliary troops of the army?'

'Have you not trodden the road to Meger, where the sky is dark by day, and is overgrown with cypresses and oaks, and with cedars that reach high heaven?[2] There are more lions there than panthers and hyenas, and it is girt about with Beduins on every side.'

'Have you not climbed Mount Shewe? Have you not trodden it, while your hands are laid upon . . . and your chariot is battered by the ropes as your horse is dragged . . .'

'Let me tell you of . . . *beret*. You shrink from climbing it and prefer to cross by the stream. You understand how it tastes to be a *mahir*, when you carry your chariot on your shoulders.'

---

[1] Near Damascus, in Syria. A Canaanite name.
[2] There were no large trees such as these in Egypt.

'When you halt in the evening, your whole body is crushed . . . and your limbs are broken . . . You waken, when it is far into the night' (i.e. the *mahir* is suddenly called to a night-alarm).

'You are alone to do the harnessing. Brother comes not to brother. The fugitives have come into the camp. The horses have been let loose. You have been ransacked in the night. Your clothes have been stolen. Your groom has awakened in the night . . . he has taken what was left and joined the ranks of the wicked' (i.e. the enemy). 'He has mingled with the tribe of the Beduins and changed himself into an Asiatic. The foe comes to pillage in secret, and they find you asleep, and when you awake you find no trace of them . . . or of your clothes and equipment. They have made away with them. Now you are a fully-equipped *mahir*, and you take hold of your ear.'[1]

Later the unfortunate Amenemope '—scribe of the Army' (i.e., quartermaster-sergeant)—has to pass through a narrow mountain pass:

'made perilous by Beduins, who are hidden beneath the bushes; some of them are of four cubits and five cubits from the nose to the sole of the foot, fierce of face, their heart not mild . . . You are alone, no helper is with you, and no army behind you. You determine to go forward, although you do not know the way. Shuddering seizes you, the hair of your head stands on end . . . your path is full of boulders and shingle, and there is no passable track. The ravine is on one side, the mountain on the other.'

Amenemope loses his chariot, and goes on on foot, leading his horse.

'The sky is open, and you fancy that the enemy is behind you. Trembling takes hold of you. Ah, that you had a hedge that you might put it on your other side! Your horse is galled by the time you find quarters for the night.'

Then Hori, the old warrior, imagines his young colleague in a predicament which has faced more than one soldier more than three thousand years after Amenemope was born.

'When you enter Joppa, you find the meadow growing green in its time' (i.e. when the season is at its loveliest). 'You find a

[1] Probably a gesture of grief.

pretty girl who keeps watch over the vineyards. She takes you to herself as companion and shows you the colour of her breasts. You are recognised and bear witness,' (i.e. betrayed to or discovered by the enemy) 'and the *mahir* is put on trial, and you have to sell your tunic of good Egyptian linen' (to facilitate his escape).

Finally, Amenemope gets back to Egypt, and, being a young officer with a position to keep up, promptly buys himself a new chariot with which to show off to his friends.

'Your yoke is put to rights . . . They give you a whip and attach it with lashes. Forth you go to fight on the field of battle, and to accomplish deeds of valour' (i.e. in the taverns of Thebes).

I have deliberately quoted this passage at some length because, in this democratic age, the war-correspondent's despatch is more highly valued than the official war communiqué. The general under whom Amenemope fought was probably Tuthmosis III, a military genius who has been justly called 'The Napoleon of Ancient Egypt'. Tuthmosis must have been one of the greatest soldiers of all time. Throughout his long, arduous life, he led his armies seventeen times into Syria and the desert wastes to the east, subduing the cities of the vassal-kings, meeting and defeating the Hittite king at Kadesh, on the Orontes, where even today the dust of his war-chariots still seems to hang over silent deserted 'tell' under the mountains which is all that is left of the Hittite city. He stormed the pass of Megiddo, riding in a chariot adorned with 'gold and electrum', following the same path which Allenby's armies took in 1916. For more than half a generation this little, squat, plump-faced man, whose mummified features can still be studied in the Cairo Museum, led and inspired his warriors, those slim-hipped, over-civilised Egyptians, the heirs of a civilisation twice as old as that of the 'parrot-faced' Hittites, and held them back. By all the rules, the Egyptians should have been too effete to resist the onslaught of the tough mountain-dwellers. But they were not.

When Tuthmosis III died, and his body was carried to his rock-cut tomb in the Theban hills (for by this time the Egyptians had abandoned the building of pyramids), Thebes was the richest and most powerful city on earth. The temple-treasuries of its god,

Amun, who was now equated with the sun-god Re (under the name Amun-Re), were crammed with the wealth of Asia—gold, silver, copper, bronze, and semi-precious stones. Most of the kings of Syria-Palestine, including those of Tyre, Sidon, Byblos, and other Canaanite cities, were vassals of the king of Egypt, sending their yearly tribute to the Pharaoh. The Cretans, too, safe behind their ocean barrier, were in close cultural contact with Thebes, and in the tomb of Rekhmire, Vizier (Prime Minister) of Tuthmosis, we can still see the dark-skinned, slim-waisted Minoans, whom the Egyptians called the 'Keftiu', bringing as offerings the typical products of their land—long, slender rhytons, vases, goblets; near the end of the line a man carries aloft a gold or silver head of the Bull. . . .

The civilisation of Egypt, the oldest in the world, had risen for the third time, more glorious than ever. To the people of Thebes, seeing the princes of Western Asia riding through their streets, educated at the Egyptian court, marrying Egyptian wives, or bringing their beautiful daughters to be espoused to the highest in the land—even the Pharaoh himself—it must have seemed that the millennium had arrived; that nothing could threaten their authority. The Babylonians of the Euphrates valley, ruled by a weak line of Kassite kings, were so subservient that they wrote pleadingly to the king of Egypt for gold, 'which, in thy kingdom, is as dust'. The 'abominable Kheta'—as described in their temple inscriptions—had been, if not destroyed, at least held in check. The Keftiu were no problem. They were fascinating foreigners from a land so remote that few Egyptians had ever seen it, who traded with Egypt on equal terms, but who also could be represented in the tomb-inscriptions as vassals of Pharaoh, bringing offerings.

'It was the confidant of the sovereign, the mayor and Vizier Rekhmire, who received this tribute'

—and the Prime Minister himself, Rekhmire, surveying the wall-panitings of his tomb, his 'House of Eternity', might say to himself —'well, that's near enough'.

And the king himself, seated in his splendid palace in Thebes, would remember the inscriptions which he had caused to be cut on the far-off cliffs of Syria, records of his conquests which would last for three thousand years, to be discovered and read by archaeologists of the twentieth century A.D. He would remember with pride the day when he led his armies across the Euphrates itself, when he went to chastise the Mittani. A strange river that. Unlike the Nile, it flowed southward, so that the Egyptians had to describe it as 'that inverted water which goes downstream in going upstream'. His conquests had opened up a new world to the Egyptians, a puzzling world in which there was a Nile in the sky, and where rivers flowed the wrong way. To 'go up' meant to leave the low-lying Nile Valley. 'To descend' meant 'to come home'. 'Foreigner' was synonymous with 'highlander'.

As for the ancestral gods of Egypt—well, Amun was king, of course; he was the god of Thebes, and as Thebes was now all-powerful, naturally Amun must be the same god as Re, who had reigned over Egypt when the pyramid-builders ruled from Memphis seven hundred years ago. The pyramids were now empty, plundered monuments lapped around by the encroaching sands. One saw them when one returned from Syria. There they were, stark against the sky as one's war-galleys swept southward to Thebes, ransacked, derelict, the home of bats. Still, they were the eternal dwellings of one's ancestors, gods such as Djoser, Khufu, and Menkaure.

But the gods of the 'Highlanders', the mountain-dwellers of Syria, and those who lived beside the Euphrates—they did not know Re, or Amun, or Osiris. Odd, that . . . still, the priests understood. That was their business. And Tuthmosis, bored and restless, tapped the arm of his throne, encrusted with gold and lapis-lazuli, thinking of the moment when once again he would mount his war-chariot and, shaking the dust of Thebes from his wheels, turn his face towards the mountains of Syria, the tented camp, the comradeship of soldiers, and 'the road to Meger, where the sky is dark by day, and is overgrown with cypresses and oaks, and with cedars which reach high heaven'.

But there were still several weeks to go; and in the meantime there was the triumphal procession to the temple of Amun-Re when he, as High Priest, must make offering to the king of the gods. One of the priests had written a poem in honour of the occasion, which would eventually be carved in deep hieroglyphs on the walls of the temple, a monument for all time. Tuthmosis glanced at the papyrus scroll on his knee.

> *I have come, causing thee to smite the princes of Zahi;*
> *I have hurled them beneath thy feet among the highlands.*
> *I have caused thee to see thy majesty as lord of radiance,*
> *So that thou hast shone in their faces like my image.*
> *I have come, causing thee to smite the Asiatics,*
> *Thou hast made captive the heads of the Asiatics of Retenu.*
> *I have caused them to see thy majesty equipped with thy adornment,*
> *When thou takest the weapons of war in the chariot . . .*

Tuthmosis, bored, lets the papyrus slip to the floor, and sits staring in front of him. His Syrian concubine comes from behind the throne, and begins to stroke his hair. He smiles.

A good poem, admittedly, and well written. But what do the priests know of war? Was it *really* like that?

In a small, dim chamber in the Temple of Amun, a scribe is writing, a sardonic smile on his grim old face. He is writing something which Tuthmosis will never see, a document which, for generations, will be used as an exercise by Egyptian schoolboys; then will lie in the earth for three thousand years until discovered by archaeologists of the nineteenth century A.D. Yet, if the king could have seen it, probably he would have smiled in sympathetic recognition.

'*Show me how to pass by Megiddo, which lies above it. You are a* mahir, *skilled in brave deeds. A mahir such as you are, is qualified to march at the head of a host! Forward, O Mahir, to shoot!*'

'*Behold there is the . . . ravine, 2,000 cubits deep, filled with boulders and shingle. You make a detour. You grasp the bow . . . You let the chieftains see what is pleasing in their eyes till your hands grow weary. And they say, "You slay like a lion, O mahir . . ."*'[1]

---

[1] All these quotations are after the translations of Erman, *op. cit.* from Egyptian documents of the New Kingdom (1555–712 B.C.) with slight modifications, e.g. substituting 'you' for the archaic 'thou'.

CHAPTER X

Clash of Empires (2)

The scene moves to Europe. Down to the first half of the Second Millennium the only civilised peoples in the world were those of Egypt and Asia—apart from the isolated kingdom of Crete, which, as we have seen, owed its origin to Anatolia and Egypt; its cultural links were with Egypt and Asia Minor. To the north, across more than one hundred miles of ocean, lay the forests and mountains of the European mainland, peopled by wandering hunters and traders. At some places—e.g. along the valley of the Danube—these wanderers sometimes formed agricultural settlements. But, here, too, men had learned bronze-working and other crafts, brought to them by travelling craftsmen,[1] the remote ancestors of the 'tinkers' of more recent times. There were trade-routes, too, linking the civilised lands of Babylonia, Egypt, and Crete with the dark hinterland of Europe.

It seems probable that such travelling traders and craftsmen would bring to the northern lands tales of the rich countries bordering the Mediterranean, where the sun shone for most of the year, where vines, figs, olives, grew in abundance, and life seemed easy. There, also, were peoples grown effete through centuries of soft living. The temptation to the northerners, inured to rain and tempest, unsettled, insecure, always on the watch for enemies, must have been great. For whatever the reason, the fact is clear that over a period of three thousand years there was a steady movement of northern peoples towards the south and the sun.

---

[1] In a tomb at Beni Hassan in Egypt there is a painted scene of such a group of craftsmen, from Palestine, visiting an Egyptian noble of the Middle Kingdom (1700 B.C.). One man is shown with a set of bellows for copper-smelting. Cf. Genesis iv. 19–22: 'And Zillah, she also bare Tubal-cain, an instructor of every artificer in brass and iron.' Tubal's half-brother was Jubal; 'he was the father of all such as handle the harp and the organ.'

In recent years doubts have been cast on the origin of the invaders. An earlier generation of archaeologists believed that they came from northern Europe and this is still standard doctrine —that they were Nordic warriors identifiable with Homer's 'fair-haired Achaeans'. Yet in fact we cannot identify who the Achaeans were in point of origin. They may have been the direct descendants of the people who invaded Greece in 1900 B.C. or they may have come into Greece at the beginning of the Late Helladic Period, *circa* 1600 B.C. Dr. Frank Stubbings, to whom I am indebted for much information on this period, reminded me that these invaders are characterised by a certain type of plain-grey pottery called *Minyan*, which has close parallels with the type of pottery found in the sixth level of Troy, also dating from the beginning of the Middle Bronze Age (1900 B.C.). It looks as if both occurrences reflect different parts of one ethnic movement, perhaps a movement *westward* through Asia Minor which led also to the establishment of the Indo-European Hittites in the centre of Asia Minor.

There is, says Dr. Stubbings, no evidence that these introducers of Minyan came from countries *north* of Greece; such evidence as there is suggests an Asiatic origin. The 'northern invaders' were never more than a philological hypothesis, at a period before pre-historic archaeology in Greece had started. Looked at broadly, one could regard (a) the Middle Helladic invasion of Greece (*c.* 1900 B.C.), (b) the establishment of Indo-Europeans in Syria, (c) the Hyksos in Egypt, and (d) the shaft-grave people of Mycenae, as *all waves of one big westward movement of peoples covering several centuries through the Middle Bronze Age.*

Within Greece itself we can see, first, an invasion of new peoples beginning round about 1900 B.C. and second, a fertilisation of this new, and apparently Greek-speaking stock (a) by Minoan culture and (b) by other cultural innovations of uncertain origin. These influences produced the Mycenean Greeks, whom we *know* were Greek-speaking, since the late Michael Ventris, a brilliant young British scholar,[1] succeeded in deciphering the 'Linear B' tablets which Evans found at Knossos. This language,

[1] Tragically killed in a motor accident shortly after this book was written.

AEGEAN SEA

THERMOPYLAE ▪

ORCHOMENOS ▪
▪ DELPHI

MARATHON ▪

SALAMIS ▪   ▪ ATHENS
CORINTH ▪
MYCENAE ▪
▪ TIRYNS

▪ SPARTA

▪ PYLOS

N

MEDITERRANEAN SEA

CRETE
KNOSSOS ▪

▪ PHAESTOS

STATUTE MILES

0   50   100

prosperous land; his ships, trading with the Aegean islands, with Asia Minor and the Levant, brought in wealth which filled the store-chambers of his towering palace at Knossos. In that great warren of white stone, scribes kept records, officials hurried along frescoed corridors, or lounged in the sun, watching the girls washing their linen in the stone rainwater tanks like Homer's princess Nausikaa in the 'Odyssey'.[1] The palace sentinels with their spears and great body-shields stood guard at the pillared porticoes; the south entrance from which flights of steps led down to the bridge and the road to Phaestos; the north entrance admitting to a corridor on the walls of which huge red bulls, with lowered horns, charged across a blue ground.

Rust-red and turquoise-blue, canary-yellow, terra-cotta, green, and splashes of vivid crimson—these were the colours which an Egyptian visitor of Akhnaten's time would see as he walked through the many-pillared corridors of the Knossian Palace. He would notice few, if any, inscriptions such as he was accustomed to see in his own country; only huge, coloured frescoes of such strange, delicate beauty that even he would have admired and wondered at them. Here a monkey was plucking saffron-flowers;[2] there a grey bird with outstretched wings soared from a rocky landscape with many-coloured veins and striations. As he descended the Grand Staircase, with its wide, shallow steps of gleaming white gypsum—there, on the wall beside him, was a procession of young Minoan men, lily-crowned and wearing tight-waisted, richly-coloured kilts. Grass and flowers waved beside their slim, muscular calves, and a butterfly hovered against the blue sky.

And, again and again, there was the Bull—sometimes alone, but more often with girl and boy acrobats leaping across its charging back; sometimes with crowds of men and women watching from a 'grandstand', the women in wide, many-flounced skirts of gay colours, puffed sleeves, bare breasts, and hair elaborately frisé.

---

[1] Sir Arthur Evans, in his *Palace of Minos*, mentions one such tank, and adds: 'the special fitness of rainwater for washing linen warrants the conjecture that the tank was used for this purpose, and Minoan Nausikaas may have made their way here from the Palace halls above'.

[2] Has any archaeologist commented on the fact that this figure of a monkey adopts exactly the same stance as the Bull?

spoken and written by the Mycenean invaders of Knossos in about 1400 B.C. was undoubtedly an early form of Greek, and 'Homeric' Greek at that. But a question which still remains unanswered is this; when did the Greeks first get to Crete, and how? They were there, writing Greek in the 'Linear B' script, by 1400 B.C. when Knossos fell. But how soon before?

Before continuing the story, I cannot resist throwing in one more subject for speculation, for those interested. We have seen how Evans was able to prove that the legends surrounding the island of Crete had a substratum of fact. Such stories are no longer brushed aside as they were by an older generation of scholars. Now consider the legend of the birth of King Minos. Zeus, king of gods, assumed the form of a bull and carried off Europa. Her son was Minos, who became king of Crete. Europa, according to legend, was the daughter of a Syrian ruler who had family connections with Egypt. Her migration to Crete is parallel, in the legend, with that of Cadmus to mainland Greece, a story too odd not to have some underlying historical event behind it. Then take Danaus, father of the Danaoi, who came to the Argolid, in Greece, from Egypt; *again* of the same family. Do these facts and fancies add up to some broad westward movement in the Middle Bronze Age? The Mycenean shaft-graves are *not Minoan*, but there is a possibility that their prototypes may be the built tombs of Ras Shamra, in Syria—more support for the odd legends of Cadmus and others invading Greece from the Levant.[1]

So much for speculation. But we do know that by 1600 B.C. when the Egyptians had begun to drive the Hyksos out of Egypt, these Greek-speaking invaders were already well established in their mountain citadels in the Peloponnese. At Tiryns, at Mycenae, and other places on the Greek mainland they had set up a number of independent settlements, each with its strong walled castle, usually on high ground, in which lived the local prince, his family and followers, who had subdued the native population, just as the feudal lords of the Middle Ages dominated and controlled the people they had conquered.

[1] I am obliged to Dr. Frank Stubbings for these suggestions.

At first these people probably remained aloof from the indigenous population, marrying within their own class, and maintaining the purity of their race. Helen, wife of Menelaus, king of Argos in the Peloponnese, was fair—according to Homer, who refers often to the 'fair-haired Achaeans'. They were a military people; war was their profession, and like other military aristocracies they probably despised the working, trading people of the land they had subdued. It is doubtful if they were even literate, but they loved poetry and music. A bard was always welcome in their halls and, like the Norman lords of the eleventh century A.D., they liked to sit over their wine in the evening and listen to a flattering recital of their heroic deeds. Such epic poems were passed on, orally, from generation to generation, until in the ninth or eighth century B.C., when writing had become more than a mere system of record-keeping, a Greek poet of Ionia set down in writing stories which had come down to him through many generations. They were stories of a world which had vanished in his day, a world in which warriors fought from chariots, carried large, heavy shields of leather, and lived in palaces of a type which, in his time, no longer existed. This poet, or group of poets, found a new way of using the traditional epic form and material; not merely to tell the tale of heroic deeds but to illustrate in that milieu the behaviour of human character. For example one of the two great Homeric epics, the 'Iliad' tells the tale of the wrath of Achilles, and the woe it brought on the Greeks when they were besieging Troy. The other poem, the 'Odyssey' is not merely an adventure-tale of the hero Odysseus, though, during his homeward journey from Troy, he suffers many hardships and dangers. It is, in essence, a moral tale of devotion to wife and home by an imperfect but very human hero.

In later years the Greeks of classical times (from 600 to 300 B.C.) regarded the events which form the background of these poems—the Trojan War and the events leading to it and following it—as history. Later generations looked upon them as legends and nothing more, even down to the nineteenth century A.D. Then Heinrich Schliemann, the German archaeologist already mentioned, went to Troy, in Asia Minor. Though some scholars scoffed at him, he began to dig at Bali Dagh, near the Dardanelles, and proved that there had existed an historical Troy; that it was not merely a myth.

Encouraged by these discoveries, he went to Greece, and in 1876 began to excavate the ancient citadel of Mycenae, near the plain of Argos. Homer had used the phrase 'Mycenae, rich in gold', and Schliemann—who was by no means uninterested in material treasure (he had made a fortune in the Californian gold rush of '49)—dug out of the rocky hill-top grave furniture of a type which the world had never seen before. In seven 'shaft-graves' he found skeletons of men and women; the men wore face-masks of gold and the women wore golden diadems and ornaments. Beside the bodies of the men lay daggers and swords of fine bronze, inlaid with hunting and battle-scenes, in which the participants carried weapons and shields, and wore armour of a type which seems to have been remembered by Homer, though he was writing at a time when they had gone out of use. For example there were representations of large body-shields, weapons of bronze, and remains of helmets made of leather sewn with slivers of boars' tusks, as described in the 'Iliad'.[1]

Schliemann believed that these objects dated from the time of the Trojan War, about 1180 B.C. But we know now that they belonged to a far earlier period, from between 1600 and 1500 B.C., when invading warrior-lords were establishing themselves in Greece, and had come into contact with the Cretan Empire across the sea. For many of the objects belonged to a type which Sir Arthur Evans had found at Crete, and which he called 'Minoan'. From later research it is now certain that these invaders, whom for convenience archaeologists call the 'Myceneans', imitated the culture of the older, Cretan civilisation. At first the contacts were probably through trade. Cretan merchants may have landed on the main-land and introduced the semi-barbaric northerners to the arts and crafts of Crete. The Myceneans began to copy the Cretans. Their women adopted the tight-waisted dresses and hooped and flounced skirts of the Minoans. Minoan craftsmen, painters of frescoes, and

[1] Recently Dr. Papadimitriou, a Greek archaeologist, has discovered yet another grave-circle at Mycenae containing rich treasures.

workers in bronze were persuaded to enliven the grim walls of Mycenean fortresses with paintings, and to make their beautifully engraved weapons—although the scenes depicted thereon (of hunting and fighting) were not the kind which the Minoans themselves liked to draw. But they introduced, in these scenes, representations of arms and weapons which were more Cretan than Mycenean. For example, on one of the daggers which Schliemann found at Mycenae is a lion-hunting scene in which one of the hunters carries the 'figure-of-eight' shield which, perhaps, came originally from far-off Egypt; it was one of the cult-signs of the Delta people whom Menes had conquered more than 1,500 years earlier.

In Egypt, after the triumphs of Tuthmosis III, a period of settled, luxurious peace descended on the land. Throughout the reigns of the Eighteenth Dynasty kings—from 1555 to 1350 B.C.—the wealth of the conquered provinces poured into Thebes. Egyptian tomb-paintings of this period show, again and again, processions of foreigners bearing offerings and, at the tail end of the line, groups of manacled captives, with their wives and children—another source of wealth. Most of this loot went to fill the treasure-houses of Amun, who had become the principal god of Egypt, equal in status with the ancient sun-god Re. In reality this meant that the priests of Amun-Re, guardians of the temple treasuries, were gradually attaining a power which almost equalled that of the Pharaoh himself. They held the keys of death and life.

The kings of Egypt and their noble followers were no longer buried in pyramids and *mastabas*. Instead, legions of workmen, who lived on the west bank of the Nile, were permanently employed in excavating huge rock-cut tombs in the limestone cliffs of Thebes, the eternal homes of the royal and ennobled Egyptians. On the walls of the long, tortuous corridors leading to the royal tombs were painted scenes representing, in minute detail, the procession of the dead monarch through the twelve caverns of the Underworld—for at this period it seems to have been accepted that, after death, the king had to pass through twelve chambers in which flowed an infernal Nile; in each of these caverns he was likely to meet gods and demons who would demand an answer to certain questions, such as these:

King: Hail, ye Gods. I know ye, and I know your names; let me not be stricken down by your blows; report not the evil which is in me to the God whom ye follow.[1]

Questioner: Who, pray, art thou? What is thy name?

King: He who groweth under the grass and dwelleth by the Olive Tree is my name.

Questioner: Pass on then.

King: I pass to a place north of the Olive.

Questioner: What didst thou see there?

King: A thigh and a leg.

Questioner: And what said they to thee?

King: That I shall see the greetings in the land there of the Fenkhu. . . .[2]

It is unlikely that these magical spells and rituals had any more rational meaning for the lay Egyptian than they have for us. Many of them dated from those infinitely remote times, more than 2,000 years before Tuthmosis III was born, when the Ancient Egyptians of pre-dynastic times lived in primitive settlements beside the great river, burying their dead in simple pit-graves in the sand. These spells, to which the rich and literate and the poor and uneducated alike were subject, were part of an elaborate trick by which the Egyptians hoped they could hoodwink the menacing powers which would try to deny them survival in the after-life. The meaning of the words was unimportant. It was their effect that mattered—like the combination which opens a safe.

But already, long before Tuthmosis III or Hammurabi or Minos, a new force had begun to stir in the human mind. Maybe it was there at the beginning, but within the historical period— i.e. after the invention of writing—we can see it in operation. Professor Breasted called it *The Dawn of Conscience*, the title of one of his most provocative books. Already, in the Pyramid Age, a thousand years before, a noble could have inscribed in his tomb the words:

[1] i.e. Osiris.
[2] E. A. W. Budge, *Book of the Dead*. Methuen & Co., London.

'*Never have I taken a thing belonging to any person.* . . .
Never have I done aught of violence towards any person.'
And a provincial governor could say:
'*I gave bread to the hungry; I clothed him who was naked
therein* . . . *I never oppressed anyone in possession of his
property.*'

Archaeologists call these statements, which can also be found
in the *Book of the Dead*, 'the Negative Confessions'. But one must
admit there was the other side of the picture. The cynical, disillusioned Pharaoh, Amenemhet I, of the Twelfth Dynasty
(1900–1700 B.C.) tells his son:

> *I gave to the beggar,*
> *I nourished the orphan.*
> *I admitted the insignificant,*
> *As well as he who was of great account.*
> *But he who ate my food made insurrection;*
> *He to whom I gave my hand, aroused fear therein.* . . . [1]

To Amenemhet the conception of 'good' and 'evil' was clear,
but the idea of returning good for evil was not. But one fact is
certain: that by this time, and probably long before, the thought
that one's behaviour in this life might be accountable in the after-
life had taken hold of the human mind. To know the combination
of the safe was not enough. What we conveniently label 'moral
values' were already in existence long before the Jewish prophets
formulated their laws.

By the time of Amenophis III, the people of Israel had already
lived in Egypt. Abraham, Jacob, Joseph, had sojourned in the
Delta with their flocks and herds, tolerated—though certainly not
loved—by the cultivated Egyptians, to whom, as the Old Testament writer says, 'every shepherd is an abomination'. [2] But the
writings of such spiritual giants as Moses and Isaiah have so
permeated our thinking that one tends to forget that the much

---

[1] *A History of Egypt*—J. H. Breasted: Hodder & Stoughton, London, 1924.
[2] Probably a reference to the 'Hyksos' invasion. The Hyksos appear to have
been nomadic herdsmen.

earlier civilisation of Egypt, with which the Israelites were in contact, also produced religious leaders.

The greatest of these was Amenophis IV, son of Amenophis III. He is better known under the name which he adopted after he broke with the Amun priesthood of Thebes—*Akhnaten*. Professor Breasted calls him 'the first individual in history'. J. D. S. Pendlebury (who excavated in Egypt as well as Crete) described him as 'the first rebel against the established order of things whom we know, the first man with ideas of his own which ran counter to all tradition, *who was in a position to put those into practice*' (my italics).

Akhnaten came near the end of a long line of illustrious kings, most of whom had been warrior-leaders, the greatest being Tuthmosis III. Successors to Tuthmosis, Tuthmosis IV and Amenophis II, maintained Egypt's power, but did not extend it. By the time of Amenophis III, active campaigning had practically ceased; the Pharaohs relied on their fleet and garrisons to hold their Palestinian and Syrian possessions from which tribute flowed into imperial Thebes, enriching the treasury of the god Amun, whose name was now incorporated in that of the king—e.g. *Amen*ophis, just as more than a thousand years before the Memphite kings of the Sixth Dynasty included in their names that of the sun-god, Re. Amenophis III, concerned at the growing power of the Amun priesthood, began to favour again the sun-god who had been worshipped by the kings of the Old Kingdom, but this time under a new name—*the Aten*, meaning 'the Disk'. The sybaritic king, living in his palace on the western bank, sailed with Queen Tiyi in their royal barge, which bore the name 'the Aten gleams', as we know from the commemorative scarab made at this period. In fact, the cult of the Aten has been traced even further back—to the time of Amenophis's predecessor, Tuthmosis IV.

'The view generally held by most modern Egyptologists is that the origin of the cult was political, and arose

(a) because of the need to set up a rival to Amun . . . and

(b) because of the need for a *universal* god who would be recognised not only in Egypt but in the Pharaoh's foreign dominions. One theory is that Amenophis III hoped that by being worshipped as *Nebmare,* the "great god", he would hold the allegiance of his subject peoples without the need for frequent displays of force'. [1]

In about the fourth year of his reign Queen Tiyi bore him a son, who was given the same name as his father. When he was twenty-one the prince married the beautiful Nefretiti, who may also have been his sister or half-sister. (Brother and sister marriages were usual within the Egyptian royal and noble families; it was probably done to ensure the right of succession to the throne, which was always through the female line.) At his *sed-festival* celebrating the thirtieth year of his accession, Amenophis III appointed his son co-regent, and for four years the two ruled jointly from Thebes. And then there was an extraordinary change—something which has no parallel in the long history of Egypt. In the fourth year of his co-regency, the young prince and co-regent began to build an entirely new capital on a virgin site over two hundred miles north of Thebes. Two years later he left Thebes for ever and established himself in his new capital, which he called *Akhetaten*—'the horizon of the Disk'. There, with Nefretiti, he lived for eleven years, surrounded by his court, nobles and officials who, like all Egyptians of their class, made tombs for themselves in their own lifetime. These tombs were cut out of the cliffs on the eastern side of the river, nearest the capital itself, unlike those at Thebes which are on the western side. From their sculptured reliefs and inscriptions, archaeologists have attempted to interpret the history of this unique period.

Sir Flinders Petrie worked there in the latter part of the nineteenth century, and the German archaeologists[2] followed him. Later, in the inter-war years, John Pendlebury and Professor H. W. Fairman, British scholars, continued the work. Practically all we know of Akhnaten and his followers is derived from a study of the tomb-reliefs of Akhetaten, and objects dug up on the site, of which the most valuable were scores of small baked-clay tablets inscribed in the Babylonian 'cuneiform'—from the diplomatic files of Akhnaten's Foreign Office.

[1] *The Lost Pharaohs*—Leonard Cottrell: Evans Brothers, London, 1949.
[2] They found the famous portrait-bust of Nefretiti, now in the Berlin Museum.

These tombs are unique in Egypt for one reason: their inscriptions and sculptured scenes refer to *one god*—the Aten—and one god only. The multifarious gods and godlings of the Egyptian pantheon—lioness-headed, jackal-headed, ibis-headed, ram-headed, even the mummified Osiris with his crook and 'flail'—are absent from these austere sepulchres. So is Amun-Re, the great god of Thebes.

Instead, in every tomb, we see carved on the wall a representation of the sun's disk, from which descend rays, each ending in a human hand, which sometimes touches the human figures of the King and Queen below. This was Akhnaten's god, the Aten. The King himself had changed his name from Amenophis ('*Amun-is-satisfied*') to Akhnaten ('*It-is-well-with-the-Aten*'). Nefretiti's name, however, was completely personal and appropriate. It means 'the beautiful woman has come'.

Although the tombs vary in size and plan, there is a marked similarity between all of them. In each appears the figure of the king and usually the queen and their daughters. In each the royal family are depicted honouring the owner of the tomb, a nobleman or official, who is usually shown (very small in comparison with the figures of the royal family) standing below the balcony of the palace receiving gifts from his royal master. In one tomb—that of a noble named Ay (of whom we shall hear later)—we see the great man's friends and followers leaping and rejoicing at the honour done to him. Hieroglyphic inscriptions record the dialogue. A sentry on duty at the palace asks:

'*For whom is this rejoicing being made?*'
and receives the reply:

'*The rejoicing is being made for Ay, the father of the God, with Tiyi*' (his wife, not the queen). '*They are being made people of gold!*'

'*You will see,*' rejoins the sentry, '*these are the beauties of the age.*'

The scene above shows Akhnaten and Nefretiti on the balcony of their palace; the lovely queen, her slim figure unconcealed beneath an almost transparent robe,[1] caresses one of her daughters, while her husband throws down gold collars and circlets to his delighted official. The accompanying inscription has preserved

[1] In some of these tomb-reliefs, the King and Queen are nude.

148

for three thousand years the homage due to one of the most beautiful women who has ever lived.

'The heiress, great in favour, lady of grace, sweet of love, Mistress of the South and North, fair of face, gay with the two plumes, beloved of the living Aten, the Chief Wife of the King, whom he loves, lady of the Two Lands, great of love, Nefretiti, living for ever ...'

The love of beauty, in nature and art, seems to have been part of the new religion which Akhnaten embraced. We know nothing of its ethical content—or even if it had any—because our sole evidence of it is contained in the famous hymn to the Aten, parts of which were inscribed on the wall of every tomb. This hymn may have been composed by the king himself, although elements in it bear a resemblance to much earlier hymns to Re. Throughout this long, religious poem there is only one object of worship—the Aten—which some authorities believe was not merely the physical disk of the sun, but its life-creating power.

> *Thou risest beautifully in the horizon of heaven,*
> *Oh living Aten who creates Life!*
> *When thou risest in the eastern horizon*
> *Thou fillest every land with thy beauty.*
> *Thou art beautiful, great, gleaming and high over every land.*
> *Thy rays, they embrace the lands to the limits of all thou hast made.*
> *Thou art Re and bringest them all,*
> *Thou bindest them (for) thy beloved son.*
> *Thou art afar off, yet thy rays are on the earth;*
> *Thou art in the faces (of men) yet thy ways are not known.*

This emphasis on the omnipresence of the sun whose rays 'embrace the lands to the limits of all thou hast made' suggests an attempt to introduce the worship of a universal god acceptable not only to the Egyptians but to the foreign peoples over whom they now ruled. This is brought out very strikingly in a further passage, already quoted:

> *All the distant lands, thou makest their life.*
> *Thou settest a Nile in Heaven that it may descend for them*

And make floods on the mountains like the sea,
In order to water their fields in their towns.

So much for the political element in the Aten-faith. But the more one reads the poem, the more it becomes apparent—to this writer, at least—that it had deeper roots. If one accepts the definition of religion as 'an habitual, all-pervading sense of dependence on, reverence for, and responsibility to a higher power', can there be any doubt of the religious quality of this passage?

Creator of germ in woman, who makest seed in man,
Who givest life to a son in his mother's womb,
Who pacifiest him so that he may not cry,
A nurse (even) in the womb.
When he comes forth from the womb . . . on the day of his birth,
Thou openst his mouth duly(?) and suppliest his needs.

Then follows the glorious salutation, like the swelling note of an organ:

'*How manifold are thy works!*
They are hidden from the face of men, O sole god,

Like unto whom there is none other,[1]

Thou madest the earth at thy will when thou was alone—
Men, cattle, all animals, everything on earth that goes on its feet,
Everything that is on high that flies with its wings,
The foreign lands, Syria, Kush, and the land of Egypt.
Thou settest every man in his place, and suppliest their needs.
Each one has his food, and their days are numbered.
Their tongues are diverse in speech, and their forms likewise,
For thou has differentiated the peoples . . .[2]

These extracts must suffice to convey an idea of this moving work. To quote it in full would require several pages.

An illusion persists in some minds that archaeologists and

[1] Our emphasis.
[2] Translated by Professor H. W. Fairman, in *Tell el Amarna* by J. D. S. Pendlebury, Lovat Dickson & Thompson, London, 1935.

scholars in general are unprejudiced men, searching for objective truth. One eminent scholar has written of Akhnaten's hymn:

'The Aten is a purely creative god. He has made all things living and provided their wants, but there his work ends. There is no feeling that he will reward good or punish evil. There is no sense of sin or even of right and wrong.'

—which is true, but the same writer adds:

'Today the impression that the art and civilisation of Amarna gives us is that of an ephemeral butterfly age with that total lack of moral standards usually associated with happy morons.'[1]

What this archaeologist really means, in the writer's opinion, is that Akhnaten and Nefretiti went around with too few clothes, that they worshipped physical beauty, valued good food and wine, and led a hedonistic existence. Also, as we shall see later, they appear to have shown a marked lack of interest in fighting other people. One feels, perhaps unjustly, that this scholar would have been happier if he had found, in Akhnaten's city, some such injunctions as those which Moses gave his followers at about the same period, such as:

And if any mischief follow, then thou shalt give life for life,
Eye for eye, tooth for tooth, hand for hand, foot for foot,
Burning for burning, wound for wound, stripe for stripe . . .
If an ox gore a man or woman, that they die; then shall the ox
  be surely stoned . . .

Judged by these austere standards, Akhnaten was not a great moral teacher, and it is absurd to try, as some writers have done, to compare him with Jesus Christ, who was born fourteen hundred years later. But, seen against the background of primitive magic and superstition from which he tried to free himself, the young king has every right to be judged as a religious revolutionary. And perhaps, even in our enlightened age, there are still a few who would not be ashamed to belong to his band of 'happy morons'.

Far to the north, across hundreds of miles of blue water, the island kingdom of Crete also seemed secure. There, as at the court of Amenophis III and of Akhnaten, the king reigned over a

[1] *Tell el Amarna*—J. S. Pendlebury, *op. cit.*

In small cult-chambers there were little faience statuettes of the Minoan mother-goddess dressed exactly like the court ladies who passed him in the corridor, but with snakes entwined round her arms, or holding them in her hands; for she was an earth-deity, and the earth-loving snake was her emblem. On sacred plinths stood the Double Axe. If only the Egyptians had been less insular and had described for us the other civilisations which they knew! Then we would have had more to feed our imaginations than a few pathetic coloured fragments of frescoes, a number of tiny bead-seals, with scenes in intaglio, a handful of statuettes of the snake goddess, and the ruins of the Palace which Evans dug from the earth.

We have, however, the Throne Room, in the heart of the palace, on the side of the Great Court opposite the domestic quarters; and here we may have an advantage over the Egyptian, who probably never saw it. For this was the Holy of Holies of the mysterious Minoan cult. It was not large—a low-ceilinged, rectangular room surrounded on three sides by a low bench, as in a cathedral chapter-house of the Middle Ages. On the far wall two painted griffins guarded a stone throne with a peculiar wavy-edged back.

It is still there—the oldest throne in Europe.

Opposite the throne a flight of steps led down to a stone-lined pit, which was never intended to hold water, for there were no outlets such as the Minoans—skilful hydraulic engineers—would have made. Other pits of this type have been found elsewhere—at Knossos, and in other Minoan palaces. Evans called them 'lustral areas', and they may have been used in some cult connected with the propitiation of the earth. Crete lies in the seismic zone, and throughout its history has suffered periodical earthquakes; this, Evans suggested, might explain the importance of an earth-deity to the Cretans.

He also pointed out that in the mythology of some ancient peoples, earthquakes are caused by a great bull beneath the earth. In a memorable passage of his book, *The Palace of Minos*, he describes his own experiences of such an earthquake:

'A dull sound rose from the ground, *like the muffled roar of an angry bull* . . . As the quickly-repeated shocks produced their cumulative effect, the crashing of the roofs of two small houses made themselves audible, mingled with women's shrieks and the cries of children . . . It is something to have heard with one's own ears—the bellowing of the bull beneath the earth, which, according to primitive belief, tosses it on its horns . . .'[1]

Evans believed that it was such an earthquake which brought about the final downfall of Knossos, which seems to have occurred round about 1400 B.C. But Pendlebury did not; he pointed out that Knossos bore the unmistakable marks of destruction by fire, and that in ancient cities earthquakes did not necessarily cause fires, such as occur in modern towns with their gas and electricity mains. Pendlebury, Evans's principal assistant, believed (as do most modern authorities) that Knossos, Phaestos, and the other nerve-centres of Cretan civilisation fell to foreign invaders.

Who these invaders were we cannot know definitely, in the absence of written records. But three facts are significant. First, we know that round about 2000 B.C., northern invaders entered Greece and that by *circa* 1550 B.C. they were firmly established at Mycenae and other centres; they were a warrior people, but their art shows strong Minoan influence. Second, after *circa* 1400 B.C., the Minoans disappeared from the scene, but for the next two hundred years the Myceneans were the leading maritime power in the Aegean Ocean. Third is the most recent—and, in some ways, most dramatic—discovery: in 1954 a young British philologist, Michael Ventris, succeeded, with the co-operation of American and British scholars, in deciphering the Minoan writing which had baffled Sir Arthur Evans for forty years. There were two forms of this writing, which Evans called 'Linear A' and 'Linear B'. 'Linear A' still defies all attempts to read it, but 'Linear B' has proved to be *an early form of Greek*—having affinities with Homeric Greek.

This 'Linear B' script also occurs on the mainland. In 1939 Blegen of Cincinatti University found 600 such tablets at the Mycenean site at Pylos, in the Peloponnese. They appear to date from about 1200 B.C., and other examples have since been dis-

[1] *The Palace of Minos*—Sir Arthur Evans: Macmillan, London.

covered by Professor Wace at Mycenae and other places. But none of the tablets discovered so far date from earlier than 1200. The oldest are those from Knossos, which appear to date from about 1400; *and only at Knossos do we find the other type of script*—the so-called 'Linear A'.

The current interpretation of these facts by Wace, Ventris, Blegen, and others, is that the Myceneans, who were of the same stock as the later Greeks of classical times, adopted the Minoan writing-system and used its characters to write in their own language—Greek. To give an over-simplified illustration, it is as if, 3,200 years from now, a future archaeologist had discovered two books, both using the Latin alphabet, but one book was in German, the other in French. If some form of the French language still survived, a philologist could probably read the French book, but if the German language had completely disappeared, it would be extremely difficult to decipher the other.[1]

What was the scene on that fatal Spring morning when the Mycenean raiders descended on Knossos? We have no written records—for the long-sought clue to the tablets which Evans found sixty years ago provides us only with a series of inventories; lists of objects—wine-jars, tripods, chariots, and occasionally slaves—of great importance to archaeologists and students of Homer, but meagre food for those who long for the poems and chronicles of that long-vanished civilisation. There remain only two elements from which to construct our picture; one is the Knossian Palace itself, with its evident marks of fire and destruction, and the mute objects which tell their own story—the block of basalt on which some craftsman was working, but left half sawn through, the over-turned ritual bowls in the Throne Room, the unctuous smoke-stains left by burning oil jars. The other element is Greek legend, especially that of Theseus and the Minotaur.

Writers who are not professional historians have to tread very carefully, lest they be accused of allowing their imaginations to falsify history. This may occasionally be permissible in an historical

[1] This is an inexact parallel because both French and German have a common root in the vanished Aryan tongue, from which most European languages are descended. 'Linear A' and 'Linear B' appear to have no such common root.

novel, but never in a work which tries—however imperfectly—to present facts. Therefore the writer has decided to leave the final word to John Pendlebury, the gifted young archaeologist whom Evans appointed as Curator of Knossos and who, had he lived, would probably have worn his mantle.

When the events which Pendlebury described took place, Akhnaten was established in his new capital; the Hittites, recovering from the blows which Tuthmosis had struck, were again advancing into Syria; in Babylon, far to the east, a feeble line of kings ruled over a kingdom whose glories seem to lie for ever in the past. The Myceneans—lusty, ambitious, their spirit still untamed by the enervating climate of the Mediterranean—were launched upon the sea, an element so unfamiliar to their ancestors that they had no name for it, and had to borrow that used by the indigenous population they had conquered—*Thalassa*.[1]

Pendlebury writes, in his *Archaeology of Crete*:

'Now there is a name which is always associated with the sack of Knossos, at least with the liberation of its subjects—*Theseus*. Names have a habit of being remembered when the deeds with which they are associated are forgotten or garbled . . . It has already been suggested that the seven youths and seven maidens may have been the mainland quota for the bull-ring at Knossos. This must be the type of detail that would be remembered, the more so in that it may well have been the sentimental reason without which no purely commercial war can ever take place . . .'

'. . . And, in the last decade of the fifteenth century B.C., when a strong south wind was blowing which carried the flames of the burning beams horizontally northward,[2] Knossos fell . . .'

'The final scene takes place in the most dramatic room ever excavated—the Throne Room. A great oil-jar lay overturned in one corner—ritual vessels were in the act of being used when disaster came. It looks as if the King had been hurried there to

---

[1] A number of other pre-Greek words survive in the Greek language—e.g. place-names ending in *-os*, like *Corinthos*, *Phaestos* and *Knossos* itself. These names are not Greek; neither are such names as *hyacinth* and *narcissus*, which have passed into our own language.

[2] Note the archaeological detective work. Pendlebury had noted the direction of the smoke stains.

undergo, too late, some last ceremony in the hope of saving the people.'

'Theseus and the Minotaur! Dare we believe that he wore the mask of the Bull?'[1]

[1] *The Archaeology of Crete*—John Pendlebury: Methuen, London, 1939.

CHAPTER XI

The End of the Eighteenth Dynasty

Before we begin the last stage of our journey, from 1400 to about 450 B.C., it is well to pause for a while and take a backward glance at the ground we have covered. At the beginning of this story, round about 4000 B.C., there was no civilised community living anywhere on earth. Eight hundred years later one such community had begun in Egypt, where a number of hitherto independent settlements had coalesced, first into two kingdoms and then into one. About five centuries later another civilisation—that of Sumer—was established in Lower Mesopotamia, also owing allegiance to one king, Sargon.

We have seen how these two valley-civilisations developed independently of each other, yet with certain common features due to similar environments. Both invented and developed systems of writing; both were familiar with irrigation, ship-building, carpentry and metal-work; both originally worshipped a large number of local gods among whom certain deities became prominent, recognised throughout the land and served by powerful priesthoods who were also the guardians of technical knowledge. Both were ruled by kings who were sometimes priests as well.

These civilisations of Western Asia both suffered changes of fortune; dynasties rose and fell; sometimes the strong centralised control was relaxed and there was anarchy and civil war. Of the two Egypt was the more stable, as, apart from the Hyksos, she did not have to suffer foreign invasion until late in her history, whereas Sumer, Akkad, and Babylon were repeatedly overrun.

We have also seen how Syria-Palestine became a battleground of states and a melting-pot of races, constantly open to waves of Semitic peoples moving northward and westward from the desert to the valley of Jordan and the fertile coast-lands. Among these wanderers two peoples stand out—the Canaanites, who established prosperous city-states along the coast of Lebanon and Syria; and the ancestors of the Hebrews, originally nomadic herdsmen who eventually settled and adopted agriculture. The Hebrews knew Egypt, and may have been among the tribes who invaded the Delta with the Hyksos, but in 1400 B.C. there was no Jewish nation. Their great period, the days of Moses and Elijah, of the Judges, Gideon, Jephthah, Samson, of the Kings, Saul, David, and the rest, were still to come. In the time of Akhnaten they were still wanderers.

To the far north, in the mountains of Anatolia, a powerful state, that of the Hittites, had arisen, which, pushing southward into Syria, had already come into conflict with the Egyptian empire. And along the banks of the northern Tigris yet another empire was rising—that of Assyria.

In the island of Crete, on the southern fringes of Europe, another great civilisation had risen, flourished for fifteen hundred years, and then been overthrown by northern invaders, the so-called Myceneans who now replaced the Minoans as the maritime power of the Aegean. They were warriors and sea-raiders, and spoke a language akin to that of Homeric Greece. They appear to have adopted the Minoan writing-system and used it to write their own language, but their only written records which have been discovered to date are inventories.

Such was the scene in about 1400 B.C. when Akhnaten ruled from his new capital of Akhetaten; a poet and a mystic who had defied the entrenched priesthood of Amun-Re, and had tried, at one stroke, to overthrow the polytheistic faith of his ancestors. Meanwhile, away to the north-east, the Hittites, recovered from the blows inflicted on them by Tuthmosis III, had begun to nibble at the fringes of the Egyptian Empire.

It is very tempting, when confronted with the written documents of Egypt, Babylonia and the Hittite Empire, to concentrate on the lives of the few human beings who can speak to us over the gulf of centuries. There is Tuthmosis and his military campaigns, and the scribe Hori who saw and described them from the standpoint of a soldier; later we shall encounter the Hittite King, Shubbuliliuma, receiving the pitiful plea of the girl-queen, Ankhesnamun, widow of Tutankhamun, that he should send her one of his sons so that she might marry him and so escape marriage to a scheming politician. The writer, hearing these faint cries from the dust-heaps of the remote past, longs to listen and to speculate ... But the temptation must be resisted, for they are only a few lone voices crying in the wilderness. Millions of ordinary men and women, who left no writings, built no tombs, lived and died through these epochs. We must consider them too.

If, then, we study the archaeological record only, as we were compelled to do during the period before the invention of writing, what does it tell us about the lives of the mute, anonymous masses at the middle of the Second Millennium? How do their lives compare with those of their ancestors who lived under Menes or Sargon? And what were their technical achievements?

Childe points out that, compared with the period 4000–3000 B.C., and the beginnings of civilisation, the innovations in science and technology during the Bronze Age were comparatively few. He cites only five; better transport and armament; the invention, in Babylon, of 'place value' in mathematical notation;[1] the invention, apparently by the Phoenicians, of an alphabetic script, probably derived from the more cumbersome hieroglyphic writing of the Egyptians; and, most revolutionary in its impact, the discovery by an unknown Armenian tribe, *of an economic process of working iron.*

In Egypt the mass of the population appears to have lived very much as their ancestors had lived in the time of the Pyramid builders. In the tombs of the Eighteenth Dynasty nobles one sees paintings almost exactly like the scenes depicted in the *mastabas* of Khufu's time—more than one thousand years earlier. The field labourers till their master's land with the same primitive tools, the butchers slaughter sheep and oxen for the sacrifice, men catch wild-fowl or harpoon fish, women reap the corn at harvest-time, or dance naked at the feast of some rich nobleman, while the guests

---

[1] A system in which the value of a sign is indicated by its position in relation to other signs—e.g. '3' by itself means three. The same figure followed by two noughts means 'three hundred'.

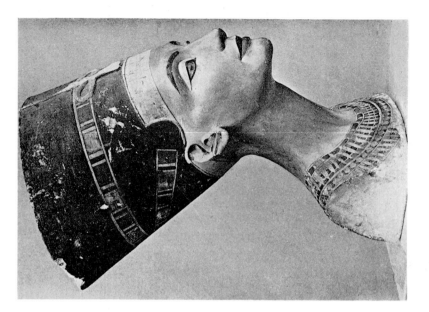

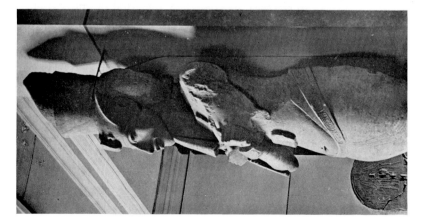

5(a) *left*: Akhnaten

5(b) *right*: Nefretiti

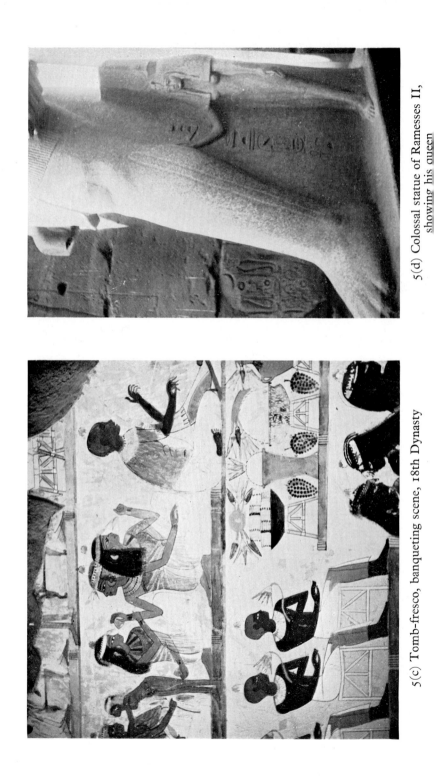

5(c) Tomb-fresco, banqueting scene, 18th Dynasty

5(d) Colossal statue of Ramesses II, showing his queen

sit with wine-cups in their hands. And above are similar texts, sanctified by the tradition of two thousand years.

Nothing seems to have changed, except that the noble and official classes, men and women, wear long robes, whereas the nobles of the Old Kingdom wore only a white kilt, leaving the breast bare. New Kingdom art, though freer than that of the Old Kingdom, still preserved the old traditions. The artist had not learned to draw in perspective; men, women and animals are drawn in profile, though the eyes are represented in full-face.

But if the lineaments of civilisation had changed very little during a thousand years, it had spread over a much greater area.

Between about 2000 and 1000 B.C. there were civilised communities living over wide areas of the Middle East and also in the Indus Valley. Even as far away as northern China, at An-Yang, there was an outpost of urban, civilised life in which men lived in cities, cultivated and irrigated a river-valley and had a writing system. But, apart from such highly-integrated societies as those of Egypt, Babylonia, and the Hittite kingdom of Asia Minor, the technical processes and manufactures produced by these societies were carried by trade to the outermost fringes of Europe, to the central Asian steppes and even as far as southern Russia.

Improved communications, by sea and land, helped this spread of knowledge. The Egyptians of the Middle Kingdom were building ships more than two hundred feet long and seventy feet wide, capable of transporting over a hundred men. These ships could also carry great loads. The Myceneans, also skilful seafarers, were building ships of 100-foot length. The Egyptians, though not a maritime people, ventured out of their river valley and coasted along the shore of the Lebanon to fetch cedar and other products of the Levantine colonies. With a following wind they could do the journey from the Delta to Byblos (an important port in the Lebanon) in four days' sailing.[1]

Land transport had also improved. A caravan on the Syrian plains could cover thirty miles in a day, but for those able to afford it, the light horse-drawn chariot was much faster. These vehicles, constructed of costly imported wood and made by highly-

[1] The return journey took longer as rowing was usually necessary.

L

skilled craftsmen, were equivalent to the luxurious car of today, except that only the highest officials, kings, princes, and officers could afford them. We have read the interesting and amusing satirical piece written by Hori telling of the joy of a young and noble Egyptian officer on receiving his war-chariot, bought for him by his parents. It draws a contrast between the fun of showing it off in the streets of Thebes and campaigning with it in the Syrian mountains 'where a Beduin lurks behind every bush' and the officer has to carry the axle-tree on his shoulder when he has lost his horses in a skirmish. 'From the nineteenth century B.C.', writes Childe in *What Happened in History*, 'horse-training was an important, even literate profession in north Syria, and chariot racing a practically useful sport.'

By the middle of the Second Millennium, trade had expanded to such an extent that Bronze Age chieftains in Cornwall were buried with faience beads and amulets made in Crete and Egypt, and Mycenean chieftains wore ornaments made in Britain. Amber from Jutland (Denmark) reached Greece and Crete, and Mycenean craftsmen sometimes used tin from Cornwall and gold from Ireland.

Before we continue our journey, two facts seem important to the writer and may be worth a thought. The first is that, in 1400 B.C., most of the features which we associate with the modern State were in being. There was centralised control of government, with a Civil Service, an elaborate system of taxation, a police force, a professional Army and Navy. States such as Egypt and the Hittite Empire had Foreign Offices, and presumably a Foreign Policy. Rulers exchanged diplomatic correspondence, which was filed (see the Tell-el-Amarna letters later in this chapter). They made and signed treaties of non-aggression—e.g. that between Ramesses II and Hattusilis III, copies of which were kept at Thebes and at Boghaz-Keui, the capitals of their respective countries. They had frontiers, with Customs barriers. They had a common language for diplomatic correspondence—Babylonian cuneiform—just as French was the language of diplomacy in the nineteenth century A.D. And their women studied and sometimes copied each other's fashions.

The second fact concerns weapons of war. When we encounter the beautiful, slender bronze rapiers which Schliemann found in the shaft-graves at Mycenae, our first instinct is to admire the beauty of the craftsmanship. But if one takes a more material view —as Childe does—they have a different significance.

In the 'Iliad', he points out, it is the well-armed heroes with their costly bronze weapons and fine war-chariots[1] who do most of the fighting; battles resolve themselves into a series of single combats, while 'the infantry are mere spectators'. That the foot-soldiers were passive onlookers I seriously doubt. Surely their masters would not have taken them all the way to Troy merely to look on? None the less it does appear from Homer's descriptions, and to some extent from the Egyptian temple reliefs of Ramesses II, that the powerfully armed and armoured warriors were the spearhead of the attack. Childe draws from this the conclusion that, as only a few could afford these costly weapons, and therefore possessed a monopoly of them, 'the masses were militarily worthless and accordingly politically impotent.'

It requires a considerable stretch of the imagination to equate bronze rapiers with nuclear weapons, and war-chariots with tanks. But if one makes the effort, the comparison with the realities of power in the twentieth century may not seem so fantastic.

Akhnaten has been described as a pacifist. One cannot be certain, as the records are so scanty, but let us look at the facts.

In 1887 an Arab woman was digging at Tell-el-Amarna (the site of Akhnaten's city) for *sebakh*, a nitrous earth which is used in Egypt as a fertiliser. She came upon hundreds of small baked-clay tablets about the size and shape of dog-biscuits. They appeared to have some form of writing on them, and Arab friends who knew the European passion for *antikas*, however unbeautiful, advised her to take them to the dealers, who might possibly give her a few piastres. She bundled them into a sack, and by the time they eventually reached M. Grebaut, head of the Antiquities Service in Cairo, many of the tablets had crumbled. Grebaut was not

[1] The varying military use of the two-horse chariot makes an interesting study. The Homeric heroes arrive by chariot, then get down to fight on foot. The Egyptians seem to have fought from their chariots, as did the Hittites.

impressed. He pronounced the tablets to be fakes. It was not until only 350 were left that someone recognised that they were genuine documents in the Babylonian cuneiform writing. Savants translated them, and a new and absorbing page in the history of Ancient Egypt was opened to the world. For the Arab peasant had stumbled on the archives of Akhnaten's Foreign Office.

There were letters to the King from Egypt's vassal-states in Syria-Palestine, and others from the kings of Babylon, Kheta, and Mittani, who wrote to the Pharaoh as equals.

Those from the Syrian vassal-states are especially interesting because they reveal clearly that the empire which Tuthmosis III had won, and which had been consolidated by his successors, was being threatened by its old enemies, the Hittites. The trouble had already begun in the reign of Amenophis III, Akhnaten's father. Tushratta, brother of the Mittanian princess whom Amenophis had married, wrote to the Pharaoh about an attempted Hittite invasion:

'Teshub, my Lord, gave my enemy into my hand, and I routed him. There was none among them that returned to his own land.'

And Aki-Izzi, lord of Katna, another Egyptian city in Syria, warns the Pharaoh of the threat from a certain Aziru the Amorite, a petty prince who seems to have been in league with the Hittites.

'O my Lord, if the trouble of this land lies upon the heart of my Lord, let my Lord send troops, and let them come!'

By the time of Akhnaten, the threat had become a reality. As the Hittites again began to push southward, some of the Pharaoh's vassals joined with them, and began attacking the still-loyal cities of Tunip, Simyra, and Gebal (Byblos), on the coast of Canaan. Their ostensible purpose was to prevent these towns falling into Hittite hands, but the reality is clear from the urgent appeals for troops which poured into Akhnaten's Foreign Office from the governors of the threatened provinces.

The governor of Tunip, a coastal city, wrote:

'My Lord, Tunip, thy servant, speaks, saying; who formerly could have plundered Tunip without being plundered by Menkheperre' (i.e. Tuthmosis III). 'The Gods of the King of Egypt, my Lord, dwell in Tunip. May our Lord ask his old men if it is not so.'

'Now, however, we belong no more to our Lord, the King of Egypt. If his soldiers and chariots come too late, then the King of Egypt will mourn over the things which Aziru has done, for he will turn his hand against our land. And when Aziru enters Simyra' (another coastal city) 'he will do as he pleases in the territory of our Lord the King.'

'. . . and now Tunip, thy city, weeps, and her tears are flowing, and there is no help for us. For twenty years we have been sending to our lord the King, the King of Egypt, but there has come not a word, no, not one . . .'

But no help came from Akhnaten, shut off in his Holy City, absorbed in the mysteries of his new religion. The worship of the god Amun was proscribed, and the king sent emissaries throughout the length and breadth of the land with instructions that they should hack out the name of the hated god wherever it appeared, even in the tomb of his own father. One can see their handiwork to this day.

'Meanwhile, from the Pharaoh's threatened Asiatic dominions the pleadings of the harassed but loyal vassal-princes swelled to an agonised chorus. From the east the Habiru, whom some historians have identified with the Jews, were pressing into Canaan. On the north the wily Hittite King Shubbuliliuma spun his diplomatic web, intriguing with the petty kings of the Pharaoh's northerly provinces and inviting them to break away from Egypt. The "Quisling" Aziru became increasingly dangerous, and while protesting his loyalty in fulsome letters to Akhnaten, was attacking the king's Phoenician cities.'[1]

All these facts have been deduced from a study of the little baked-clay tablets which the Arab woman dug out of the ground at Tell-el-Amarna. Within the old sack which she slung over her back were the voices of great kings, the intrigue of politicians, the despair of betrayed and abandoned cities. An exaggeration? Read this letter, dictated at white-heat by Ribbadi, the loyal governor of Gebal (Byblos), when the enemy was nearing his gates:

'Behold Aziru has fought my chiefs, and the chiefs whom I

[1] *The Lost Pharaohs*—Leonard Cottrell: Evans Brothers, London, 1949.

despatched to the city Simyra he has caused to be seized in the city. Both the city Beruta (Beirut) and the city Ziouna are sending ships to the city. All who are in the land of the Amorites have gathered themselves . . . I need men to save the rebellion of this land . . . Give me soldiers!'

And this one, evidently written later, when ruin had come to Simyra:

'Grievous it is to say what he hath done, the dog Aziru. Behold what has befallen the lands of the King on account of him; and he cried peace unto the land, and now behold what has befallen the city of Simyra—a station of my Lord, a fortress . . . and they spoil our fortress . . . ah, the cries of the place . . . a violent man and a dog . . .'

Still the old warrior held out at Gebal, while city after city fell. 'Now Abdeseherah is marching with his brethren', he wrote to the Pharaoh, and appealed to him to:

'. . . march against him and smite him . . . the land is the King's land, and since I have talked thus you have not moved and the city of Simyra has been lost. There is no money to buy horses, all is finished, we have been spoiled . . . give me thirty companies of horse with chariots, men, men . . . there is none of this for me . . . not a horse . . .'

No letters from the king to his vassals have ever been found. Perhaps he never sent any; perhaps the court officials who dealt with diplomatic correspondence kept the truth from him. For example, there is a letter from the traitor Aziru written to one Dudu (or Tutu), Akhnaten's Foreign Minister, which contains the words:

'Thou art in that place (Egypt) of my father, and whatever is the wish of Dudu my Father, write it and I will surely give it. Behold thou art my Father and my Lord. . . . The lands of Amor are thy lands, and my house is thy house; and whatever thou desirest, write, and lo! I will assuredly grant thy wish. Lo, now, thou sittest before the King, my Lord, and my enemies have spoken slanders of me to my Father before the King, my Lord. Do not thou allow it to be so . . .'

In other words: 'Assure the King of my loyalty. Speak well of me; don't let the King believe what my enemies say; and I'll see that *you* are looked after . . .' The situation could well be contemporary.

The end of the Eighteenth Dynasty was not far off. Akhnaten's great experiment had failed. Apart from the King and the Court party, there is no evidence to show that the new, purified religion ever took hold of the mass of the Egyptian people. Perhaps its most lasting influence was on Egyptian art. The rigid formalism of traditional Egyptian sculpture and painting was abandoned. The King, the Queen, and their daughters were shown not as gods but as human beings, in human attitudes. One relief on the wall of a tomb at Amarna shows the King kissing the Queen as they drive in their chariot. Another represents Akhnaten dandling one of his daughters on his knee. In another scene, depicting the royal family driving in their chariot, one of the daughters is poking the horse's rump with a stick. Even the King's physical defects were shown—indeed, possibly exaggerated. He had an unusually long skull and a swollen belly; these are always emphasised.

Such candour in Egyptian art had never been known before; nor did it ever occur again. But the freer, more naturalistic style introduced in Akhnaten's reign (which some scholars have suggested may have been due to refugee Cretan artists who may have come to Egypt after the fall of Knossos) continued to influence Egyptian sculpture and painting long after the 'Heresy Period' was over.

The end of Akhnaten, and of the Eighteenth Dynasty, is obscure. The late John Pendlebury, with Professor Fairman, dug at Amarna just before the Second World War and, from their excavations, made some interesting deductions which I have space only to summarise. Their researches provide the most up-to-date information we have on the Heresy Period and dispel a number of misconceptions concerning Akhnaten which occur in earlier books on the subject. For instance, Arthur Weigall and James Baikie state that the King ascended the throne in his early 'teens, achieved his religious revolution before he was twenty, and died at about the age of thirty. This is now known to be incorrect. Akhnaten was about twenty-five when he became co-regent, thirty when he became King, and he died at about the age of forty-one.

His body has never been found. The mummy found at Thebes, near the tomb of Tutankhamun, which earlier writers believed to be that of Akhnaten, is not his. It may be that of his half-brother, Smenkhkare.

It seems possible that Nefretiti was the real driving-force behind Atenism. Excavations have shown that after the fourteenth year of Akhnaten's reign, the King lived in one part of his capital with Smenkhkare and Meritaten, his eldest daughter, while on a number of monuments the name of Nefretiti has been deliberately obliterated, and replaced by that of Meritaten. As we know that Nefretiti survived the King, Nefretiti's disgrace is the most reasonable explanation.

Why was she disgraced? We cannot be sure, but certain facts may be significant. At Hermopolis, in 1938, archaeologists found an inscription which states:

'*The King's daughter, whom he loves, Ankhsenpaaton the younger, born of the King's daughter Ankhsenpaaton.*'

This indicated that Akhnaten married his daughter, Ankhsenpaaton, while Nefretiti was still living, and that she bore him a child who was also named Ankhsenpaaton.

Smenkhkare married Akhnaten's eldest daughter, Meritaten, and then went to Thebes where he reigned as co-regent while Akhnaten remained at Amarna. In the third year of his co-regency, Smenkhkare began to restore some form of Amun-worship at Thebes. The proof of this is provided by Hieratic *graffiti* in the tomb of Per-Re at Thebes.

The interesting point to notice is that Smenkhkare's successor, the now-famous Tutankhamun whose tomb was discovered by Howard Carter in 1922 was called Tutankh*aten* on his accession; he changed his name later, probably under duress, but his tomb contained a number of objects in which the Aten-symbol (the sun's disk with descending rays) occurs—e.g. the golden throne. Tutankhamun must have been an Atenist when he succeeded Smenkhkare, yet, as we have seen, the latter king had already begun to compromise with the older faith.

Where does Nefretiti fit into this picture? After Year Fourteen of Akhnaten's reign, the Queen retired to her own palace, taking with her Tutankhaten, who was little more than a boy even when he came to the throne. (In his tomb Carter found a box with a sling, some pebbles, and simple mechanical toys.) Objects bearing Nefretiti's name, with that of Tutankhaten, dated *after* Year Fourteen of Akhnaten's reign, have been found by Pendlebury and Fairman in the Northern Palace at Tell-el-Amarna.

Professor Fairman interprets these clues as follows—as a theory only, but in the writer's view a valid one, bearing in mind the known facts. Near the end of Akhnaten's reign there was a split in the court; some urging a return to Thebes and re-adoption of Amunism, others determined to be loyal to the new faith. These differences (and perhaps others) led to a rupture between Akhnaten and his Queen. Akhnaten made Smenkhkare co-regent, and sent him to Thebes to effect some compromise with the older faith. Nefretiti remained at Akhetaten, the new capital, but lived apart from her husband, taking with her her son Tutankhaten, whom she nurtured in the new faith. What Akhnaten's view was we cannot know, but one suspects that he was a broken and disillusioned man, who did not care very much what happened but was determined never to return to Thebes.

Akhnaten died at the age of forty-one, in the seventeenth year of his reign. Almost simultaneously Smenkhkare also died, leaving a vacant throne. This gave Nefretiti her opportunity. She produced Tutankhaten, married him to Ankhsenpaaton, Akhnaten's widow, and so legitimised his accession (which had to be through the female line). Still a child, the boy reigned from Akhetaten for a time but was eventually compelled or persuaded to return to the ancestral capital and adopt a new name—'Tutank*hamun*'. His wife also changed her name to Ankhesn*amun*. They were both little more than children. Thus the wheel had come full circle and the priests of Amun resumed their former power.

How did this happen? We do not know, but the presumption is that Nefretiti was then dead. Soon afterwards the priests of Amun regained full authority. The old religion was restored, and the name of the 'heretic king' was hacked out of his monuments—as he had attempted to destroy that of Amun. Akhetaten was deserted and left to fall into ruin. It was never occupied again.

We have little documentary evidence for this tragic story, apart from a few inscriptions and the deductions of the archaeologists from the ruined foundations of Akhnaten's city. Yet it has the ring of truth.

There is also a postcript so dramatic that readers may suspect that the writer has allowed his imagination to distort historical truth. Yet the facts are there and may be checked.

We have encountered the Hittite King Shubbululiuma, who had intrigued with the vassal-kings of Egypt in Syria, and who was steadily gnawing away the outer edges of the Egyptian Empire. Some years ago archaeologists discovered at Boghaz Keui, the Hittite capital, a cuneiform tablet recording a series of letters which passed between Shubbululiuma and an unknown Egyptian princess. Professor Sayce translated it. The tablet describes the sacking of Amka (on the plain of Antioch). Then it goes on:

'Then their ruler (i.e. of the Egyptians) just at that moment died; now the Queen of Egypt sent an ambassador . . . she said thus . . . "My husband is dead; I have no children; your sons are said to be grown up; if you give to me one of your sons, he will be my husband; he will be a help; send him accordingly, and thereafter I will make him my husband. I send bridal gifts." '

Obviously, a marriage alliance between the Hittites and Egypt would have been greatly to the former's advantage. Still, Shubbululiuma was cautious. He sent a letter of inquiry to the Egyptian Queen, to which he received the following reply:

'What is this you say, "She has deceived me"? . . . Now you say to me thus, "there is thy husband"; but he is dead; I have no son; so I have taken a servant . . . and to another country this matter I have not written; to you, however, I have written; your sons are said to be grown up; so give me one of your sons, and he shall be my husband and King of Egypt.'

Who was this Egyptian Queen, and who was her husband? One of Tutankhamun's names was *Neb-kheperu-Re*, which is not unlike the name given in the Hittite tablet. His widow was the same Ankhsenpaaton, daughter-wife of Akhnaten, who later changed

her name to *Ankhesnamun*. The German philologist Herr E.
Edel, had definitely identified this king and queen with the Hittite
inscriptions. The dates fit, and there is little doubt that the Queen
who wrote so desperately to the Hittite king was the young widow
of Tutankhamun.

If we consider these two letters in relation to the known facts
concerning the last years of the Eighteenth Dynasty, they tell a
pathetic story. Already twice-widowed, the 24-year-old girl saw
her scheming courtiers struggling for power. There was Ay, her
father's former chief minister; there was Horemhab, who had
commanded his armies. Either, by marrying her, could make himself King of Egypt. But marriage could not take place until
Tutankhamun was buried; and the process of embalmment took
ninety days. Those three months gave Ankhesnamun her last
chance. She smuggled out a letter to the Hittite king pleading with
him to send one of his sons . . . 'and he as my husband in the land
of Egypt shall be king.'

Eventually Shubbuliliuma did send one of his sons; but he never
reached Thebes. No doubt someone saw to that, for the next
Pharaoh who appears on the king-list is Ay, Tutankhamun's
successor.

More than three thousand years later two British archaeologists,
Howard Carter and Lord Carnarvon, began to excavate in the
Valley of the Kings at Thebes—the burial place of the Pharaohs
from the Eighteenth to the Twentieth Dynasties. More than
thirty of the greatest of Egypt's kings were buried in these deep
rock-cut tombs, hollowed out of the limestone cliffs. All but one
had been plundered in antiquity; indeed, most had been standing
open for more than two thousand years, showplaces even in Greek
and Roman times. But on the 1st of November, 1922, Carter, after
seven seasons of fruitless search, came upon a flight of stone steps
leading down into the rock, just below the entrance to the tomb
of Ramesses VI. This area had been covered by stone chippings
and rubble thrown down by the excavators of Ramesses's tomb
and had escaped detection.

When Carter and Carnarvon had removed the stones which
blocked the passage, they made the richest archaeological discovery

of modern times, an almost intact tomb of a Pharaoh who died more than thirty centuries ago. The body was encased in a coffin of solid gold, so heavy that it required four men to lift it. This inner coffin was surrounded by two outer coffins of wood encased in gold, these in turn being placed within a series of gold-encased shrines, one inside the other like a Chinese nest of boxes.

In adjoining chambers were the king's funerary furniture—his beds, chairs, boxes of clothing, palace ornaments of gold and semi-precious stones, his arms and hunting-gear, his chariots, even the child's chair and the toys he used as a boy. The tomb was that of Tutankhamun. On the back-panel of his golden throne was a plaque of electrum (gold and silver alloy) set with carnelian, lapis-lazuli, and other stones, and embossed with a scene set in the garden of the royal palace; the young king, seated on a chair, is attended by his queen, Ankhesnamun, who anoints his body with perfumed oil from a jar. Above the couple the Aten-disk, Akhnaten's 'sole god' sends down his rays. The faces of the king and queen have the unmistakable 'Amarna' stamp—delicate, sensitive, languid, the product of generations of inbreeding which had purified and rarefied the royal stock to the point of degeneracy. This inbreeding ended by producing an unstable genius—Akhnaten—and then finally flickered out. When Tutankhamun, the last of his line, died in about 1350 B.C. the Eighteenth Dynasty, the most glorious epoch in Egypt's long history, ended.

The Empire which Tuthmosis had won was crumbling. The Hittites and their vassals controlled the former Egyptian dominions in Syria-Palestine. In the capital there was unrest and dissension, as rival parties intrigued for power. A detached observer would have been justified in thinking that after more than two thousand five hundred years of civilisation Egypt's greatness was at an end. But he would have been wrong. For the third and last time, under a new line of kings, the peoples of the Nile Valley roused themselves, shook off their enemies, and regained their Empire.

CHAPTER XII

The Iron Age Revolution

There are many ways of interpreting history, but the two extremes are represented by what one might call the 'Churchillian' school, in which human events are moulded and directed by strong personalities; and the determinist school, to whom individuals matter far less than material factors such as climatic conditions, technical inventions, trade and commerce. These factors, say the materialists, dictate the course of history; the human beings who appear to shape it—men like Imhotep, Sargon, Hammurabi, Tuthmosis, to name a few who have appeared in this story—are 'produced' automatically to meet the needs of their times. If they had not appeared, others like them would have.

This, of course, is a broad generalisation, but readers looking for a more detailed view of the historical landscape will find that in general professional historians tend to accept one or the other view. For example, Sir Winston Churchill, in his *History of the English-Speaking Peoples*, devotes a whole long chapter to Alfred the Great, and another to Edward I. On the other hand, Professor Childe, in his *What Happened in History*, devotes twenty pages to the social revolution brought about in Greece and Asia Minor by the cheap production of iron tools and weapons, and the introduction of metal coinage; but Aristotle gets less than a page, and Plato is hardly mentioned.

There is no such animal as an 'objective' historian. They all have—indeed, must have—a point of view; in the writer's opinion both schools should be studied, so that the human bias of one can counterbalance the materialist tendency of the other. My own view is summed up in the words of Herman Melville in that wonderful passage from *Moby Dick* in which the hero, sitting on the deck of a whaling-ship, watches the Indian Queequeg making a mat:

'I was the attendant or page of Queequeg while busy at the mat. As I kept passing and repassing the filling or woof or marline between the long lines of the warp, using my own hand as the shuttle, and as Queequeg, standing sideways, ever and anon slid his heavy oaken sword between the threads, and idly looking upon the water, carelessly and unthinkingly drove home every yarn . . . it seemed as if this were the Loom of Time, and I myself were a shuttle mechanically weaving and weaving away at the Fates. There lay the fixed threads of the warp, subject to one single, ever-returning, unchanging vibration, and that vibration merely enough to admit of the crosswise interblending of other threads with its own. This warp seemed necessity; and here, thought I, with my own hand I ply my own shuttle and weave my own destiny in these unalterable threads. Meanwhile, Queequeg's impulsive, indifferent sword, sometimes hitting the woof slant-ingly, or crookedly, or strongly, or weakly, as the case might be; and by this difference in the concluding blow producing a corres-ponding contrast in the final aspect of the completed fabric; this savage's sword, thought I, which thus finally shapes and fashions both warp and woof; this easy, indifferent sword must be chance— aye, chance, and free-will, and necessity—no wise incompatible— all interweavingly working together.'

This apparent digression has been introduced because, for the next five centuries of our journey—i.e. from 1350 to 850 B.C.—the materialist school, apostles of Necessity, can help us better to understand the broad sweep of history. With their aid we can with-draw ourselves, temporarily, from the fascinating but perhaps irrelevant faces of individuals like Tuthmosis, Akhnaten and Ankhesnamun, and try to survey the main trend of events in several countries.

This is what we see.

In 1350 B.C., in Egypt, a new, powerful line of kings—those of the Nineteenth Dynasty, had begun. Their names—Horemhab, Sethi 1st, Ramesses II, Ramesses III—were great in Egyptian history. They won back their former dominions, threw back (but did not destroy) the Hittites, built tombs and temples greater and richer than any of their predecessors. The tomb of Sethi 1st, which Belzoni re-opened in the early nineteenth century, was the largest and most elaborate in Thebes. The Hypostyle Hall of the temple of Amun at Karnak, remains one of the most stupendous buildings in the world. Ramesses II, Sethi's successor, crossed the Orontes, and commemorated, in enormous sculptured reliefs on his temples, his alleged victory over the Hittite king at Kadesh (though the Hittite historians tell another story). In 1275 he signed a treaty of non-aggression with Hattusilis III, King of the Hittites, copies of which were kept both at Thebes and at Boghaz Keui, the Hittite capital. And Egypt had never been more wealthy.

In about 1200 Ramesses III, another great warrior, defeated a coalition of peoples—Libyans, Semites from Syria-Palestine, and the 'sea-peoples' of the islands—in a series of great land and naval battles. This invasion, at one stage of which the attackers reached Heliopolis, was much more than an attack by professional armies. It was a migration of peoples, moving down the Palestinian coast with their women and their baggage-wagons. 'The Isles,' wrote Ramesses's priestly historian in a great temple inscription at Medinet Habu, 'were in tumult.' And in the same inscription, recording the names of the tribes who took part in the invasion, occur 'the Danua' and 'the Achaiwasha'—strangely like the Danaoi and the Achaeans of the Homeric epics.

In the Greek mainland and in Crete, the Myceneans had taken over the old Minoan Empire, and their trade-goods, pottery vessels, tools and weapons, were spread over an area which stretched from Sicily in the west to Syria in the east.

Round about 1200 B.C. they were still firmly established at Mycenae, where they had built great 'beehive' or 'tholos' tombs of stone, much more elaborate than the simple shaft-graves within the Citadel. These later tombs, shaped like huge stone beehives twenty feet high and approached by entrances flanked by high walls, are not unlike the built tombs of Ras Shamra, in Syria. The Myceneans' art continued to reflect the 'Minoan' culture of the Mediterranean peoples whom they had overthrown, and whose system of writing they had adopted.

Their predominance was due mainly to their valour and skill and to the fact that their military aristocracy possessed the expensive bronze rapiers and daggers, and the costly war-chariots which only they could afford—also, they had mastered the sea. In about 1190 B.C. they sent an expedition to Asia Minor and, some historians say, tried to force the Dardanelles in an effort to secure control of the Black Sea trade-routes. Their long and finally successful siege of Troy (Ilios)—the key point—became the subject of epic poetry, originally oral, which an Ionian poet was to set down in writing about four centuries later in the '*Iliad*'. But Homer's epic does not mention trade-routes. He says that the cause of the war was the abduction of the beautiful Helen. This story is naturally rejected by the prim materialist school as being too frivolous a pretext for a war. I am not so sure. H. G. Wells may have been right when he wrote:

'The *Iliad* makes it clear that destruction came upon Troy because the Trojans stole Greek women. Modern writers, with modern ideas in their heads, have tried to make out that the Greeks assailed Troy in order to secure a trade-route to Colchis or some such fine-spun commercial advantage. If so, the authors of the *Iliad* hid the motives of their characters very skilfully . . . The Homeric Greeks were a healthy, barbaric Aryan people with very poor ideas about "trade-routes"; they went to war with the Trojans because they were thoroughly annoyed about this stealing of women.'

The Hittites, chief enemies of Egypt and their equals in power at this time, eventually controlled a great Empire which stretched from the homeland in the mountains of Armenia, southward as far as Syria, westward to the coast of Asia Minor, and eastward to the Euphrates. Their mountain-fortress at *Hattusas* (Boghaz Keui) girdled with massive protective walls, was the citadel and nerve-centre from which they controlled their subject-provinces. In about 1400 the kingdom of Mittani, on the 'great bend' of the Euphrates, whose kings hovered nervously between allegiance to Pharaoh (see the Amarna Letters) and loyalty to their powerful

6(a) Part of processional way, Babylon, built by
Nebuchadnezzar, showing wall reliefs

6(b) View of excavations, Babylon

6(c) Assyrian relief showing hunting scenes

6(d) Winged bull of Assyria

northern neighbours, had been sacked by the Hittite king, Shubbuliliuma, after which he penetrated southward as far as Abina (the Hobah of Genesis xiv. 15) and even claimed the Lebanon as his frontier.

Then came the revival of Egypt under the Nineteenth Dynasty kings, who won back most of their Empire, and one of whom—Ramesses II—signed the treaty with the Hittite king, Hattusilis III. Yet the Hittites were not defeated and remained powerful. The mountain-peoples and the Nile Valley peoples faced each other, as equals, across the subject-peoples of Syria-Palestine. Meanwhile, one of these tribes of wandering nomads, the Hebrews, had settled in Egypt, and probably round about 1250 (during the reign of the Pharaoh Mereneptah), had left the country under the leadership of the patriarch Moses and begun their long sojourn in the wilderness of Sinai. They were poor people, wandering herdsmen who counted for nothing in comparison with the mighty powers of Egypt, Hatti, and Babylon, yet already their prophets had lit a flame which, growing brighter throughout the centuries, would burn and continue to burn long after the military achievements of Sethi, Hattusilis, and the Mycenean kings had become merely the subjects for archaeological research.

At this period (1250 B.C.) Jaweh, the Hebrew god, was still a tribal deity, a god of war who watched jealously over the fortunes of his chosen people, a god more powerful even than Pharaoh himself:

'For Pharaoh will say of the children of Israel that they are entangled in the land, and the wilderness has shut them in.'

'And I will harden Pharaoh's heart, that he shall follow after them; and I will be honoured upon Pharaoh, and upon all his host; that the Egyptians shall know that I am the Lord. And they did so . . .'

'. . . But the Egyptians pursued after them, all the horses and chariots of Pharaoh, and his horsemen, and overtook them encamping by the sea, beside Pihahiroth, before Baalzephon . . .'

'. . . And the Angel of God, which went before the camp of Israel, removed and went behind them; and the pillar of cloud went before their face, and stood behind them. . . . And Moses stretched out his hand over the sea; and the Lord caused the sea to go back by a strong east wind all that night, and made the sea dry land, and the waters were divided.'

'And the children of Israel went into the midst of the sea upon the dry ground; and the waters were a wall unto them on their right hand and on their left.'

'And the Egyptians pursued, and went in after them in the midst of the sea, even all Pharaoh's chariots, and his horsemen. . . . And Moses stretched forth his hand over the sea, and the sea returned to his strength when the morning appeared; and the Egyptians fled against it; and the Lord overthrew the Egyptians in the midst of the sea . . .'

A myth, no doubt, which served to hearten the Israelites throughout the years of tribulation. Like the war-like achievements of the Achaeans at Troy, the story was taken up by poets and sung in the camp.

'And Miriam the prophetess, the sister of Aaron, took the timbrel in her hand; and all the women went out after her with timbrels and with dances.'

'And Miriam answered them, *Sing ye to the Lord, for he hath triumphed gloriously; the horse and the rider he hath thrown into the sea!*'

From about 1380 onwards, the Assyrians began to dominate the Upper Tigris by 1250, under Shalmaneser I, they were ruling Babylon as well. On the Phoenician coast, Tyre replaced Sidon as the ruling city, but the Phoenician city-states strung along the Lebanese coast were still prosperous, though owing nominal allegiance to Pharaoh. At this time, too, the mid-thirteenth century, a marriage took place between Ramesses II and a Hittite princess, thirteen years after the signing of the famous Egyptian-Hittite treaty which guaranteed peace and security throughout the Levant.

And yet, after about 1200 B.C. a Dark Age began, not merely in one state but in most of the civilised world. A fresh wave of invaders—in the Dorian Greeks—swept into Greece and destroyed the civilisation of the Myceneans. Round about the same time the empire of the Hittites came to an end; they were driven out of

Asia Minor, although a people calling themselves Hittites continued to rule in northern Syria; these, however, may have been former dependents of the Anatolian Hittites who had adopted the culture of their conquerors. In Babylon the weak Kassite dynasty ended, and the Assyrians came down from the northern reaches of the Tigris and occupied Hammurabi's city. In Egypt there was at first fierce resistance. The Pharaohs, Mereneptah and then Ramesses drove the invaders from the Nile, but before long Egypt too fell to foreign conquerors; the ancient enemies of Egypt, the Libyans of the west, and the Nubians of the south, prevailed; their rulers sat on the throne of Pharaoh.

What was the reason for this decline, almost simultaneously, of four flourishing civilisations? If it had happened in only one of them one might ascribe the catastrophe to the weakness or incompetence of individual rulers. But for such widespread changes we must look for a deeper cause, and here the materialist school can help. In the first two chapters of this book we described how the inventions of metal tools and weapons, and the development of new techniques, enabled mankind to settle in self-sufficient communities, to improve their control over their environment and so increase their stock of natural wealth. This inevitably led to over-population of the settled areas, so that in time people over-spilled into new territories—or, as in the Nile Valley and Mesopotamia, organised themselves into larger units.

But there came a point beyond which natural wealth did not increase, although the population did. One of the results was that great states made war on each other, partly for the glory of their rulers, but also for loot. If you could not produce any more wealth yourself, you stole it from your neighbour. As States became more highly organised and more scientific, such struggles became more and more costly, both to victors and vanquished, though the use of captives as slaves helped to compensate for this. But by the Second Millennium, rulers like Ramesses III and Hattusilis had begun to use foreign mercenary troops, mainly from the Greek islands and from Syria-Palestine, probably to make good the losses among their own population. Such mercenaries served their masters for one reason—the prospect of plunder.

Incidentally, it is now, for the first time, that we can see the operation of two contradictory sets of moral values regarding murder and theft. Moses told the Israelites, 'Thou shalt not kill . . . thou shalt not steal . . . thou shalt not covet thy neighbour's house.' But that applied only to the family and the tribe. It was quite in order to attack the land of Canaan, kill its citizens and appropriate their homes in the name of Jaweh. That was war, which was different. We do not know, but from his conduct of foreign affairs, it may have been that Akhnaten thought that such moral laws should apply to nations as well as individuals—hence his failure. The problem is still with us.

There was, however, another more potent cause for the revolution which took place during the twelfth and eleventh centuries. Somewhere in the Armenian mountains a barbarian tribe whom the Hittites called the *Kizwadana* invented a process of producing bulk *iron* of good quality. Iron was no new discovery. Iron tools were occasionally used, both in Egypt and Mesopotamia, as early as the Third Millennium. (Petrie discovered pieces of wrought iron in the Great Pyramid which had evidently been used by its builders.) But it was costly and difficult to produce in quantity because, with the low furnace temperatures in use at that time, iron was extremely difficult to melt, and reduction left only a mingled mass of iron and 'slag' which then had to be purified and beaten into 'blooms' by hammering. Yet, if only these difficulties could be overcome, iron was a far better metal for tools and weapons than bronze—harder, more durable, and, above all, available in much greater quantities. It is one of the commonest ores in the earth's crust.

Some time in the fourteenth century, the *Kizwadana* learned the trick; the Hittites, their conquerors, discovered the secret and for a time guarded it jealously. When one of the Pharaohs made curious inquiries of his 'brother', the Hittite king, all he got in return was one specimen dagger. Incidentally, such a dagger was found in the tomb of Tutankhamun. It must have been a rare treasure, far more valuable at the time than the costliest implements of gold.

But inevitably, in time, the secret leaked out, and gradually the process spread all over Western Asia, and thence into Europe, until eventually it was known as far away as Britain.

The ultimate result of that invention by some obscure barbarian tribe was to change the face of history. For now anyone could have durable weapons with a hard cutting-edge, far superior to the expensive bronze swords which had been practically a monopoly of the war-lords. Any little farmer could have iron ploughshares which enabled him to tackle land which had been uncultivable before, axes for felling trees and clearing new ground, and iron scythes for reaping. All these made his work easier and his land more productive. Similarly, the barbarians who had been kept beyond the frontiers of civilised lands by the superior weapons of their owners now had the power to achieve military equality with them.

These two factors—the exhaustion of the old Bronze Age Kingdoms by over-population and warfare, and the dissemination, among barbarian peoples, of the secret of iron-working—were probably the main reasons for the social changes and shifting of power which we see after *circa* 1200 B.C.

Of course, these changes did not take place everywhere, or at the same time. Indeed, in Western Asia the new Iron Age aristocracies simply took over the old divine kingships of the earlier Bronze Age rulers, with their complex administrative machinery, and society changed very little. The Hittite kingdom, for instance, merely contracted. It lost its hold over its old homeland in Asia Minor and instead ruled from Carchemish on the Upper Euphrates, where it controlled trade routes between east and west. This withdrawal from Asia Minor may well have been due to the incursions of the Mycenean sea-rovers, who at this time were feeling the pressure of new barbarian peoples thrusting down into Greece from northern Europe, just as the Myceneans themselves had fought their way into Greece some five or six centuries earlier.

Here is a point where archaeology and legend appear to meet. Homer, who wrote round about 900–800 B.C., described the Trojan War, which was fought near the beginning of the twelfth century B.C. He describes the Greek host as 'the bronze-clad

Achaeans'. From the fact that some of the armour and weapons found by Schliemann at Mycenae are very like those described by Homer, and for other reasons, we can be certain that these 'Achaeans' were, in fact, the Mycenean warriors and sea-rovers.

In the temple and palace of the Egyptian king, Ramesses III, at Medinet Habu, in Thebes, occurs a list of tribes whom the Pharaohs defeated in 1200 when 'the isles were in tumult'. Among these tribes are 'the Danura' who may possibly be Homer's 'Danaoi', and the 'Achaiwasha', who could be his 'Achaeans'. The similarity is interesting, but it could be a coincidence.

But in 1924 Mr. E. Forrer, a specialist in Hittite archaeology, announced that he had found in Hittite documents references to the Homeric Greeks, or Achaeans, and even the names of individuals such as Eteocles of Orchomenos and Atreus of Mycenae. His findings were criticised, notably by Friedrich in 1927, after which F. Sommer undertook an exhaustive study of the material. The matter is still in some doubt, but the fact remains that the Hittite texts of this period refer to a country called *Ahhiyawa* or Ahhiya. One of them refers to the fact that relatives of the king of Ahhiyawa were sent to Hatti for lessons in chariot-driving. (We know how important the chariot was in Homeric warfare.) Another speaks of a certain 'man of Ahhiyawa' named *Attarisiyas*, who apparently had attacked a vassal-prince called Maduwattas and driven him out of his kingdom. Later the Hittite king sent a detachment which fought *Attarisiyas*, who commanded one hundred chariots and an unnamed number of foot-soldiers, defeated him, and reinstated the exiled Maduwattas. If we look at the map of Asia Minor we see at once how accessible were its western shores to Mycenean sea-rovers. We know also that the Myceneans were familiar with this country—their pottery has been found there,[1] and on the north Syrian coast. Though scholars are rightly cautious and non-committal, it is tempting to think that the *Ahhiyawa*, who gave so much trouble to the Hittites, were Homer's Achaeans.

And if one is prepared to go a step further, is it not remarkable

[1] Chiefly at Troy and Miletus.

that the name *Attarisiyas*, the troublesome foreigner who drove a Hittite vassal-prince from his land, resembles *Atreus*, father of Agamemnon, who led the Achaean host to Troy?

But if the Myceneans were troubling the Hittites and the Egyptians, they themselves were in equally great difficulty in Greece. New waves of invaders were sweeping down from the north; these were the Dorians, ancestors of the Greeks of classical times. The fact that during the thirteenth and twelfth centuries B.C. the Myceneans were raiding, colonising and plundering throughout the Aegean and beyond may be due to two reasons: (a) pressure of invaders of kindred Greek-speaking stock, and (b) the Mycenean population had increased to such an extent that Greece could no longer support them and they were forced to emigrate. The Achaeans of Homer's epics were a seafaring people—raiders and pirates. The world of the *Iliad* and the *Odyssey* is the Mycenean world. The adventures of Jason in his search for the Golden Fleece, of Odysseus and his wanderings are splendid myths based on the lives of real people in real situations.

They did not know that they were driven by economic necessity. They had not heard of the tribe in the Armenian mountains which had cheapened iron. No Marxist historian had told them that overpopulation and warfare had weakened the Bronze Age States, and that their descendants were to become the founders of western civilisation. Enough for them the comradeship of soldiers in battle; the swift sharp encounter when the broad blades flashed, and when Diomedes 'of the loud war-cry' slew like a lion. Enough for them the council of war when the cunning Odysseus gave them counsel, or the sage Nestor tempered their youthful ardour with the wisdom of years. Enough for them the chuckle of water under the swift keel; when they shipped their oars and lay back as favouring winds bellied the broad sail:

'*And now, like a team of four stallions on the plain who start as one horse at the touch of the whip and break into their bounding stride to make short work of their course, the ship lunged forward, and, above the great dark wave that the sea sent roaring, her stern began to rise and fall. With unfaltering speed she surged ahead, and not*

183

even the wheeling falcon, the fastest thing that flies, could have kept her company . . .'[1]

Ahead lay the blue sea, dimpling in the sunlight; ahead lay storms and tides and unknown perils; the Sirens 'who bewitch everybody that approaches them', the dread monsters, Scylla and Charybdis, ready to strike as the ships passed through the narrow straits. But the Greeks had a leader, the resourceful Odysseus who would guide them through every peril.

'Oarsmen, stick to your benches, striking hard with your blades through the broken water, and we may have the luck to slip by and avoid disaster. Helmsman, your orders are these. Get them by heart, for the good ship's steering-oar is under your control. Give a wide berth to that smoke and surf you see, and hug these cliffs, or before you can stop her the ship may take it into her head to make a dash over there and wreck us.'[2]

The ordinary Greek of the Mycenean period knew nothing of Egyptian architecture, of Babylonian mathematics, or the curious little signs with which the Oriental scribes set down the dull conquests of their masters. Some of them had heard of Egypt and the land of the Kheta. A few had even served in Oriental armies. But for the most part theirs was a world of high mountains, of green valleys beyond which gleamed the sea, of simple settlements beside a stream in which the white-armed maidens washed their linen. And there were the high-walled citadels of Mycenae, Tiryns, Orchomenos, Pylos, in the shield-hung halls of which the warriors lounged, nodding over their wine, while a bard sang of long-dead heroes, of sirens and sea-monsters, and dangerous voyages by sea and land.

No one wrote down these poems, but from generation to generation they were passed on by word of mouth until, during a Dark Age, long after the Mycenean palaces were in ruin and a new people occupied the land, Homer wove them into his epics, for scholars to analyse, and romantics to dream over.

According to the materialist school of history, 1200–1100 B.C.

[1] *The Odyssey*—Homer: Translated by E. V. Rieu, Penguin Books, London, 1951.
[2] *op. cit.*

was a period of change, when new technical processes were altering the structure of society—for the better. The barbarian invaders from the north, with their iron weapons, overthrew the overblown Mycenean aristocracy and laid the foundations on which a new world could be built. There was no one to tell the Myceneans this, of course, which was a pity, for then they would have realised that their heroic gestures were futile, and their opponents the instruments of inevitable economic and social change. But the Achaeans, unaware of this, did their best with their allotted life-span, made due offerings to the gods, without expecting much in return; defended their land when they could; took other people's lands when they had to; and in the brief intervals of peace, hunted, drank, feasted, and made love.

There are worse ways of living and dying. At least they never assumed that their plundering was sanctified by an exclusive god, and at best they gave Europe its two greatest epic poems.

CHAPTER XIII

'Babylon, the Mighty City'

The time sequences into which this book is divided are, of course, quite artificial. Even the millennia—3000 to 2000 B.C., 2000 to 1000 B.C.—though convenient for latter-day historians, are quite meaningless in relation to the people who lived through them. But sometimes dates are convenient landmarks; for instance, 1100 B.C., when a great wave of Dorian invaders swept down into Greece and overthrew the Mycenean civilisation, and 525 B.C., when the Persian king, Cambyses, conquered Egypt.

The six-hundred-odd years which separate these two events saw Egypt first conquered by Nubians and Libyans, then absorbed into the Assyrian Empire, freeing itself for a short while, only to be conquered again by the Persians. For Egypt it was a period of decline. But during the same period the Phoenicians became the greatest maritime power in the Mediterranean, until supplanted by the Greeks. On the northern Tigris the Assyrians rose to power in the twelfth century, declined, arose again in the ninth, eighth and seventh centuries, became for a time a greater empire than Egypt herself, until in 612 B.C. Nineveh fell and a revived Babylon took its place as the ruling power in southern Mesopotamia.

Meanwhile, in western Asia Minor a new power, the Lydians, were dominant for about two hundred years, down to 546, when Lydia became part of the new Persian Empire. Throughout this period the Greeks were founding city-states in Greece itself, and colonising far and wide throughout the Mediterranean; in Asia Minor, Syria, Egypt, North Africa, Cyprus, Rhodes, and the islands, and even as far west as Italy, Sicily, and southern France.

The Phoenicians established their great commercial colony at Carthage in the ninth century, another at Tarshish (Cadiz) in

Spain, passed through the Straits of Gibraltar, traded with Britain and even sailed round Africa.

In Syria-Palestine the Hebrew tribes, after generations of wandering, established themselves in the Judean hills and became a nation, ruled first by Judges such as Jephthah, Gideon, and Samson, until, in about 1025, they crowned their first king, Saul. His successor, David, established the capital of Jerusalem, and was followed by Solomon (*circa* 970–933), who built a palace and temple with the aid of Phoenician workmen and imitated in a small way the luxuries of the great Oriental monarchies of Egypt, Babylon and Assyria. Then the kingdom was divided into that of Ephraim and Judah. During the repeated wars between Assyria and Egypt, between Babylon and Assyria and Egypt and Babylon, the petty Jewish states sided first with one side, then with the other, and as a result were frequently mauled. In about 930 B.C. the Egyptian King Sheshonk (*Shishak* of the Bible) invaded Judah and 'came up against Jerusalem. And he took away the treasures of the house of the Lord, and the treasures of the King's house; he even took away it all . . .' In 701 Sennacherib, the Assyrian king, also attacked Judah.

The usual lamentations followed.

In 612, Nineveh, the Assyrian capital, fell before a combined assault of the Babylonians, Medes and Scythians. In 597 the Babylonian king, Nebuchadnezzar, conquered Judah and carried the Jews into captivity. This happened again in 586 (the Second Deportation), after which the Jewish religion might well have perished had it not been kept alive by its exiled prophets. Finally, in 538, when the newly-risen Persian power overthrew that of Babylon, the exiles were allowed to return to their ruined city. From this time onwards a line of Persian kings—Cyrus, Darius I, Xerxes, Artaxerxes I, Darius II, and Artaxerxes II—ruled most of western Asia and Egypt and, but for the valour of the Greeks, would probably have conquered southern Europe as well.

Those are the bald facts; a mere catalogue of dates and dynasties, conquests and re-conquests; 'official history', in fact. We owe our knowledge of it partly to the work of archaeologists working in Egypt, Assyria, Babylonia, Asia Minor and Greece, partly to the

Old Testament, and for the latter part to Greek historians such as Herodotus and Thucydides. To chronicle each phase in detail would be possible in a much longer book, but impracticable in this one—not only for reasons of space, but because in the writer's opinion much of this later history repeats in a different form the pattern of events in the Third and Second Millennia. For instance, Assyria of the eighth century and Babylon of the seventh were typical Oriental despotisms of the kind with which we have become familiar in Egypt and Mesopotamia more than a thousand years earlier, although there had been technical developments, chiefly in warfare, which made military action more efficient and devastating. Iron weapons replaced those of bronze; mercenaries were used in large numbers, and the Assyrians in particular developed heavy cavalry, siege-engines, and a technique of terrorism which makes the earlier Egyptian and Hittite empires seem almost benevolent by comparison.

In all the annals of human conquest, it is difficult to find any people more dedicated to bloodshed and slaughter than the Assyrians. Their ferocity and cruelty have few parallels save in modern times. The kings were generals; their nobles belonged to a military caste; their trade was war. Such culture as they possessed had been borrowed from Babylonia, and apart from the brutal vigour of their art—exemplified by the famous winged bulls and carved reliefs in the British Museum and the Paris Louvre—their main contribution to human progress was in preserving, in the royal libraries, much of the literature of ancient Babylonia.

The Assyrians, the 'children of Ashur', were a Semitic race, originally colonists from Babylonia, and at first its subjects. Later they conquered Babylon round about 1300. In the ninth century they descended on Syria and Canaan and reached the Mediterranean. In 722 their king, Sargon, besieged the northern Jewish kingdom and destroyed its capital, Samaria. Twenty years later came Sennacherib, whose terrible advance, as described in the Old Testament, inspired Lord Byron's famous lines:

> *The Assyrian came down like a wolf on the fold,*
> *And his cohorts were gleaming in purple and gold,*

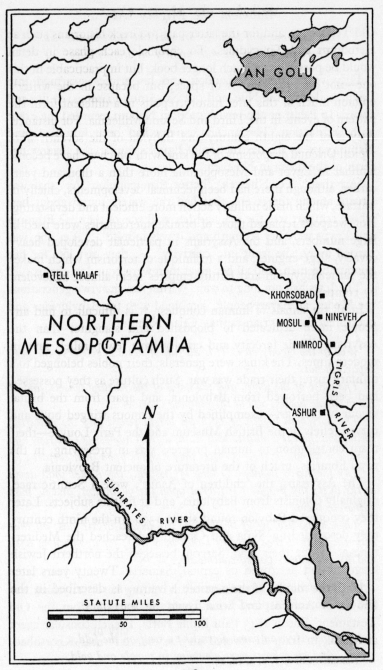

VAN GOLU

TELL HALAF

KHORSOBAD

MOSUL ■ ■ NINEVEH

NIMROD

ASHUR

TIGRIS RIVER

NORTHERN MESOPOTAMIA

EUPHRATES RIVER

STATUTE MILES

0   50   100

'Babylon, the Mighty City'

And the sheen of their spears was like stars on the sea
Where the blue wave rolls nightly on deep Galilee . . .

Fifty years later Ezarhaddon and his armies swarmed into
Egypt, sailed up the Nile, and put No-Amun (Thebes) to fire and
sword. In Palestine the Jewish prophet Nahum recorded the event
with satisfaction. The ancient enemy had been humbled, and
Nahum saw, in the destruction of Egypt's capital, the shadowing-
forth of the doom of Nineveh.

'Art thou' (i.e. Nineveh) 'better than populous *No*, that was
situate among the rivers, that had the waters round about her;
whose rampart was the sea, and her wall was of the sea? Ethiopia
and Egypt were her strength and it was infinite . . . Yet she was
carried away, she went into captivity . . . they cast lots for her
honourable men, and all her great men were bound in chains . . .'

The Jews had not long to wait. Within less than two generations
the Medes, an Aryan people, combined with the Babylonians and
overthrew the Assyrian capital. Cried Nahum:

'Woe to the bloody city! It is all full of lies and robbery; the prey
departeth not.'

'The noise of the whip, and the noise of the rattling wheels, and of
the prancing horses, and of the jumping chariots.'

'The horseman lifteth up both the bright sword and the glittering
spear; and there is a multitude of slain; a great number of carcases; and
there is none end of their corpses; they stumble upon their corpses . . .'

'Thy shepherds slumber, O king of Assyria; thy nobles shall dwell
in the dust; thy people is scattered upon the mountains, and no man
gathereth them.'

'There is no healing of thy bruise; thy wound is grievous; all that
hear the bruit of thee clap the hands over thee; for upon whom hath
not thy wickedness passed continually?'[1]

Until the middle of the nineteenth century hardly anything was
known of Assyria, save what could be learned from the Old
Testament. But in 1843 Paul Emile Botta, French consular agent
at Mosul, in Iraq, discovered an Assyrian city near Khorsobad.

[1] Nahum—Ch. 3. 1, 2, 3, 18, 19.

The accumulation of centuries of occupation had buried it, leaving only a huge, shapeless mound of earth. Digging into this mound, Botta was astonished to find himself tunnelling into chambers lined with stone slabs, vigorously carved with spirited scenes showing men with thick, curled beards, tall head-dresses, and proud, cruel lips. Sometimes they were standing in war-chariots watching their soldiers attacking a walled city with siege-engines; flames leaped from burning buildings, decapitated corpses floated in the river, women and children were being taken away captive. There were processions of gods too, and above them, inscriptions in a language which could not, at that time, be understood. Botta sent to his superior, Mohl, a message which caused a sensation when it reached Europe.

'I believe myself', he wrote, 'to be the first who has discovered sculptures which with some reason can be referred to the period when Nineveh was flourishing.'

When Botta cut his first excavation trench he found first the buried chambers of the Assyrian king's palace, but as he went further he came upon doorways, each flanked with a pair of huge human-headed bulls or lions, winged and terrible. These, with infinite labour, he prised loose from their foundations, and, with the heavy carved slabs, dragged them on rollers to the river, floated them on rafts down to Basra, and sent them via a French warship to Paris.

A few years after Botta had unearthed the Assyrian town of Dur Sharrakin, Austen Henry Layard, an Englishman, discovered and excavated Nineveh itself. His anticipatory dreams, as described in his book *Nineveh and its Remains*, give us the full zestful flavour of mid-Victorian archaeology.

'Visions of palaces underground, of gigantic monsters, of sculptured figures, floated before me. After forming plan after plan for removing the earth, and extricating these treasures, I fancied myself wandering in a maze of chambers from which I could find no outlet. Then, again, all was re-buried, and I was standing on a grass-covered mound.'

Layard too found sculptured bulls and many superbly carved reliefs, which he also removed and transported to the British

Museum where they now stand. These sculptures, when they arrived, awed and excited the Victorian public, accustomed as they were to stimulating Biblical descriptions of the vile Assyrians. In fact there was something about the Assyrians which appealed to the Victorians, just as the Ancient Egyptians attract us in the twentieth century. Perhaps, as Seton Lloyd has observed 'these enormous Assyrian bulls had something in common with the ponderous conservative philosophy of the mid-Victorian period, with its unshakeable faith in the best of all possible worlds.'

Anyone who has visited the British Museum, where hundreds of tons of Assyrian sculpture clutter up some of the largest galleries, will recognise immediately what Lloyd means. One of the reliefs depicts, in loving detail, the torture of a captive king. Another Assyrian inscription reads:

'I slew one of every two. I built a wall before the great gates of the city; I flayed the chief men of the rebels, and I covered the wall with their skins. Some of them were enclosed alive within the bricks of the wall, some of them were crucified with stakes along the wall; I caused a great multitude of them to be flayed in my presence, and I covered the walls with their skins.'

Some modern scholars, who deprecate the 'popularising' of archaeology, would do well to read the works of their Victorian predecessors. There are passages in Layard, Maspero, and even Petrie, which the editor of *Life* magazine would probably have blue-pencilled as being too highly-coloured.

But they were remarkable men. They endured hardships and dangers which would turn some modern archaeologists grey; no air-conditioning, no laboratories and quiet libraries for them; no kite-balloons for aerial photography, no jeeps for transport; and hardly any financial support from governments or private institutions. Botta, admittedly, received a magnificent response when he appealed to the French Government for funds, but when Layard wrote to Canning, the ambassador at Istanbul, suggesting that his finds were of such importance as to merit support by the British Museum, all Canning managed to obtain for him was two thousand pounds. The result was that Layard was forced to raise money by selling antiquities.

Yet within two years he excavated Nineveh, establishing the existence of at least one Assyrian palace there, besides discovering eight Assyrian palaces connected with such kings as Ashurnasir-pal, Sargon, Shalmaneser, Tiglath-Pileser, Ezarhaddon (conqueror of Egypt) and Sennacherib. He was also responsible for shipping to England the hundreds of tons of Assyrian sculpture which now grace the British Museum.

In return he was made unpaid attaché to Her Majesty's Embassy at Constantinople.[1]

The other great archaeological adventure in Mesopotamia was the excavation of Babylon. Like Nineveh it was familiar from the Bible. Isaiah had written:

Alas, alas that great city Babylon, that mighty city! for in one hour is thy judgement come.

And the merchants of the earth shall weep and mourn over her; for no man buyeth her their merchandise any more;

The merchandise of gold and silver, and precious stones, and of pearls, and fine linen, and purple, and silk, and scarlet, and all thyine wood, and all manner vessels of ivory, and all manner vessels of most precious wood, and of brass, and iron, and marble.

And cinnamon, and odours, and ointments, and frankincense, and wine, and oil, and wheat, and beasts, and sheep, and horses, and slaves, and the souls of men.

Readers will remember that in 1792 B.C. Hammurabi ruled from this city an empire which stretched from Assyria to the Persian Gulf, and from the Mediterranean in the west to Elam in the east. (See Chapter VII.) His rule did not last long, and after his death Babylon fell a victim to invaders from the north and east, and later it was ruled by a weak line of Kassite kings until, in the early part of the thirteenth century B.C., it became a tributary state of the Assyrian Empire. But throughout its long history, Babylon clung on to the culture which it had inherited from the long-vanished Sumerians. In spite of conquests and re-conquests, war and devastation, the arts and sciences survived; and since

---

[1] For this information the writer is indebted to Mr. Seton Lloyd's book, *Foundations in the Dust.*

some of these reached the Greeks and were transmitted by them to us, Babylon has a greater claim to our respect than Assyria with its winged bulls.

Their greatest achievements were in astronomy, mathematics and literature. They catalogued the stars. In the royal library of the Hittite capital of Hattusas, archaeologists found copies of this catalogue, which by 1200 B.C. had become known even as far west as the Aegean. A century later the Assyrian scribes had revised the list, and by 800 B.C. the Babylonian astronomers had attained such a degree of accuracy that they had begun to give the stars' positions and helical settings. Even more remarkable is the fact that from 747 B.C. they gave up dating events from the 'nth year of a certain king, and instead to count the years from a fixed point, as we count them from the birth of Jesus Christ. The Babylonians used as their conventional point 'the era of Nabonassar'.

A genuine science of mathematics began in the temple schools of Babylon, apparently in the time of Hammurabi (*circa* 1800 B.C.). The extant documents which illustrate it are mainly concerned with the division of property, inheritance and business operations. Like geometry in Egypt, where it was necessary to formulate rules for the parcelling of land, or the building of monuments, Babylonian mathematics fulfilled a practical need.

Sheer pressure of business forced the Babylonian clerks to simplify their mathematical signs, just as much later the Phoenicians, a trading people, devised a simple alphabet to facilitate their commercial dealings. 'The Babylonian temple scholars . . . invented a system that enabled them to operate with fractional quantities that cannot be represented on the fingers or with counters, and that without the tedious calculations entailed in the unit fractions or aliquot parts that their forerunners had been forced to employ. This purely technical improvement in the instrument used in reckoning gave man mastery over—almost— the whole domain of real numbers.'[1]

Throughout this long span of time Babylonian literature developed in many forms; their epic poems, some of which owe their origin to the Sumerians, tell heroic stories of gods and

[1] *What Happened in History*—Gordon Childe: London, 1942.

heroes. Their religious poetry greatly influenced the Hebrews, as did their folk-tales explaining the origin of the earth and of mankind—e.g. Genesis. But one misses the note of tender lyricism which one finds in Egyptian love-poetry.

But unlike the Egyptian hieroglyphic and hieratic writing (hieratic was the cursive form of hieroglyphic), Babylonian cuneiform—the wedge-shaped signs which had been invented by the Sumerians—spread throughout western Asia, so that Babylonian culture spread to many countries outside Babylon itself.

For a brief period between 612 and 539 B.C., Babylon again became a great military power. This was the period of Nebuchadnezzar, who carried the Jews into captivity, who thrust Shadrach, Mesach and Abednecho into the fiery furnace, and Daniel into the lions' den. One of his successors, Belshazzar, is chiefly remembered as the villain of one of the most dramatic stories in the Old Testament.

Some of the Jews, carried into captivity by Nebuchadnezzar, were brought to Babylon, 'the mighty city', with its streets paved with marble, its bridges across the Euphrates, its great walls on top of which two chariots could drive abreast, and houses of three and more stories. It would seem to them as New York would appear to the inhabitants of a small mid-Western town who had never seen a great city.

Then, one day, Belshazzar, son of Nabonidas, gave a great feast in his palace, at which the Jews were compelled to be present. The writer of the Book of Daniel describes the scene, with all the fascinated horror of the outraged puritan:

'*Belshazzar the king made a great feast to a thousand of his lords, and drank wine before the thousand.*'

'*Belshazzar, whilst he tasted the wine, commanded to bring the golden and silver vessels which his father Nebuchadnezzar had taken out of the temple which was in Jerusalem; that the king, and his princes, his wives, and his concubines, might drink therein.*'

'*. . . They drank the wine, and praised the gods of gold, and of silver, of brass, of iron, and of stone.*'

'*In the same hour came forth fingers of a man's hand, and wrote over against the candlestick upon the plaster of the wall of the king's palace; and the king saw the part of the hand that wrote . . .*'

'*. . . And this is the writing that was written. MENE, MENE, TEKEL UPHARSIN . . . "God has numbered thy kingdom, and finished it . . . Thou art weighed in the balances and art found wanting . . . Thy kingdom is divided, and given to the Medes and Persians".*'

'*. . . And in that night was Belshazzar the king of the Chaldeans slain.*'[1]

It is ironical that the best-known work of literature which can evoke for us the splendour and sumptuousness of the Babylonian court, and the terror of its destruction, is by the exiled spokesman of a small Semitic tribe, one of many whom the conqueror had swept before him like chaff. Yet through his angry eyes we can see it, and what he does not tell us we can imagine; the shimmer of light from massed candles, the courtiers in scarlet and gold, the wives and concubines drinking from gold and silver vessels, the massed clash of armlets and anklets as near-naked dancers swirl and stamp before the great idols—'gods of gold, silver, brass, iron, wood and stone, which see not, nor hear, neither do they know . . .'

The site of ancient Babylon has never been lost. During the eighteenth and nineteenth centuries, generations of travellers pottered about among the dusty mounds near Hillah, on the Euphrates, usually taking away with them a few inscribed bricks. In Lord Byron's *Don Juan* occur the malicious lines:

> *Though Claudius Rich, Esquire, some bricks has got,*
> *And written lately two memoirs upon 't.*

Claudius Rich was one of the pioneers of Mesopotamian research; he was succeeded by James Silk Buckingham, Austen Henry Layard, Paul Emile Botta, Henry Rawlinson, Hormuzd Rassam, and others. But it was not until 1899 that the German archaeologist, Dr. Koldewey, began a systematic excavation of

[1] Daniel, ch. 5.

Babylon, a work which continued up to the outbreak of the First World War. He trained his Arab helpers with such care and skill that they were able not only to trace baked-brick walls, but even the more fragile sun-dried walls.

After years of slow, painstaking work the great German scholar revealed the whole plan of Babylon. Where previously there had been only a confused mass of mounds, ditches and broken walls, there appeared the fortifications (including remains of the great wall and the monumental gates), the processional avenue flanked by huge sculptured reliefs of lions and dragons, the Palace of Nebuchadnezzar, the Ishtar Gate[1] and even the foundations of the famous Hanging Gardens with the remains of the well from which water was pumped to them. Where the buildings themselves had perished, Koldewey by 1914 had been able to make a reliable reconstruction.

The city which he and his staff discovered was mainly the Babylon of Nebuchadnezzar, although it stood on much earlier foundations. The excavations found the Sacred Way which ran through the city from north to south. This magnificent street was raised more than forty feet above the level of the plain. It was paved with slabs of red and white stone, each over three feet square. Its flanking walls were covered with glazed tiles of bright colour, ornamented with friezes of lions, bulls and dragons. Near the centre of the town stood the great temple with its enclosure. The Sacred Way crossed the Euphrates by a massive bridge (which Herodotus mentions) and then passed to the western quarter of Babylon.

The temple itself, called E-temen-anki, had a tower about 250 feet high, with a triple staircase leading to sanctuaries dedicated to the various Babylonian gods. Of this temple Herodotus, who visited Babylon in the sixth century B.C., wrote:

'On the summit of the topmost tower stands a great temple with a fine large couch in it, richly covered, and a golden table beside it. The shrine contains no image, and no one spends the night there except (if we may believe the Chaldeans who are the priests of Bel) one Assyrian woman, all alone, whoever it may be

---

[1] Subsequently reconstructed in Germany from the original materials.

that the god has chosen. The Chaldeans also say—though I do not believe them—that the god himself enters the temple in person and takes his rest upon the bed.'[1]

This tower or 'Ziggurat' was almost certainly the Biblical Tower of Babel, though some archaeologists suggest that Birs Nimrud, which also had a high ziggurat, may have been the Tower. The reader will note that Babylon in the seventh century B.C. retained many features of the Sumerian cities of two thousand years earlier, described in Chapter IV.

None of these monumental splendours survive today, of course; our knowledge of them is derived partly from Herodotus, and partly from the work of the German archaeologists who for fifteen years painstakingly counted and measured baked or sun-dried bricks and, from a dust heap, reconstructed on paper a city which was the glory of the ancient world. But twentieth century tourists who visit Babylon will find it much as the eighteenth and nine-teenth century travellers saw it; a few huge mounds of mud-brick and broken pottery heaped beside the great river which flows majestically across the sombre plain, past silted canals and scrubby little fields where once were acres of waving wheat, vine-yards and olive-groves, the economic foundation of the second oldest civilisation on earth.

It may seem fanciful, but it seems to me that this transitional period—the seventh century—in human history is like the end of the Third Movement in Beethoven's Fifth Symphony. There is a moment when the Third Movement has ended, but the Fourth and final movement has not begun. One waits, hushed and ex-pectant, while a sinister figure on the strings weaves back and forth across a slow, insistent, rhythmic beat from the tympani. E. M. Forster, in his novel *Howards End*, likens this passage to a march of goblins.

'It was as if the splendour of life might boil over and waste to steam and froth. In its dissolution one heard the terrible, ominous note, and a goblin, with increased malignity, walked over the

[1] Herodotus, *The Histories*. Translated by Aubrey de Selincourt. Penguin Books, London, 1954.

universe from end to end. Panic and emptiness! Panic and emptiness! Even the flaming ramparts of the world might fall.'[1]

To an Egyptian priest living in 600 B.C., who knew of the
great civilisations of the East which had flourished and decayed
through nearly three thousand years, it might well have seemed
that 'the splendour of life' had 'boiled over and wasted to steam and
froth'. Admittedly the Egyptian colossus still stood. There was
still a Pharaoh on the throne, ruling from Sais, in the Delta, the
place in which the earliest civilisation of the Nile Valley had
originated; but though he campaigned in Asia with the aid of
foreign mercenaries, his victories were short lived. It was now the
Twenty-sixth Dynasty, two thousand six hundred years after
Menes, who founded the First. Yet the Pharaoh still wore on his
crowns the double insignia—the cobra and the vulture—which
Menes had used to signify his dominion over Upper and Lower
Egypt. The same gods—Re, Osiris, Isis, Horus, and the rest—
were worshipped, though Neit, the tribal goddess of Sais, with her
crossed spears, had returned to favour after some three thousand
years. Workmen still sculptured, on tombs and temples, similar
scenes to those which had adorned the monuments of the Old
Kingdom. There was even a religious and cultural renaissance.
The Saites studied and reproduced the ancient religious texts,
revived the ritual, and imitated the art of that far-off age. But,
unlike the European renaissance of the fifteenth century A.D., it
was not a starting point for new ideas, but a last backward glance
at glories which would never return.

Looking eastward our Egyptian priest would see the ruins of
empires. The Hittites were a memory. The maritime greatness of
the Phoenicians had ended, though their colonies survived. The
dreaded Assyrians who, only seventy years earlier, had sacked
Thebes, had themselves been destroyed. Babylon alone of the
ancient kingdoms remained great, but she too had not long to live.
Sixty years later Cyrus the Persian would ride in triumph along
the Sacred Way, and Babylonia would be absorbed into the Persian
Empire.

As for the Greeks, *they* were everywhere, of course—in Egypt,

[1] *Howards End*—E. M. Forster: Edward Arnold & Co., London, 1932.

Syria, Asia Minor, in hundreds of colonies scattered throughout the Aegean Islands, and along the coasts from Marseilles to the Black Sea. They were an intelligent people, good mercenary soldiers, keen traders and skilful craftsmen. But there was something irritating about their perpetual curiosity. They were always asking the *reason* for things. They poked about among one's monuments, scrawled their names on the walls, pestered one with their eternal questions, and chattered all the time.

How could one take them seriously? They were brave warriors and expert sailors but, far from falling into line behind a king like the obedient Egyptians or Babylonians, they could rarely be persuaded even to follow their own clan-leaders for long; and they were perpetually quarrelling among themselves. The trouble was that they *would* argue, and regarded themselves as 'free men'—whatever that meant.

The Greeks were children. Clever, of course, but still children.[1] And the priest would return to his temple to perform once again the sacred rites which his predecessors had been practising since the beginning of Egyptian history. *He* did not ask questions. His ancestors had provided all the answers more than two thousand years ago.

[1] This statement was made by an Egyptian priest to Solon the Athenian law-giver.

CHAPTER XIV

The Dawn of Western Civilisation

Stereotypes are the bane of any writer who attempts to portray the peoples of past civilisations. For many, the words 'Ancient Egypt' immediately evoke a picture of rows of little brown-skinned people, always seen in profile, with legs and arms in stiff, grotesque attitudes; and a comic sign-language consisting mainly of birds, beetles and serpents. With the Ancient Greeks it is worse, for we know all about the Greeks. They wore long white robes; their women were either draped and bosomy, with hair piled on top of their heads, or else undraped, heavy-limbed and voluptuous —and sometimes without arms. The men were always handsome— 'like gods'—and spent their time either in deep-browed meditation against a vague background of columns, or else charging naked behind huge round shields, and wearing firemen's helmets.

They were also 'classical', of course—which means that they wrote plays in which nothing happened and robed women moaned in chorus—and produced statuary which, though the subjects were occasionally scandalous and the characters usually nude, could safely be shown to school-parties in any well-conducted art gallery. This had something to do with 'the human form divine', but whatever it was, it was perfectly respectable. It was Art.

We are not suggesting that readers of this book see the Greeks in this way; nor are we being superior because, if one examines one's own mental picture, fragments of the stereotype may still linger there. That is the trouble with stereotypes—there is an element of truth in most of them. But any who feel offended by this absurd caricature are never likely to understand the real Greeks, who loved a joke and would have been the first to laugh at the ridiculous picture which later generations—mainly the Victorians—had pasted over the original.

There are so many contradictions in the Greek character that no single view of it is possible. Take as one example their superb courage in battle, and the high respect which they gave to the military virtues. Here is a passage from Homer's *Iliad* in which the Trojan hero, Hector, rejects his wife's plea that he should not expose himself to danger on the battlefield:

'*I should feel great shame before the Trojans and the Trojan women of the long robes if like a coward I should linger away from battle. Nor do I find that in my heart, for I have been taught to be brave always, and to fight in the forefront among the Trojans, winning great glory for my father and myself.*'

How typically Greek, we think! But so is this poem, by an Ionian poet named Archilochus. To get the full flavour of its impudence one must remember the injunction which the Spartan mothers gave to their sons before they went to war: 'Come back with your shield—or *on* it!'

> *Some lucky Thracian has my warlike shield.*
> *I had to run; I dropped it in a wood,*
> *But I got clear away, thank God! So hang the shield.*
> *I'll get another just as good!*[1]

That is Greek too, and just as typical.

Then take their undoubted reverence for their gods, always consulting them before making decisions, and making due thank-offerings to them afterwards. Yet Herodotus tells a story concerning Themistocles, the Athenian hero, who more than any other statesman was responsible for the Greek victory over the Persian fleet at Salamis. Themistocles sent messengers to the people of the Greek island of Andros who, with other Greeks, had been asked to subscribe to the cost of the fleet, and backed his demands with the hint of force.

'He put it to them,' says the Greek historian, 'that they would be unable to avoid paying, because the Athenians had the support of two powerful deities, one called *If-you-please*, and the other *Oh-but-you-must*, and the Andrians replied that Athens was very

---

[1] Translated by H. D. F. Kitto. *The Greeks*. Penguin Books, 1951.

lucky to have two such useful gods, who were obviously responsible for her wealth and greatness; unfortunately, however, they themselves in their small and inadequate island, also had two deities in permanent possession of their soil—and by no means such useful ones, for their names were *Haven't-a-penny* and *Sorry-I-Can't* .'[1]

This story illustrates two aspects of the Greek character, their capacity for irreverence, and their sense of humour. Can one imagine the Hittites or the Assyrians behaving like this?

But the most perplexing contradiction to modern minds is between their capacity for rational thought and their adherence to what we regard as the grossest superstition. They were probably the most intelligent and knowledgeable people who ever lived. They were the founders of what we call 'science'; they observed, studied, and reasoned things out. 'Nothing can arise out of nothing,' wrote one of their philosophers in the sixth century, 'naught happens for nothing, but everything has a ground in necessity.' In two or three generations they discovered the true theories of eclipses, that the earth was round, and that, like the other planets, it revolved round the sun. Two of their watchwords were 'save the phenomena' and 'give a reason'.

Professor Burnet wrote, 'No sooner did an Ionian philosopher learn half a dozen geometrical propositions, and hear that the phenomena of the heavens recur in cycles, than he set to work to look for law everywhere in nature, and with an audacity amounting to *hubris*[2] to construct a system of the universe.'

Such thinkers rejected the primitive Babylonian fables which said that the universe began in primeval chaos, and looked for a primary substance which remained permanent amid change. They called this fundamental substance *physis* (nature, hence our word 'Physical') and conducted deep inquiries into its nature and origin.

The word 'atom', for instance, is Greek (*atomos*, meaning 'indivisible') and was used to elucidate one of their theories of matter. Anaxagoras and Aristotle believed that matter was finite and continuous. Others such as Democritus and Epicurus taught

---

[1] Herodotus, *op. cit.*

[2] A Greek word, almost untranslatable, but meaning roughly 'spiritual pride'.

that matter was *grained*—that it consisted of minute particles which could not be divided.

A century before our time such scientists as Darwin and Huxley examined fossils of animals, and postulated that the world was far, far older than Man, and that over a period of millions of years there had been changes in the earth's crust; so that what had once been under the sea was now on a mountain-top. More than two thousand five hundred years before Huxley, a Greek philosopher, Xenophanes, found fossilised remains of sea-shells in the mountains of Sicily, and the imprint of seaweed and fishes in a quarry near Syracuse, and correctly interpreted them.

'These men', writes Kitto, 'were quite capable of using their eyes and their minds together, and we need not suppose that Thales' answer' (to the question 'what is the world made of?') 'was based on nothing but abstract reasoning.'

Yet these brilliant people respected Oracles, and could base vital decisions—such as whether or not they should resist the invading Persians (and, therefore, whether Western civilisation should survive) on the babblings of an old woman squatting in a cave at Delphi, chewing laurel-leaves.

The Greeks were such an original people that each age and every nation sees them differently. The French, naturally, were attracted by their intellectual gifts, whereas some British Hellenists of the Victorian and Edwardian periods were so attracted by the Greek cult of athletics that they seem to have seen the Hellenes mainly as jolly nice chaps, who had been to Public Schools, and were awfully good at games (which they were). The Germans tended to see them as tall 'blond beasts' from the North. The modern Greeks, equally naturally, see them as a small, dark Mediterranean people like themselves. Is it possible to look at the Greeks freshly, forgetting for a moment what our ancestors have said and thought about them?

We derive our knowledge of Greece from two main sources—written history and archaeology. Unlike the language of the Egyptians, the Babylonians and Assyrians, the Greek language never died. It was preserved under the Romans, then by the Roman Catholic Church, and revived under the Renaissance.

Medieval monks read Aristotle and Plato; Shakespeare read contemporary translations of Homer and other Greek writers and used them as material for his plays. From the sixteenth century onwards, Greek literature and art were one of the principal bases of drama, poetry, sculpture, and painting throughout western Europe.

But until less than a century ago we had no idea of the origins of Greek culture. To scholars of the eighteenth and early nineteenth centuries it seemed to have sprung out of nothing—like the warriors who leaped, fully-armed, from the furrows in the story of Jason and the Golden Fleece. As recently as 1846, the historian Grote could write:

'. . . I begin the real history of Greece with the first recorded Olympiad, or 776 B.C. . . . For the truth is, that historical records, properly so called, do not begin until after this date. . . .'

Grote believed that Homer, whose writings the classical Greeks regarded as history, was a mere spinner of fairy-tales. Schliemann, the German archaeologist, was the first to upset this theory when he discovered, at Troy and later at Mycenae, relics of a civilisation remarkably like that described in the *Iliad* and the *Odyssey* (see Chapter X). Then, at the beginning of the present century, Sir Arthur Evans discovered, at Knossos in Crete, evidence of a civilisation which had a clear affinity with that of the so-called 'Myceneans', but was far older. (See Chapter VIII.) Eventually the historians had to admit the existence of what they called a 'pre-Hellenic' civilisation, long before the days of classical Greece (roughly 600–300 B.C.), but that after about 1100 B.C. this civilisation collapsed, giving way to a 'Dark Age' which was illiterate. Nowadays even this theory is beginning to be discredited, although it still has its adherents.

But the British archaeologist, Professor Wace (University of Princeton), who has directed some of the most recent and important excavations at Mycenae, writes:

'We can no longer speak of pre-Hellenic Greece, because from 2000 B.C. onwards the Greeks were in Greece, and Mycenean art is the first great manifestation of Greek art.'

As for the language, the mysterious Minoan writing, which

Evans called 'Linear B', and which baffled him for forty years, turned out to be a primitive form of Greek. As already mentioned,[1] Michael Ventris, a young British architect (who had heard Evans lecture on the Minoan tablets when Ventris was a schoolboy at Stowe), eventually deciphered it in 1954, and other scholars eagerly supplied him with material. Professor Blegen of Cincinnatti University, who had excavated at Pylos (the home of Nestor, one of the heroes of the *Iliad*) wrote to Ventris in 1953:

'Since returning to Greece I have spent much of my time working on the tablets from Pylos, getting them properly ready to be photographed. I have tried your experimental syllabary on some of them. Enclosed for your information, is a copy of Pylos No. 641, which you may find interesting. It evidently deals with pots, some on three legs, some with four handles, some with three, and others without handles. The first words by your system seem to be *ti-ri-po-de*, and it occurs twice as *ti-ri-po*. The four-handled pot is preceded by *que-to-ro-we*, the three-handled by *ti-ro-o-we* or *ti-ri-yo-we*, the handle-less pot by *an-no-we*.'
(All these are Greek words. L.C.)
'All this seems too good to be true. Is coincidence excluded?'

It was not a coincidence. 'Linear B' was Greek, and Homeric Greek at that. Chadwick, another young Englishman, and a colleague of Ventris, found that among the names given in the tablets were some which, by Ventris's system, could be read as *Hector* and *Achilles*, and also the names of a number of later Greek gods, which were evidently known in Greece more than three hundred years before the traditional date of Homer's birth, and five centuries before the earliest date of 'classical' Greece (776 B.C.). Some of the tablets also described articles of furniture which are mentioned in Homer's poems. For example in the *Odyssey*, Homer relates how:

'They put a chair for Penelope to sit by the fire, wrought with ivory and silver; the craftsman Ikmalios made it long ago, and fitted it with a footstool for the feet.'

At Pylos, Blegen found in 1953 a long list of furniture which, when translated by Ventris and Chadwick, read:

[1] See pages 116 and 117

'*One chair of ebony inlaid with ivory on the back; the footstool inlaid with ivory figures of a man, a horse, an octopus and a griffin.*'
Such furniture was unknown in Homer's day (*circa* 900–800 B.C.), let alone in the time of the 'classical' Greeks.

Nowadays, scholars are not even certain if the art of writing, which the Myceneans learned from the Minoans, ever died out completely in the so-called Dark Age. It seems certain that elements of the old Mycenean culture survived—for instance, the art of making pottery on the wheel, bronze-working and other crafts. The influence of Mycenean art can also be traced in later Greek art. But fashions changed. For example, the chariot went out of use as an instrument of war; and so did the big Mycenean body-shield. Although there are references to these in the poems of Homer, he obviously wrote during the Iron Age when his heroes used iron weapons and carried small round shields, not unlike those used by the Greeks of classical times. Also, they cremated their dead, whereas the Myceneans buried theirs. But, like flies in amber, elements of the vanished Mycenean culture—its palaces, furniture, arms, and method of warfare—survived in the 'Iliad' and the 'Odyssey', inherited by the poet from earlier oral poetry of Mycenean times.

What can be tolerably certain is the later 'Dorian' invaders who began swarming into Greece during the Twelfth and Eleventh centuries were of kindred Greek-speaking stock to the Myceneans. Neither they nor their Mycenean predecessors destroyed the indigenous population, who were of the aboriginal 'Mediterranean' stock—small, dark, and long-skulled. Indeed these people are still there—from Spain to Asia Minor—having absorbed their conquerors. But they were dominated by the invaders.

As successive waves pushed down through the Balkans and into Greece, there was fighting for land, and sometimes the defeated clans would take to the sea and found colonies elsewhere, in the islands, or along the coasts of Asia Minor, Syria, North Africa and Italy. Over-population produced the same result.

There was never a unified Greek State. Partly because of the geography of the country, divided as it was by high mountains and sea-channels running deep inland, and partly because of the character of the people themselves, the Greek ideal of government became the small, independent city-state, which they called the *polis*; it is from this, incidentally, and related Greek words such as *polites* (citizen) and *politeia* (citizenship) that we derive our words 'political'—appertaining to the State of its Government—and 'politician'—one allegedly skilled in politics. To the Greeks the State was the City and its surrounding land. Most of these were very small.

It was the same in the numerous Greek colonies which were set up in the islands and along the coast of the Mediterranean. The Myceneans also had colonised, but the later Greeks did so on a much larger scale. From about 1000 B.C. onwards, for more than six hundred years, parent cities solved their population problems by sending out groups of men and women to found colonies; the very word is of Greek origin, derived from *kolon*, meaning 'limb'. These settlements, too, were independent owing no political allegiance to the parent-city, though bound to it, sometimes, by sentimental ties.

The Greeks were not the only Mediterranean people to form colonies; the Phoenicians founded Carthage in North Africa, and Tarshish (Cadiz) in Spain; and another people, who may have come from Asia Minor, settled in Italy. These were the Etruscans, who developed a unique and brilliant civilisation of their own; they came into conflict with the Greeks but were ultimately overcome by the Romans at a much later period.[1]

Except for Sparta, the most conservative of Greek states, the Greeks were not ruled by kings. They experimented with various forms of government, usually elective; sometimes an oligarchy (rule by the few), sometimes an aristocracy which originally meant 'rule by the best' (from *aristos*—best—and *kratia*—rule); but often one man would seize power for a time and become an absolute ruler (autocrat). The Greeks rarely tolerated these for long, even when—as sometimes occurred—they were benevolent. The Hellenic peoples discovered—as who has not?—that such men often became corrupted by power; then the Greeks gave them the less complimentary name of *turranikos* (tyrant), meaning a

---

[1] The Etruscan civilisation will be described in a later volume.

cruel and oppressive ruler; and it became an act of patriotism to destroy them. The most popular form of government—in every sense of the word—was *demokratia* (rule by the people), which reached its greatest glory in fifth century Athens. From it comes our word 'democracy'.

It is significant that practically all our words describing systems of government come from the Greek language.

But if there is one fact of which we can be quite certain it was that the Greeks were not egalitarian, in the sense of believing that all men are equal. They would have been the last people to accept this view. One of the Greek ideals was the full, complete man; daring, adventurous, successful in many fields of activity in which wealth, if acquired, was merely incidental. There has probably never been such a race of individualists, to whom the 'Welfare State' would have been anathema. But this was both a strength and a weakness, for while the Greek love of freedom gave full play to the growth of the spirit and the intellect, encouraging the gifted and intelligent, it hindered them from uniting and sinking their differences in the face of a common enemy, except on one rare and wonderful occasion.

Also, lest we tend to over-idealise the Greeks, it is well to remember that their economy was based partly on slave-labour, though a slave in fifth century Athens enjoyed privileges which would not have been permitted under any of the Oriental despotisms. They enjoyed more legal protection than did American Negro slaves. The Spartans, a military people who scorned trade and agriculture, sneered at Athens, where, they said, 'you cannot distinguish between slave and free man; you cannot take a stick to a slave in an Athenian street because you may be striking a free man. They all wear the same clothes.' The Spartans were less scrupulous. They encouraged their martial youth to hunt down and kill their *helots*, partly for the exercise and also to prevent the serfs becoming too numerous. But the Spartans were unlike any other Greeks.

The 'classical' Greeks, then, were a different kind of human being from any described in this book (save, perhaps, the Myceneans)—different in their art, their literature, moral outlook, political and social organisations, in their way of thinking and feeling about life. The question which remains can be summed up in that useful American phrase—'how did they get that way?'

There is, of course, no final and definite answer to such a question. One can only express a point of view. First, there was the so-called 'genius of the race'. Theories of racial superiority tend to be discredited nowadays, but I believe that the Greeks of this period possessed special qualities of mind and character which enabled them to make full use of the opportunities presented to them. These opportunities were many. In the first place the Greeks, unlike the Egyptians and Sumerians who created the first great civilisations on this planet, had to travel widely. This was forced upon them by the fact that the settlements they formed in the mountain valleys and bays of continental Greece, could not support a large population; as their numbers increased, and as new invaders came down from the north, they were compelled to emigrate.

Secondly, they did not carry with them too many legacies of the Bronze Age. Their minds were untrammelled by too many earlier traditions; and such traditions as they possessed encouraged self-reliance, an adventurous spirit, and the will to fight, and if necessary, die bravely. The compulsion to travel and colonise made them into a nation of seafarers and traders, and wherever they went they came into contact with the remains of earlier, older cultures, which they approached with fresh, curious minds. Seafaring and service as mercenaries in the armies of Egypt and Asia taught them many things. For instance, they learned from the Phoenician traders their simplified alphabet, and adapted it to write their own language. (The Phoenician script itself may have been derived from the Egyptian hieroglyphs.) But they improved on the original, adding vowel sounds.

Then they visited Egypt and Babylonia, both of which, though decaying, were still in being when the Greeks first came in contact with them. Egypt especially fascinated them, and their writers paid tribute to the debt which they owed the oldest of civilisations. Herodotus, the 'father of history', who was born between 490 and 480 B.C., spent his early life travelling over much of the known world, visiting Egypt as far south as Assuan, Meso-potamia, Palestine and southern Russia. In Egypt he did not only do what we can do today—visit the pyramids, tombs, and temples —but he was able to talk to the priests who kept the temple records and knew the history and traditions of their land. In his *History*, he describes the geography of Egypt, why the Nile floods, Egyptian astronomy, religious practices, their burial customs (including the method of embalming), and tells us much about Egyptian history and social customs. There is no doubt that elements of Egyptian culture—for example, medicine, astronomy, geometry, and the art of working in stone—were absorbed by the Greeks. But, as with the Phoenician alphabet, they improved on them.

The Greeks also penetrated into Syria-Palestine (the Jews knew them; the Old Testament calls them *Javan*, a corruption of 'Ionian'), and to Babylonia, from which they derived some of their mathematical knowledge. Herodotus's description of Babylon itself is one of the most fascinating chapters of his book; for through the eyes of this youthful Greek, we see one of the oldest civilisations, not in ruins, but still in being. Here was the new world looking at the old with respect and admiration, but not always uncritically. He writes:

'Babylon lies in a wide plain, a vast city in the form of a square with sides nearly fourteen miles long and a circuit of some fifty-six miles, and in addition to its enormous size it surpasses in splendour any city of the known world. It is surrounded by a broad deep moat full of water, and within the moat there is a wall fifty royal cubits wide' (about 80 feet) 'and two hundred high' (about 320 feet) . . . There are a hundred gates in the circuit of the wall, all of bronze with bronze uprights and lintels.'[1]

Koldewey has since proved the Greek historian's figures to be inaccurate; the total area of Babylon enclosed by walls was about 14 square miles, but the breadth of the walls was correct (80 feet). The original height may have been that of a 20-storey building.

Of course it was not only men of means, such as Herodotus, who saw the ancient world. Thousands of ordinary Greeks— traders, seamen, and soldiers—also saw it, and sometimes lived in

[1] Herodotus' *Histories*, op. cit.

it, or along its fringes. And yet they were not absorbed and turned into imitation Egyptians or Asians. They remained Hellenes (their own name) whether they lived in Sicily, Syria, Asia Minor, or Egypt. What held them together was their language and culture. They seem always to have regarded themselves as different from other people. To them there were the Hellenes, who spoke Greek, and the *barbaroi*, who did not. We translate this word as 'barbarians', but to the Greeks it did not necessarily imply contempt. Even the Egyptians and the Babylonians, people of a far older culture, which they respected, were still *barbaroi* to the Greeks; it simply meant people who did not speak or think like a Greek, and whose language sounded like 'bar-bar'. That was all.

CHAPTER XV

Myths and Morals: Literature and Art

In Western universities there is a branch of study—now, alas, less popular than it was—called 'Humane Studies', or, more succinctly, 'the Humanities'. It means the study of ancient Greek and Roman literature. The name is significant, because if there is one factor which distinguishes Greek thought from that of previous civilisations it is its concern with human beings, their relation with each other, with the world of nature, and with God.

One finds this running, like a golden thread, through Greek poetry, drama, sculpture and painting, and even through Greek religion, whose gods and goddesses are far more human than any deities have a right to be. The amorous Apollo pursues the nymph Daphne until she turns into a laurel-bush; Zeus, king of the gods, seduces so many girls that one loses count; Aphrodite, goddess of love, married to the ugly smith, Hephaestos, seizes the opportunity of her husband's absence to invite the war-god Ares to her bed; but Hephaestos entangles them in a cunning net, and then summons the rest of the gods to be witnesses of his wrong and his wife's shame. But they were only amused:

'*And when they saw Hephaestos' clever device, unquenchable laughter came over them. Apollo, son of Zeus, turned to Hermes and said "Hermes, son of Zeus, was it worth it?" And the giant-slayer said "Yes, I would change places with him at this very moment".*'

Some prim pedants claim that this and similar Homeric passages are the work of later interpolators, writing in a period of decadence. But there is little evidence for this; the Greeks of the 'classical' period certainly knew and relished these tales, and modern anthropologists, delving into the origin of Greek myths, have found more scandalous examples dating from a period far earlier than

Homer. Does this mean that the Greeks were less moral than other peoples? By no means. As Professor Kitto writes:

'. . . the bulk of classical poetry and art is notably serious. It is very far from lacking in gaiety and charm; nevertheless the outstanding quality is a sense of moral responsibility.'[1]

What, then, is the explanation of this apparent dichotomy? To find an answer we shall have to forget for the moment the pretty stories of Zeus, Apollo, Aphrodite, Hermes and Poseidon with which generations of European writers and artists have entertained us; we must go further back into European history.

The first fact to recognise is that Greek religion is a mixture. Like the Egyptians, the Sumerians, and other ancient peoples, the inhabitants of Greece in historic times had their nature-deities, local gods of mountains, streams, and forests, and primal gods of earth, sun and sky. We have seen that in prehistoric Crete the inhabitants seem to have worshipped an earth-goddess (see Chapters I and VIII). We have also seen that the earliest deities seem to have been female. These aboriginal Mediterranean peoples, who also occupied the mainland, worshipped an earth-deity. For example, the temple and shrine of Apollo at Delphi, the most renowned oracle of the Greek world, which played such an important part in the shaping of Greek history, was originally the shrine of the earth goddess Ge (or Gea). Themis, who is associated with her in tradition as her daughter and partner, is probably another manifestation of the same deity.

Greek legends told how Apollo, the 'Far-darter', the vigorous god, came to Delphi and made it his sanctuary, killing the serpent (Pytho) which had previously occupied it. (Remember that the Cretan earth-goddess had snakes, emblem of Earth, wreathed round her arms.) In some versions of the legend, for instance in the Third Homeric Hymn, Apollo occupies Delphi by force. In others, such as that in the *Eumenides* of the poet Aeschylus, he does it in a more civilised way.

'*In the third place, willingly and not perforce after her*' (*Themis*) '*sat another child of Earth, the Titaness Phoebe. She gave it as a birthday gift to Phoebus (Apollo) who took his name from hers.*'

[1] *The Greeks*—H. D. F. Kitto, *op. cit.*

Delphi must stand as an example of what took place in other parts of Greece. Originally there is a native deity, usually a goddess connected with nature. Then comes another god and takes possession. Sometimes he destroys the earlier deity, but usually he marries her; or he may even become her son. We have heard of the goddess Pallas Athene, the principal deity of Athens, and 'Argive Hera' the wife of Zeus. The interesting point is that neither of these goddesses is Greek; they are both pre-Greek;[1] moreover, both Athens and Argos were originally Mycenean settlements. But the 'Olympians'—such deities as Zeus, Poseidon, Hermes, and Ares—were not originally of the Mediterranean; they were gods of the sky, and of the tribe, brought down from the north by the Greek invaders. And they are nearly all *male* deities.

From these facts archaeologists, philologists, and anthropologists have deduced that just as the Greeks invaded and subdued the earlier inhabitants of the country, so their own gods supplanted or, more often, became associated with the deities of the earlier peoples. This inevitably led to confusion, but the Greeks (unlike the Egyptians, who never threw away anything) loved order and unity. Also they had to *explain* everything, and with their lively dramatic sense they were very good at explaining.

Professor Kitto thinks that many of the Greek myths are 'explanations of things'. For instance, the Greeks arrive and settle in a land which already has a god. They have brought their god too, but such a situation cannot endure for long. A time comes when people begin to ask themselves, 'what relation exists between these two gods? One could be the son of the other. But the son must have a mother, too. Who could she be?' It would not be long before an explanation was found. The incoming god fell in love with a local maiden, or an attractive nymph bathing in a stream 'kindled his amorous fires'; the result was rapid and inevitable.

Greek mythology is full of such incidents, but in the dim remote past, long before the beginnings of Greek civilisation as

[1] Philologists tell us that the Greeks retained in the language many names which they took over from the Mediterranean races whom they conquered. For instance, names ending in *-nth*—e.g. *Corinth*, *hyacinth*—are pre-Greek. So are names ending in *-os*—e.g. *Knossos*, *Pylos*, *Phaestos*, etc.

we know it, these amorous exploits were probably attributed to a large number of different gods. But a time came when the Greek love of order and simplicity compelled them to rationalise their theology. The many local gods began to be identified with one or other of the Olympians—with Zeus or Heracles or Poseidon. This was much tidier and easier to comprehend, but it meant inevitably that a few major deities were saddled with the responsibility for a great number of indiscretions. The majority of the Greeks, being human, did not mind this, and probably respected the gods all the more for their virility. But some of their philosophers and poets raised moral objections, even doubting if gods existed. Euripides writes of 'the wretched tales of poets', and says that if a god commits an evil deed he cannot be a god. Plato condemns poets who represent the gods as fighting each other, making love, and indulging in human emotions like fear or grief. Even Homer is banned from his 'Republic'. But Plato had himself been a poet in his youth.

There are also more sinister and horrible Greek myths which cannot be explained as the light-hearted inventions of poets. Readers of Fraser and, more recently, Robert Graves, will be familiar with these, and their explanation.

Some of them were primitive fertility-gods, who were sacrificed in the spring to ensure the fruitfulness of the earth; others were attempts to explain the origins of things—e.g. out of Chaos came Earth, mother of gods and men, and she produced Ouranos (note the pre-Greek name) or Sky. He in turn was overthrown by Cronos, his son, to whom Rhea (another earth-deity) was 'subject in love', as the ninth-century poet Hesiod writes. He goes on:

'*Rhea . . . bore splendid children, Hestia, Demeter, and gold-shod Hera and strong Hades, pitiless in heart, who dwells under the earth, and the loud-crashing Earth-shaker, and wise Zeus, father of gods and men, by whose thunder the wide earth is shaken. These, great Cronos swallowed as each came forth from the womb of his mother's knees with this intent, that no other of the proud sons of Heaven should take kingly office amongst the deathless gods.*'

Eventually Rhea outwits Cronos by giving him a stone to swallow, and then rears Zeus in secret in a cave on Mount Ida in Crete. Many of these myths are probably Minoan in origin, or rather came from the primitive Mediterranean people who occupied the mainland and the Aegean islands, including Crete, before the Greeks came.

The Greeks also adopted gods of other lands; for instance, Adonis is the Syrian god, Thammuz, the young lover whose death the Syrian women lamented every year, and whose sacred stream, which flows red, can still be seen in the Lebanese mountains. Dionysus, whom the coarser Romans turned into a mere god of wine, was originally a god of frenzied 'possession', whose worship seems to have originated in Asia Minor. The cult of Dionysus swept over Greece, and during his festivals bands of Greek women and girls—the Maenads—would leave their homes and go to the mountains to celebrate orgiastic rites at which no man could be present on peril of his life. Orpheus, sometimes a god of music and at other times of the Underworld, was torn to pieces on one of these occasions.

One could fill page after page with such illustrations, for the subject is endlessly fascinating; but the temptation must be resisted because one could not adequately explain the origins of Greek religion even in a book, let alone a single chapter. Readers will find in the Bibliography suggestions for further reading.

But it is necessary to include this slight sketch, if only to compare Greek religion with the religious development of the earlier civilisations described in this book, and, even more important, try to understand how the genius of Greek poets and philosophers used these frequently amoral myths to illustrate great spiritual and moral truths. The nature and tribal gods of the Greeks were no better or worse than the gods of Egypt—Anubis, Sekhmet, Thoth, and the rest, or the nature-gods of Sumer, Anu, god of the sky, Ki, the earth goddess, and Enki, god of the waters. They were certainly different from Jaweh, the Jewish tribal god for, unlike him, they were not exclusive to one nation. When the Greeks came to Egypt and were told about Amun, they sensibly identified him with Zeus; in Babylonia they encountered a goddess of love and beauty, Ishtar. Who could she be but Aphrodite? It was so simple.

What they would have thought of Jaweh (Jehovah) it is difficult to imagine. They certainly would not have found it easy to fit him into their pantheon. He approved of war against his peoples' enemies, ('the Lord is a man of War') but one could hardly identify him with Ares, who shared a bed with 'Aphrodite the golden'. He was all powerful, like Zeus, but it was difficult to imagine him turning himself into a bull in order to seduce Europa. If they had heard that he was a universal god, the source of all life, the First Cause—as Plato saw God—they would have shown him the same reverence that they afforded him much later when his worship was introduced by St. Paul and other Christian missionaries (a great German scholar wrote that the teachings of Jesus were never fully understood until they had been translated into the Greek language). But in 500 B.C. he certainly was no such deity. He was the god of an obscure Semitic tribe, and nothing more.

If the Greeks had been able to read the writings of the Jewish prophets at this time, their intelligence and imagination might have shown them that here was a conception of God which could develop into something much greater than a tribal deity. But that did not happen until much later.

The finest in the Greek spirit showed itself in other ways. It took the dross of barbaric myth and the earth of folk-tale and transmuted them to the pure gold of poetry; nor was this poetry only the word-distillation of the sensual pleasures of living— though these played an important and rightful part. In the hands of the Athenian dramatists such as Aeschylus, Euripides and Sophocles, poetic myth became an instrument which searched men's hearts and souls, making them see the splendour and meanness, the tragedy and the comedy of human life, and hinting at spiritual verities of which most men become aware only through art or prophecy. But the teachers in this case were not priests but artists.

The *Oresteia* of Aeschylus, his great trilogy consisting of the 'Agamemnon', the 'Libation-bearers' and the 'Furies', takes as its subject the terrible story of the *Atridae*, the sons of Atreus; of Agamemnon, sacker of Troy, returning to Mycenae to be murdered by his wife Clytemnestra, who was slaughtered in turn by her son

Orestes, who was then driven mad by the avenging Furies. It is a story of cannibalism, human sacrifice, murder and matricide. Yet Aeschylus transforms it into one of the greatest tragedies of the world, exploring the heights which the human spirit can attain, and the miry depths to which it can sink; its message, the futility of revenge, of violence breeding violence, war breeding war, is as pertinent today as it was two thousand five hundred years ago. Yet the basis is a folk-myth as barbarous and inhuman as any which came out of Egypt or Babylonia.

That may give some measure of the 'difference' of the Greeks.

Aeschylus, admittedly, belongs to a later period of Greek history, the fifth century, the time of the full Athenian glory. But already, as far back as the ninth century, we can see this moral force at work. We can see it in Homer. In the *Iliad* and the *Odyssey* the Gods are, for the most part, an amusing, almost irrelevant decoration (though not completely irrelevant, because they sometimes interfere capriciously with the affairs of men). The description of Hera, wife of Zeus, borrowing Aphrodite's jewellery to help allure her own husband (and so distract him from her attempt to aid the Trojans) is delightful:

> *. . . then ponders deep*
> *The stag-eyed Queen, how best she might beguile*
> *The wakeful mind of aegis-bearing Zeus;*
> *And, musing, thus appeared the*
> *readiest mode;*
> *Herself with art adorning, to repair*
> *To Ida; there, with fondest blandishment*
> *And female charm, her husband to enfold*
> *In love's embrace; and gentle, careless sleep*
> *Around his eyelids and his senses pour.* [1]

But one feels that it is only there to amuse Homer's hearers and remind them that the consort of the King of Gods uses exactly the same wiles as their own wives to achieve her ends. It was not such passages as this which the Greek schoolboys had to learn at school, but sterner lines such as:

[1] This coy Victorian translation has been chosen deliberately.

Myths and Morals: Literature and Art

As is the life of the leaves, so is that of men.
The wind scatters the leaves to the ground; the
vigorous forest puts forth others, and they
grow in the spring-season. Soon one generation
of men comes and another ceases.

—which is very like the Hebrew, '*As for man, his days are as grass* . . .'

In Homer's world the emphasis is always on man. The gods are indifferent; you must accept fate and do what you can, even resisting the gods if necessary, knowing that you must lose. It was no use whining to them that life had treated you unfairly, nor hope that by your good deeds you would 'store up treasure in heaven'. There was no heaven, only the dim shades, in which the spirits of the dead wandered without hope. Yet the Greeks accepted this stern code and lived by it. Not only schoolboys, but men, learned by heart such Homeric phrases as:

'*Endure, my heart; far worse hast thou endured.* . . .'

and:

'*Hateful to me is he who speaketh one thing with his lips but another in his heart.*'

We know from later Greek literature that travelling teachers, called 'Sophists', went around reciting Homer and instructing youth by moral examples drawn from the poems. Plato draws a vivid picture of one such man, who was evidently a bore.

'*It must be marvellous, Ion, to go about, as you do, from place to place, to draw a great crowd wherever you go, and have them hanging on your lips.*'

and he adds:

'*—and you in your best clothes too.* . . .'[1]

How one admires that keen thrust, like a stiletto between the ribs! The Greeks hated pseudo-piety.

But if the Homeric gods are frivolous and amusing, they acquired moral values later. Apollo, 'the golden-haired, lord of the silver bow', from his shrine at Delphi, became the guardian of law, as well as patron of artists and writers, thousands of whom have

[1] H. D. F. Kitto, *op. cit.*

drunk from his clear 'Castalian spring' under Mount Parnassus, and prayed for the God's inspiration.[1] Zeus punished wickedness. Artemis became the protector of virgins. 'Gold-shod Hera' also had her powers and attributes. The gods of Greece developed, as indeed did Jaweh (compare the god of Moses with that of Ezekiel). But Egyptian and Babylonian gods did not, which is why we still read of Zeus, Apollo and Jaweh, but not Amun-Re or Baal.

But one must not overdraw the picture, and in an endeavour to counteract the myth of Greek amorality and irresponsibility paint them as a race of intellectuals and mystics, absorbed in Higher Things. Aesthetic they certainly were, but not in any self-conscious way. Their art, the richest flowing of the human spirit, seems to spring as spontaneously from their soil as the wild asphodel and narcissi which spangle the rich grass of their valleys; flowers which seem to glow with an inner light and throw a perfume which make such hackneyed 'poetic' words as *ambrosia* and *nectar* real and vivid for the first time.

Unfortunately, very little remains of the sculpture of Hellas in its prime. Most of the statues one sees in European and American galleries are three times removed from the originals. First, they are often plaster casts, Second, these casts are usually taken from late Alexandrian or Roman copies of the originals. Third, many belong to a later period of Greek history, the fourth or third centuries. The famous, but overrated, Venus de Milo at the Paris Louvre is such a work. But, happily, some examples remain, which can stand as examples of Greek sculpture at its finest; among these are Zeus hurling a thunderbolt (460 B.C.), in the National Museum in Athens; Hermes carrying a ram (500 B.C.), in the Boston Museum of Fine Arts; the splendid Apollo from the western gable of the Temple of Zeus at Olympia (460 B.C.), the Elgin Marbles from the frieze of the Parthenon in Athens, now in the British Museum; Athena letting fly an owl (460 B.C.), in the Metropolitan Museum of Art, New York; the 'Winged Victory of Samothrace' in the Paris Louvre; and my personal favourite, the bronze charioteer at Delphi, in Greece.

Even so, there is still something unreal and artificial about

[1] Including the present writer.

cunningly lighted and carefully labelled for visitors to gaze at and admire. It is difficult, in such settings, to imagine them as they once were—not 'works of art', beautiful, but with no relation to contemporary life, but part of the adornment of one's native city, the background of one's life, as Grant's Tomb belongs to New York, and Nelson's Column to London. There is a difference, of course. It is doubtful if Americans revere Grant's Tomb for its artistic merit, or Londoners go into raptures over Nelson's statue —whereas the Greek Dio Chrysostom, in the first century A.D., could write of the statue of Zeus at Olympia that:

'*A man heavy-laden, who had drained the cup of misfortune and sorrow, if he were to stand and gaze at this statue, would forget the heavy and weary weight of this unintelligible world.*'

Of Greek poetry we shall say little, because it is available in the original or translation, in any good library. Greek-speaking Hellenists say—and no doubt they are right—that no translation, however fine, can give the full flavour of the original Greek. Who was it said that 'the only thing that improves by translation is a Bishop'?

However, a great number of people have come to love Greek verse, even in translation; and as some poets—e.g. Louis Mac-Neice, and F. L. Lucas—are also Greek scholars, we can sometimes enjoy the advantages of both worlds. In selecting a translator, the only advice which the writer can give is that passed on to him by a noted Hellenist: it was that, in general, it is better to avoid most older verse-translations—not that these are bad in themselves (some are brilliant)—but because each age inevitably adds something of itself to a translation of a Greek poem. An example is Lord Derby's verse-translation of part of the *Iliad*, quoted earlier in this chapter. [1]Figuratively speaking, Chapman's Homer wears Elizabethan doublet and hose, Pope's Homer a periwig. Lord Derby's Hera clearly wears stays. A good modern translation, though imperfect, at least gives us the poet at only one remove.

The other point to remember is that the examples of Greek literature which have come down to us are only fragments of what must once have existed. The originals, of course, perished long

[1]P. 219.

these sculptures in their present setting, isolated and set apart, ago. What we possess is the legacy of generations of scholars who have lovingly copied and recopied the words which were originally written perhaps on Egyptian papyrus—more than twenty-five centuries ago.

The following poems were chosen, not principally for their literary quality, but partly because they illustrate aspects of Greek life and thought which we have discussed in the two preceding chapters, and partly because they appeal to me personally.

SORROW

The exiled aristocrat, Theognis of Megara (*circa* 540 B.C.), thinks of his lost lands:

> *I hear, O Polypiades, I hear the bird's shrill crying,*
> *That comes to tell the tiller that time has come to plough,*
> *And it stabbed the heart in me, to think that my lands are lying,*
> *My flowered fields, in keeping with other masters now:*
> *That no team of mine goes straining against the yoke this day,*
> *Since by its cursed pilots our city's cast away.*

PRIDE OF BLOOD

> *Ne'er yet from the root of a squill did rose or hyacinth wave;*
> *Nor came a son of freedom from out the womb of a slave.*
>
> (Theognis of Megara)

HAPPINESS IN YOUTH

> *Now is the time to surrender our hearts to merry-making,*
> *While life's fair things can give us a joy that is not vain.*
> *For the glory of youth goes by us, swift as a thought, o'ertaking*
> *Even the speed of steeds whose charging hoofs amain*
> *Whirl some king in his car to the press of the spear-fought fray,*
> *Over the green furrows, exulting on their way.*
>
> (Theognis of Megara)

It is interesting to notice the Homeric echo of 'the king in his car' and 'the spear-fought fray'. Theognis wrote more than three centuries after Homer.

As a tart contrast, two bitter lines by Hipponax of Ephesus, a sort of Greek François Villon, who lived among criminals and outcasts, and used their slang in his verse:

Two days a woman's best—the day she's wed,
The day she's carried from your doorway—dead.

YOUTH AND AGE

Ah, what is life, what is joy—but Aphrodite the golden?
Let me die, when I am gladdened no more by things like these—
Her gifts honey-sweet, and the bed of love, by none beholden,
And all the flowers of youth, that are so sweet to seize,
For the hands of man and woman. But he who is once o'ertaken
By grim old age, that makes him ugly at once and base
With misery and anguish his heart without cause is shaken,
No more to the sun rejoicing, thenceforth, he turns his face.
Hateful he grows to boyhood, a scorn to women's gaze,
Such is the bitter burden God made life's latter days.

(Mimnermus of Colophon. Late seventh century)

TO A GREEK SOLDIER, RETURNED AFTER SERVING IN THE ARMY OF NEBUCHADNEZZAR OF BABYLON

Homeward from earth's far ends thou art returned
With gold-and-ivory swordhilt—ay, and well
By service to thy comrades that was earned,
The men of Babylon; who saw thee quell
So stout a champion, in single fight.
Of five royal cubits, in his giant's height,
But one short span he fell.

(Alcaeus of Mytilene, born 620 B.C.)

LOVE

When love is temperate, nothing is more enchanting,
But save me from the other kind!

(Euripides)

Like the sweet apple that reddens upon the topmost bough,
A-top on the topmost twig—which the pluckers forgot somehow—
Forgot it not, nay, but got it not, for none could get it till now.

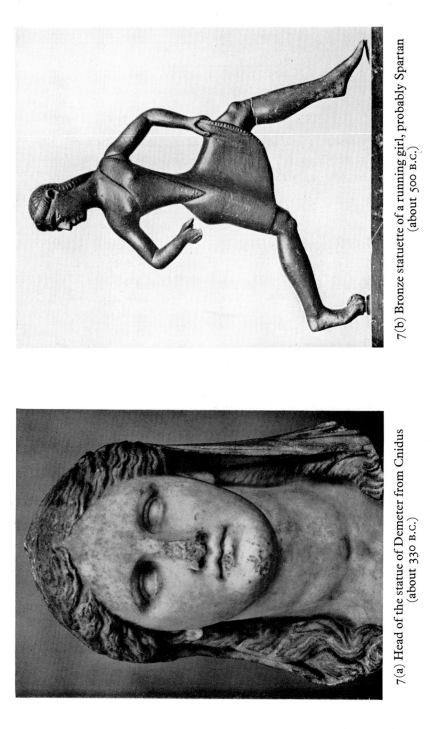

7(a) Head of the statue of Demeter from Cnidus
(about 330 B.C.)

7(b) Bronze statuette of a running girl, probably Spartan
(about 500 B.C.)

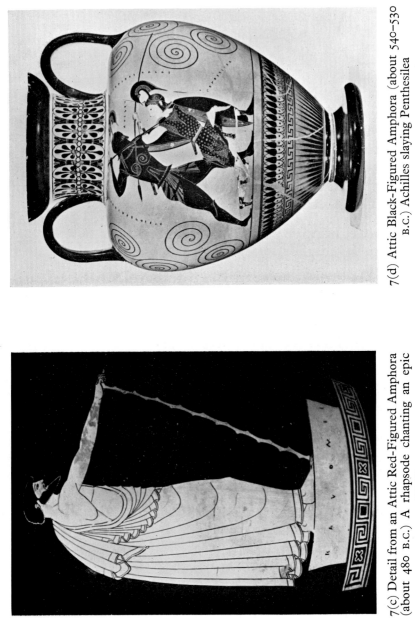

7(c) Detail from an Attic Red-Figured Amphora (about 480 B.C.) A rhapsode chanting an epic poem

7(d) Attic Black-Figured Amphora (about 540–530 B.C.) Achilles slaying Penthesilea

Like the wild hyacinth flower which on the hills is found,
While the passing feet of the shepherds for ever tear and wound,
Until the purple blossom is trodden into the ground.

(Sappho—born 610 B.C.—translated
by Dante Gabriel Rossetti)

SATIRE

The satirist Semonides of Amorgos (*circa* 600 B.C.), wrote a
poem on women, in which he compares them with various species
of brutes. Here is one which will be familiar to some of us:

Another's born of the dainty, long-maned filly,
Shying away from trouble and drudgery—
Never ask her *to grind flour, or to finger*
Dishes, or empty slops.
As for an oven—lest a smut fall on her
She'll not go near it. Her love's tyranny.
Ne'er a day but twice or thrice she bathes
And daubs herself with perfume; and her hair
Flows deep, smooth-combed, all shaded o'er with flowers.
A lovely thing to look at, such a woman,
For other men; but a curse to him that has her—
Unless he be a king or a dictator
To glorify his fancy with such toys.

I suspect that Semonides, in spite of his spleen, was not averse
to 'the long-maned filly'—if he could have afforded one.

SCEPTICISM

If oxen, or lions, or horses had hands like men, they too,
If they could fashion pictures, or statues they could hew,
They would shape in their own image each face and form divine,—
Horses' gods like horses, like kine the gods of kine.
'Snub-nosed are the Immortals, and black' the Ethiops say;
But 'no' the Thracians answer, 'red-haired, with eyes of grey.'

— — — —

Of the Gods and these other matters none knows the verity—
No man that lived before us, no man that yet shall be.

However well-perfected the system he hath made,
Its maker knoweth nothing. With fancy all's o'erlaid.
> (Xenophanes of Colophon, *circa* 564–470 B.C.)

With the exception of the Rossetti translation of Sappho, all the above translations are by F. L. Lucas.[1] To end, I am going to quote one of the best-known and best-loved poems in the English language, although its translator, William (Johnson) Cory, is by no means in the first rank of poets. It is not a great work, this translation of a late Alexandrian poet named Callimachus of Cyrene, but it seems to me to typify so much of the Greek spirit—its capacity for joy and pain, its courage and its resignation to fate:

> *They told me, Heraclitus, they told me you were dead,*
> *They brought me bitter news to hear and bitter tears to shed.*
> *I wept as I remembered how often you and I*
> *Had tired the sun with talking and sent him down the sky.*

> *And now that thou art lying, my dear old Carian guest,*
> *A handful of grey ashes, long, long ago at rest,*
> *Still are thy pleasant voices, thy nightingales awake,*
> *For Death, he taketh all away, but these he cannot take.*

---

[1] *Greek Poetry for Everyman.* J. M. Dent & Sons., London.

CHAPTER XVI

'The King with half the East at heel'

Before beginning this chapter it is as well to study a map of Greece and its neighbours This will help to make clear how geography helped to fashion the character, culture and political history of the Greek people. One notices how the long sea-channels bite deep into the land; the Gulf of Aegina in the east, the Gulf of Thessaloniki in the north, and the great Gulf of Lepanto which, joined to the Gulf of Aegina by the Corinth Canal, now makes the Peloponnese, the southern part of Greece, into an island. But in ancient times, this canal did not exist, and the town of Corinth, standing at the edge of the narrow isthm us, was of high strategic and commercial importance.

Again, the high mountain ranges tended to split the country into separate states, and also made a landward entry into the country from the north extremely difficult; hence the historic importance of such places as Thermopylae, where a small force could hold back large armies.

The innumerable islands—Chios, Andros, Syros, Naxos, Samos, Lesbos, and many others, large and small—again encouraged separatism; so did the colonies scattered along the western and southern coasts of Asia Minor, on the opposite side of the Aegean. Ionia, for example, with such towns as Ephesus and Miletus, was the oldest of Greek colonies, and produced its own distinctive type of art, softer and more elegant than the more masculine 'Doric' of the mainland. The famous 'Three Orders' which every student of architecture learns remind us of these regional differences: Doric, with its broad-based, fluted columns and simple capitals, Ionic, in which the capitals turn out in volutes, and Corinthian, with capitals decorated by acanthus-

227

leaves. You still see these architectural forms in thousands of towns throughout the United States and Europe.

The next point to consider is the landward approach from the north and north-east. Northward of Thessaly lies mountainous Macedonia, but at the period of which we are writing—600–400 B.C.—no threat came from this direction. To the north-east, beyond the northern shores of the Aegean, lay Thrace, also mountainous, though an invader from Asia might force a passage between the mountains and the sea. However, before he could do so he would have to cross the Hellespont, a narrow but still formidable sea-channel linking the Mediterranean with the Black Sea. Just south of this channel stood ancient Troy, which the Achaeans had sacked in about 1190 B.C.

It would seem, therefore, that any landward approach to Greece would be difficult and perilous, unless the invading army was supported by a powerful fleet which, sailing along the coast, could turn the Greek defences. Throughout the thousand years and more during which Greek-speaking peoples were swarming into continental Greece and occupying the islands, no such threat materialised. We have seen how the Hittite king, Mursilis III, powerful though he was, could do very little against the *Ahhiyawa*, who seem to have been Homer's 'Achaeans'—even when the latter invaded Asia Minor and drove out one of the Hittite monarch's vassals, Maduwattas (see Chapter XII). The reason, almost certainly, was that the Achaeans had command of the sea, and therefore could not be got at. The Hittites were no seafarers.

No Asiatic power threatened the Hellenic world until the middle of the sixth century B.C. The Hittites lost control of their mountain homeland and moved into northern Syria. The Assyrians' power, as we have seen, was overthrown in 612 by the Babylonians; and in any case neither of these powers showed much interest in the sea or what lay beyond it. In Asia Minor, after the decline of the Hittites, there were powerful states, one of which, Lydia, is mentioned in an inscription of the Assyrian king, Ashurbanipal (*circa* 660 B.C.) under the name *Luddi*. The inscription records that Ashurbanipal received tribute from Gyges, first of the Mermnad dynasty of Lydian kings.

The moment one reads the name *Gyges*, 'official history' with its dates and dynasties, battles and conquests, fades into the background and, as in the case of Akhnaten and Ankhesnamun, human beings emerge from the crowd, plucking at one's sleeve and insisting on being heard. If any reader complains that this interrupts the 'sweep of history', let him blame Herodotus, greatest of historians, who gently insists that history is about human beings and, unlike some of his modern successors, is quite ready to halt the grand march of his narrative to tell a human story. Here it is in his own words:

'Now Candaules' (king of Lydia) 'had a passion for his own wife, and thought she was the most beautiful woman on earth. To this fancy of his there was an unexpected sequel.'

'In the king's bodyguard was a fellow he particularly liked whose name was Gyges, son of Dascylus. With him Candaules not only discussed his most important business, but even used to make him listen to eulogies on his wife's beauty.'

'One day the king (who was doomed to a bad end) said to Gyges: "It appears you don't believe me when I tell you how lovely my wife is. Well, a man always believes his eyes better than his ears; so do as I tell you—contrive to see her naked." '

'Gyges gave a cry of horror. "Master," he said, "what an improper suggestion! Do you tell me to look at the queen when she has no clothes on? No, no; 'off with her skirt, off with her shame'—you know what they say of women. . . . I do not doubt that your wife is the most beautiful of women; so for goodness' sake do not ask me to behave like a criminal." '

But the uxorious king was insistent. He devised a plan by which Gyges, against his will (though no doubt not without a terrified curiosity) was secreted in the royal bedchamber:

' "Look," (said Candaules) "I will hide you behind the open door of our bedroom. My wife will follow me in to bed. Near the door there's a chair—she will put her clothes onto it as she takes them off, one by one. You will be able to watch with perfect ease. Then, while she's walking away from the chair toward the bed with her back to you, slip away through the door, and mind she doesn't catch you." '

Gyges did as he was told, but unfortunately the queen saw him though she said nothing at the time. But the next morning she sent for Gyges, who 'answered the summons without any suspicion that she knew what had occurred the previous night'.

' "Gyges," she said, as soon as he presented himself, "there are two courses open to you, and you may take your choice between them. Kill Candaules and seize the throne; or die yourself on the spot, so that never again may your blind obedience to the king tempt you to see what you have no right to see. One of you must die; either my husband, the author of this wicked plot; or you, who have outraged propriety by seeing me naked." '[1]

Gyges took the sensible course, killed Candaules, ascended the throne of Lydia, and founded a new dynasty. Later he had his power confirmed by the Oracle of Delphi—a wise precaution.

A successor of Gyges, King Croesus, has become part of current mythology. One still hears the phrase 'as rich as Croesus' in 1957; but Croesus, king of Lydia, was an historical personage, a man of fabulous wealth, in whose reign metal coinage first came into use, and was promptly adopted by the Greeks. Every time we jingle coins in our pockets we owe the existence of that convenient medium of exchange to the Lydians of 700 B.C. Before then trade was by barter, or sometimes by the exchange of unwieldy bars of metal. But the invention of metal coinage had revolutionary consequences.

'The peasant can convert his small surplus of farm produce into an easily divisible medium of exchange which he can reconvert into manufactured goods . . . The workman is no longer condemned to eat his wages. The small producer or the retailer can exchange his goods for coins, which can be added together till substantial values are accumulated.'[2]

So writes Professor Childe, rightly emphasising the economic basis of history. But he does not mention Candaules and his beautiful wife. Understandably.

Lydia has another claim on our attention. The Greek hero,

[1] This and subsequent quotations from Herodotus' *Histories*, translated by Aubrey de Selincourt. Penguin Classics, 1954.

[2] *What Happened in History*—V. Gordon Childe: Pelican Books, London, 1942.

Heracles, strongest of men, who strangled a serpent in his cradle, slew the Nemean lion with his bare hands, and performed other prodigious feats, was enslaved by the Lydian queen Omphale, who set him to work among her hand-maidens and, on more intimate occasions, dressed him in her clothes, while she wore his armour and carried his great club. The familiar Freudian 'deviations' are clearly indicated in the legend—masochism, transvestism, etc. All that are lacking are the psychiatrist's couch and case-book.[1]

Lydia, and another state in Asia Minor, Phrygia (from which came Midas, whose touch turned everything to gold), were in friendly contact with the Greek colonists in Ionia, and maintained relations with them. Even when Croesus subdued the Ionian cities, conquest was no calamity for the Hellenes. Croesus was something of a phil-Hellene and ruled the Greek cities through rulers friendly to himself. But all this changed when, in 546 B.C. Cyrus, king of Persia, overthrew Croesus and added Lydia to his empire.

Cyrus was the founder of the last Oriental Empire of pre-Christian times, and by far the greatest. The imperial triumphs of Sargon, Hammurabi, Ashurbanipal, Nebuchadnezzar, and the rest, are nothing compared to those of Cyrus and his successors.

> *It was of Destiny decreed*
> *As now the years unfold*
> *Battle should be the Persian's deed*
> *Yea, God ordained of old,*
> *With troops and horse encompassing*
> *He tower and town to earth should bring,*
> *And Empire be his meed.*[2]

So wrote a Greek poet in the fifth century. To him, as to most of his contemporaries, the Persians were the great Asiatic enemy; an enemy whom they respected and even admired—but one who must be resisted because he sought to absorb them into a slave-

---

[1] Gluck's tone-poem, 'Le Rouet d'Omphale', is a delightful musical illustration of this legend.

[2] *The Ancient World*—T. R. Glover: Cambridge University Press, London, 1936.

state which, while it might be all very well for the *barbaroi*, was anathema to them. They were Greeks and free men.

This did not mean that the Hellenes rose as one man and united against the danger from the east. Far from it. Many of the Greek cities of Asia Minor and the islands 'Medized'[1]—to use the contemptuous expression which the recalcitrant Greeks used to describe those who had compromised with the *barbaroi*. Looking back, one can hardly blame them. For Cyrus, whose people came from the mountains which overhang the Persian Gulf on the north-east, first conquered the Medes, a kindred Aryan people living south of the Caspian, then moved across Western Asia, overthrowing Babylon and then Lydia, until, at his death in 528 B.C., the Persian Empire extended from the Caspian Sea in the north to the Arabian desert in the south, and from the Aegean Ocean to the Hindu-Kush. His successor, Cambyses, added Egypt to his empire, so that for the first time in history the civilisations of the Nile and the Euphrates were united under one crown.

Cambyses was succeeded by the great Darius I, who further extended and consolidated the Empire.

The Persian monarch called himself 'King of Kings'—and this was no mere empty boast, but the truth. Moreover, the Persian despots had a genius for administration and organisation, superior to any who had gone before them. They not only conquered these old, proud kingdoms, but exploited their resources more efficiently than ever the Egyptians or Assyrians had done. The wealth of the subject-states poured into the Persian treasury; their men were organised into twenty *satrapies* (vice-royalties), each under a *satrap*, or military governor, with a separate civil administrator, all under the vigilant surveillance of a high official known as 'The Eye of the King', at Susa, the state capital.

The year 499 B.C. was a critical date in the history of the world, for in that year the Ionian cities, which, after the conquest of Lydia, had come under Persian rule, revolted against Darius. Aristagoras of Miletus went to Sparta in the Peloponnese and asked for help, but Cleomenes, king of Sparta, was not impressed,

---

[1] The word indicates that this tendency had begun during the ascendancy of the Medes, before the rise of Persia.

particularly when Aristagoras unwisely told him how far was the Persian capital from the coast of Asia. 'Milesian guest', said Cleomenes, 'leave Sparta before sunset, for you say things disagreeable to the Spartans, trying to lead them a three-months journey from the sea.'

Aristagoras had better luck with the Athenians, a more intelligent and less insular people. They provided some ships, as did the city of Eretria in Euboea; and with their help the Milesian leader sacked the city of Sardis, in Asia Minor, then under Persian control.

The revolt was a failure, but at least it made Darius realise that he could not hope to hold Ionia unless he could intimidate the mainland Greeks who were encouraging their fellow-Hellenes in Asia. So, in 490, with ships provided by the Phoenicians (who were, of course, now part of the Persian Empire) he landed an army on the island of Euboea, sacked Eretria, then crossed to the coast of Attica, and landed at Marathon.

The name is like a trumpet-note. Few people have not heard of it, or of the battle in which a small force of Greeks, mainly Athenians, with a contingent of 1,000 men from Plataea, beat the Persian host back to the ships, losing 192 men. These Greeks were not professional soldiers in the modern sense, though skilled in war. It was the duty of every able-bodied man in the *polis* to take arms in defence of his city. Among the Athenians who carried shield and spear that day was the poet Aeschylus and his brother. The brother was killed, but Aeschylus survived to write *The Seven Against Thebes*, *The Prometheus*, and, what many believe to be the greatest tragedy in the world, the *Oresteia*.

The Persians retired, but it was obvious to thinking minds that it was only a question of time before they tried again. Not everyone realised this, of course, but a few far-seeing men, able to look beyond the boundaries of the *polis*, recognised the danger and began to act. One of these was the Athenian statesman, Themistocles. When, at this time, a rich vein of silver was struck at Sunium, near Athens, Themistocles managed to persuade his fellow-citizens to spend the money on a fleet, ostensibly for use against the neighbouring island of Aegina, with which Athens was contemplating war, but Themistocles was thinking of a far deadlier enemy.

Fortunately for the Greeks, Darius died before he could mount a fresh attack, and a revolt in Egypt and other troubles kept the Persians occupied for ten years. Meanwhile, Xerxes, successor to Darius, made his preparations for the greatest military and naval operation which had ever been attempted, involving a total force which Herodotus estimates as nearly *five million* men. The aim was, first, the conquest of Greece; after that all Europe would be at the Persian's mercy.

In the meantime, Themistocles, the Athenian statesman, continued to make ready. The rise of Athens, greatest of Greek cities, 'the school of Hellas' as Pericles called her, will be described in the final chapter. Here it is only necessary to know that by the beginning of the fifth century Athens, after a stormy century of constitutional change, had become a democracy in which alien residents were admitted to full citizenship, and all sections of the community fully represented in the Government. Thus, 'when the tide of invasion burst upon Greece at the dawn of the fifth century, Athens was able to confront the crisis with an outfit of political institutions worthy alike of the temper of her citizens and her new-won status in the commonwealth of Hellenic city states.'[1]

In 481 the Persian colossus began to move. There has probably never been a greater, more fascinating drama in human history than this David-and-Goliath struggle between the East and the West, the Old and the New, with the future of western civilisation hanging in the balance. On the one hand was the Persian king, the most powerful man on earth, representing the older, Oriental despotisms—no different from those of Ashurbanipal, Tuthmosis, or Nebuchadnezzar, except that Xerxes' military empire was technically more up-to-date and better organised. There is dramatic symbolism even in the constitution of his great army, for in its ranks marched representative detachments of nearly all the nations who have figured in this story. The Egyptians were

[1] *The Legacy of the Ancient World*—de Burgh: Macdonald and Evans, London, 1947.

there (their engineers helped to construct the great bridge of boats across the Hellespont). So were the Libyans and the Nubians—Egypt's old enemies. The Assyrians, with their bronze helmets 'of outlandish shape' (Herodotus), marched in company with Lydians, Bactrians, Phrygians, Arabians wearing the *zeira*, a long flowing garment. And the Phoenicians provided the ships and sailors.

Also, it must be admitted, there were Greeks serving in the Persian forces—the conquered Ionians were compelled by Xerxes to join him in an attack on their fellow-Hellenes, and among the Persian king's staff were exiled aristocrats who hoped that a Persian victory would reinstate them in their former positions of power.

Fortunately for us, two of the world's greatest historians, Herodotus and Thucydides, were alive at this time, so that one does not need to piece facts together from a few inscriptions and potsherds; the whole glorious epic is available to anyone who cares to read one of the excellent modern translations of these writers.[1] To attempt to summarise it would be an impertinence; we shall, therefore, only quote a few passages to give some idea of how the Greek world saw this drama.

Here is Herodotus describing the two great bridges, each seven furlongs in length, which Xerxes' engineers constructed across the Hellespont.

'The method employed was as follows; galleys and triremes' (warships with triple rows of oars) 'were lashed together to support the bridges—360 vessels for the one on the Black Sea side, and 314 for the other. They were moored head-on to the current—and consequently at right angles to the actual bridges they supported —in order to lessen the strain on the cables. Specially heavy anchors were laid out both upstream and downstream . . . to take the strain when it blew from the west and south. . . . Once the vessels were in position, the cables were hauled taut by wooden winches ashore. . . .'

This work was done while Xerxes and his army were in Sardis, on the coast of Asia Minor. Then they marched to the Hellespont, and Xerxes 'poured wine into the sea out of a golden goblet, and

[1] e.g. de Selincourt (Herodotus), and Rex Warner (Thucydides).

with his face turned towards the sun, prayed that no chance might prevent him from conquering Europe or turn him back before he reached its utmost limits. His prayer ended, he flung the cup into the Hellespont and with it a golden bowl and a short sword. . . .'

Then the crossing began.

'The infantry and cavalry went over by the upper bridge—the one nearer the Black Sea; the pack animals and underlings by the lower one towards the Aegean. The first to cross were the Ten Thousand' (picked Persian troops) 'all with wreaths on their heads, and these were followed by a mass of troops of all sorts of nationality. Their crossing occupied the whole of the first day. On the next day the first over were the thousand horsemen, and the contingent which marched with spears reversed—these, too, all wearing wreaths. Then came the sacred horses and the sacred chariot, and after them Xerxes himself with his spearmen and his thousand horsemen. The remainder of the army brought up the rear, and at the same time the ships moved over to the opposite shore.'

'From the European shore Xerxes watched his troops coming over under the whips. *The crossing occupied seven days and nights without a break.*[1] There is a story that some time after Xerxes passed the bridge, a native of the country thereabouts exclaimed: "Why, O God, have you assumed the shape of a man of Persia, and changed your name to Xerxes, in order to lead everyone in the world to the conquest and devastation of Greece? You could have destroyed Greece without going to that trouble." '

When he reached the town of Doriscus, Xerxes decided to count the number of his troops. Herodotus says:

'As nobody has left a record, I cannot state the precise number provided by each separate nation, but the grand total, excluding the naval contingent, turned out to be 1,700,000. The counting was done by first packing ten thousand men as close together as they could stand and then drawing a circle round them on the ground; they were then dismissed, and a fence, about navel-high was constructed round the circle; finally other troops were marched

[1] Our italics.

236

into the area, and thus enclosed and dismissed in turn, until the whole army was counted.'

The fleet, including triremes, galleys, horse-transports, and other vessels, numbered about 3,000 ships. They were provided by several nations, including the Egyptians, Cyprians, Sicilians, Lycians, Ionians, and others. All these ships carried soldiers in addition to their crews, and Herodotus estimates the total sea-borne force as 517,000 men, and that the grand total of land and sea forces brought over from Asia was nearly two and a half million. In addition to these there were soldiers provided by the east European countries Xerxes had subdued—Thracians, Macedonians, etc.—together with camp-servants, and camp-followers, bringing the grand total to over five million.

Modern historians have thrown doubts on Herodotus' skill at arithmetic, but even if Xerxes' forces were only half of the Greek historian's estimate, it was still one of the most formidable concentrations of military and naval power the world has ever seen.

A Greek historian relates the story of how one of the Greek soldiers was told that the Persian archers were so numerous that their arrows darkened the sky. To which the soldier replied:

'So much the better—we shall be able to fight in the shade.'

What could the Greeks do against such a world in arms?

Naturally, a great many of the Greek states 'Medized', sending back to Xerxes the formal offerings of earth and water which his Ambassadors demanded of them as tokens of submission. But not the Athenians, who imprisoned the Persian king's messengers, nor the Spartans who flung his Ambassadors down a well, saying that if they wanted earth and water, that was the place to find them.

This was tough on the Ambassadors, but one cannot blame the Spartans.[1]

Nor does this mean that the Greeks were not aware of the immense forces marching against them. They had sent spies to Asia, who were captured by the Persians, and after being carefully

---

[1] Years later the Spartans tried to make amends for this hot-tempered act by sending two of their best citizens, Sperchias and Bulis, to the Persian king to be sacrificed. Xerxes sent them back unharmed.

shown the strength of the army, were sent back to Greece to report. The Athenians, determined to resist, obtained the support of Sparta, the most powerful military state in Greece, whose king, Leonidas, became commander-in-chief. They also applied for help to Gelo, ruler of the great Greek colony of Syracuse, in Sicily, but Gelo refused aid unless he could command either the land or the sea forces. This neither Athens nor Sparta could accept, so the embassy sailed away empty-handed. Though the allies managed to enlist the help of some of the other Greek states, the main responsibility for defence rested with the Athenians and the Spartans.

Meanwhile, Xerxes pursued his unhurried course, halting to review his great fleet (and enjoying a rowing-match between some of its members), and surveying from a white marble throne 'the whole of his army and navy at a single view'.

'. . . and when he saw the whole Hellespont hidden by ships, and all the beaches of Abydos and all the open ground filled with men, he congratulated himself—and the moment after burst into tears.'

On being asked the reason, Xerxes replied:

' "I was thinking, and it came to my mind how pitifully short human life is—for of all these thousands of men not one will be alive in a hundred years' time." '

Xerxes, who obviously enjoyed playing the philosopher-king, was curious about the reaction of the Greeks to his advance. He sent for an exiled Greek lord, one Demaratus, and asked him:

'Tell me . . . will the Greeks dare to lift a hand against me? My own belief is that the Greeks and all the other western peoples gathered together would be insufficient to withstand the attack of my army—and still more so if they are not united.'

Demaratus, first emphasising that he had but little affection for his countrymen, who had robbed him of his hereditary power and driven him from his lands, and warning Xerxes that what he had to say would probably displease the king, went on:

'. . . should it become necessary—should there be a great cause to urge me on—then nothing would give me more pleasure than to stand up to one of those men of yours who claim to be a match for three Greeks. So it is with the Spartans; fighting singly, they are as good as any, but fighting together they are the best soldiers in the world. They are free—yes—but not entirely free; for they have a master, and that master is Law, which they fear much more than your subjects fear you. Whatever that master commands, they do; and his command never varies; it is never to retreat in battle, however great the odds, but always to stand firm, and to conquer or die. . . .'

The truth of Demaratus' words was proved when the Persian host met the Spartans at Thermopylae, a narrow pass through the mountains near the head of the Gulf of Euboea. To the north, Thessaly had fallen, since the Thessalians, who had first been willing to fight, gave way to the Persians when the Allies withdrew to the south. At first they had planned to make a stand at Tempe, in northern Thessaly, but fearing that they might be outflanked, took their stand at Thermopylae, while their fleet concentrated at Artemisium on the coast of Histiaea.

'The Greek force', writes Herodotus, 'which here awaited the coming of Xerxes was made up of the following contingents; 300 heavy armed infantry from Sparta, 500 from Tegea, 500 from Mantinea, 120 from Orchomenos in Arcadia, 1,000 from other Arcadian towns; from Corinth there were 400, and from Mycenae 80.'

There were also small contingents from Boeotia, Thespiae, Thebes, Locris and Phocis, bringing the total to about 6,000 men at most. The Athenians provided most of the fleet, in alliance with their old enemies from the island of Aegina.

The Persian host, which, like a swarm of locusts, had consumed the corn and cattle of the lands through which it had passed, and, according to Herodotus, 'drunk rivers dry', came clanking and sweating up the mountain passes, until at Thermopylae it had its first sight of the Greeks. Herodotus takes up the story:

'Xerxes sent a man on horseback to ascertain the strength of the Greek force and observe what the troops were doing. . . . The Persian rider approached the camp and took a survey of all he could see—which was not, however, the whole Greek army; for the men on the furthest side of the wall . . . were out of sight.'

'He did, none the less, carefully observe the troops who were stationed on the outside of the wall. At that moment these happened to be the Spartans, and some of them were stripped for exercise, while others were combing their hair. . . .'

The puzzled spy reported all this to Xerxes, who again summoned the Greek Demaratus, and asked him for an explanation. Demaratus replied:

'These men have come to fight us for possession of the pass, and for that struggle they are preparing. It is the common practice of the Spartans to pay careful attention to their hair when they are about to risk their lives.'

Xerxes waited for four days, hoping that the Greeks would withdraw. But they stayed. So, on the fifth day he launched his attack. In the narrow pass his great numbers were of little advantage, since only a limited force of men could advance along it at a time. These, score by score, the Spartans grimly hewed down.

'On the Spartan side it was a memorable fight; they were men who understood war pitted against an inexperienced enemy, and among the feints they employed was to turn their backs in a body and pretend to be retreating in confusion, whereupon the enemy would come on with a clatter and a roar, supposing the battle won; but the Spartans, just as the Persians were on them would wheel and face them and inflict in the new struggle innumerable losses. The Spartans had their losses, too, but not many. . . . Xerxes was watching the battle from where he sat; and it is said that in the course of the attacks three times, in terror for his army, he leapt to his feet.'

Day after day the struggle for the pass went on:

'. . . but the Greeks never slackened; their troops were ordered in divisions corresponding to the states from which they came, and each division took its turn in the line except the Phocians, who had been posted to guard the track over the mountains.'

That track was the undoing of the Greeks. A traitor, one Ephialtes of Trachis, showed the Persians the way across the mountains, and the secret pathway by which they could take the Greeks in the rear. The Phocians were overwhelmed, and the Greeks realised that they would soon be outflanked.

8(a) View from near the site of the Temple of Delphi, Greece

8(b) The Acropolis of Athens seen from the Theseum

8(d) *right*: Temple of the Four Winds, Athens

8(c) Base of the Parthenon, showing 'entasis'

'At once a conference was held, and opinions were divided, some urging that they must on no account abandon their posts, others taking the opposite view. The result was that the army split, some dispersed, the men returning to their various homes, and others made ready to stand beside Leonidas.'

The Spartan leader had decided to stand firm, as Demaratus had warned Xerxes. In the morning the Persian king poured out a libation to the rising sun,[1] and ordered his army forward.

'As the Persian army advanced to the assault, the Greeks under Leonidas, knowing that the fight would be their last, pressed forward to the wider part of the pass much further than they had done before . . . they left the confined space and battle was joined on open ground. . . . The Greeks, knowing that death was inevitable, fought with desperate courage, exerting every ounce of strength that was in them. . . . By this time their spears were broken, and they were killing the Persians with their swords.'

Leonidas was killed, and a bitter struggle took place over his body. Finally, as the Persian troops, with Ephialtes, swarmed down from the mountain track, the Greeks knew that the end had come:

'the character of the fighting changed. They withdrew again into the narrow neck of the pass, behind the walls, where the stone lion of Leonidas stands to this day. Here they resisted to the last, with their swords, if they had them, or if not, with their hands and teeth, until the Persians, coming on from the front over the ruins of the wall and closing in from behind, finally overwhelmed them.'

The road into Greece lay open, and the Persian army moved south, while their great fleet, sailing along the coast, accompanied them. This fleet had met with a serious disaster at Sepias, when a storm destroyed a great number of its vessels. But those that remained still vastly outnumbered the small Greek fleet, which on hearing of the disaster at Thermopylae moved southward towards Athens, though some of its ships fought skirmishing actions with the Persian vessels. There was now nothing to stop Xerxes on land, and the Athenians knew it. They evacuated their population

[1] The Persians were sun-worshippers.

to the island of Salamis, from which they watched while the Persians put their city to the flames. Men recalled what the Oracle of Apollo at Delphi had said in reply to the question whether or not the Greeks should resist the invaders:

> *Why sit you, doomed ones? Fly to the world's end, leaving*
> *Home and the heights your city circles like a wheel.*
> *The head shall not remain in its place, nor the body,*
> *Nor the feet beneath, nor the hands, nor the parts between*
> *But all is ruined, for fire and the headlong God of War*
> *Speeding in a Syrian chariot shall bring you low.* . . .

If one man can be said to have saved Athens and Greece and Europe, it is Themistocles. It was he who persuaded the Athenians not to divide the new-found silver of the Laurion mines among themselves, but to spend it on a fleet. It was he who pointed out to his despairing countrymen two statements in the Oracle's reply, which might mean hope; they were:

> *Yet Zeus the all-seeing grants to Athene's prayer*
> *That the wooden wall shall not fall, but help you and your*
>   *children.*

and:

> *Divine Salamis, you will bring death to women's sons*
> *When the corn is scattered, or the harvest be gathered in.*

By 'wooden walls', Themistocles said, the God meant the fleet. And when his opponents pointed out that Apollo had also said that 'Salamis . . . will bring death to women's sons', the shrewd statesman, knowing Apollo's reputation for ambiguity (one of his names was *Loxias*, 'the ambiguous'), pointed out that if the God had meant disaster for the Greeks at Salamis he would have said 'wretched Salamis' or 'accursed Salamis'. But he had said '*Divine* Salamis', therefore it must be the Persians who would suffer. No doubt Themistocles was also aware that the Delphic priests had the best foreign intelligence system in the world. . . .

The last act of the drama is set in the island of Salamis, on a dark night, when Themistocles and the other Greek leaders, men from Athens, and Sparta, and other cities, are holding a desperate council of war. Thucydides tells us that at one moment the argument grew so heated that Eurybiades, the Spartan general, raised his staff to strike the Athenian, and Themistocles said, 'Strike, but hear me!'

He knew that there was still a chance, though a desperate one. The great Persian fleet was anchored in the bay. Athens was a burned-out ruin. The Corinthian leader even said that the Athenians no longer had any right to take part in the debate, since they no longer even possessed a town. Themistocles replied that they still had a fleet. He said to the Corinthian:

'As for you, if you stay here and play the man—well and good; go, and you'll be the ruin of Greece. In this war everything depends on the fleet. I beg you to take my advice; if you refuse, we will immediately put our families aboard and sail for Ciris in Italy—it has long been ours, and the oracles have foretold that the Athenians must live there some day. Where will you be without the Athenian fleet? When you have lost you will remember my words.'

This silenced Eurybiades.

During all this time Themistocles must have been on tenterhooks, wondering if his last gamble would succeed. For, knowing that unless the Persian fleet were brought to action soon the allies would melt away, he had sent a trusted follower to the Persian king, telling him that he, Themistocles, was Xerxes' friend, that the Greeks were going to retreat by night by the western exit to the Bay of Salamis; if only the Persians would block this exit they would have the Greeks trapped.

Xerxes fell for the trick. In the early hours of the morning, while the Council of War still argued, someone told Themistocles that a visitor wished to see him. The Athenian left the conference. Outside stood a certain Aristeides, a former enemy of Themistocles, who had been sent into exile. We owe Herodotus a debt for this story.

The two faced each other. Then Aristeides said:

'You and I have been the bitterest enemies; now our rivalry is, which of us can do Athens the greatest service. I have slipped between the Persian lines to tell you this; we are surrounded by the Persian fleet. Go in and tell them.'

And, according to Herodotus, Themistocles replied:

'Thank God! But you go in and tell them. They will believe *you*!'[1]

For this was exactly what the Athenian statesman had wanted. The Persian fleet had crowded itself into the narrows, where the Greeks, much more skilful seamen, would have them at their mercy. And as the exits were now blocked, the reluctant Greek allies had no option but to stand and fight with Athens. There was no escape.

The rest of the story is well known. Hemmed in between land and sea, the Persian ships could not use the advantage of their superior speed and powers of manœuvre. The Greeks, in their slower vessels, but with superior seamanship, bore down on them, boarded them, captured them, sank them, or set them on fire. It was all over in a day and a night. '*And in the morning where were they?*'

Bereft of naval support, the great Persian Army began to retreat. A strong force, under Mardonius, remained behind until the following year, but was defeated by the Spartans at Plataea. The rest straggled back to Asia as best it could (the Greeks conveniently left the Hellespont bridges undestroyed), but thousands died on the way of starvation or disease. Xerxes got back to Susa and continued to reign. But the great invasion was over. Triumphantly the Greeks liberated their Ionian colonies, and the Athenians, who had emerged as the leaders of Greek independence, founded a league of Hellenic states for the purpose of preventing any further invasions from the east.

It was, perhaps, the greatest triumph of western man, and the anti-climax which followed—when the Greeks weakened and almost destroyed themselves by internecine warfare—cannot dim its glory. It proved the fundamental falsity of Napoleon's cynical jibe—God is not necessarily 'on the side of the big battalions'.

Xerxes and his millions are almost forgotten, but Thermopylae and Salamis are still imperishable names. A. E. Housman has

[1] H. D. F. Kitto, *The Greeks*.

'The King with half the East at heel'

crystallised the emotions aroused by those names in a poem which, although written by an Englishman, is in spirit essentially Greek.

The King with half the East at heel is marched from lands of morning
His fighters drink the rivers up, their shafts benight the air
And he that dies will die for nought, and home there's no returning;
The Spartans on the sea-wet rock sat down and combed their hair.

CHAPTER XVII

Athens: Glory and Decline

The first part of our journey is nearly over. We have travelled from 4000 to 480 B.C., watched the earliest civilisations develop in the Nile Valley, Mesopotamia, and Crete, seen the Myceneans, the earliest Greek-speaking peoples to enter Europe, absorbing elements of Cretan culture, replacing the Minoans as the dominant maritime power in the Aegean, and then being overwhelmed by new peoples of kindred stock, the ancestors of the 'classical' Greeks. In Western Asia we have witnessed the conflict between the Hittite Empire and Ancient Egypt, and later between Egypt and the 'sea-peoples'. We have seen the rise of the Assyrians, only to be destroyed in their turn by a combination of Medes and Babylonians. We have watched the Greeks spreading throughout the islands and coastlands of the Mediterranean, absorbing like eager children the culture of the ancient civilisations with which they were brought into contact by war, trade and commerce, learning mathematics from Babylonia, architecture, geometry and medicine from Egypt, the alphabet from Phoenicia, but adding to these elements of their own northern character—curiosity, independence of mind, and a spirit of free inquiry.

Finally, we have seen an Aryan people, the Persians, founding the most powerful of all Oriental empires, and conquering one by one all the ancient lands of the Middle East, spreading to the Mediterranean, and only prevented from occupying Europe by the courage, intelligence, and cunning of a relatively small number of Greeks, determined to be free.

If, for the last time, we change our lens from 'close-up' to 'long-shot', and look at the area which we have called the Anvil, what do we see during the first half of the fifth century B.C.? From the Hindu-Kush in India to the shores of the Mediterranean, from the Armenian mountains to the Arabian desert, one great Oriental power is in control—Persia.

Xerxes still reigns from Susa, his capital, and his successors, Artaxerxes I, Darius II, Artaxerxes II and Artaxerxes III, will continue to rule until the Persian Empire is overthrown by a Hellenised Macedonian—Alexander the Great. But that event is still more than a century and a half ahead.

Egypt is merely a Persian province, though the ancient civilisation of the Nile still survives. The colossus lies with its back broken, though life still flickers in its aged body; the old gods are worshipped, and the ancient language is still written and spoken.

In south-western Asia Minor the Greek colonies are throwing off the Persian yoke, and further west, across the great sea, the Hellenic city-states are free of Persian interference; free, in fact, to continue to fight and quarrel among themselves. In the Aegean, Athens, after her triumphs over Persia, is now ascendant, and other Greek states are beginning to ally themselves with her in defence against a renewed Persian attack. To the west, Syracuse, in Sicily, has become one of the richest and most powerful of Greek city-states. So has Acragas (Girgenti), also in Sicily; each has more than 20,000 citizens, but Syracuse is the more important, standing second only to Athens as a centre of Hellenic culture. There are flourishing Greek colonies also in North Africa (especially Cyrene) and Italy. At Herculaneum, near modern Naples, there is an important Greek city, substantial remains of which can still be seen. There is also one at Sybaris, in Italy, from which we get our word, *sybarite*. In fact, the Greeks called southern Italy 'Great Hellas'.

There were other Greek cities even further west—modern Marseilles stands on the site of a Greek town. The only non-Greek colony of any consequence was Carthage (near modern Tunis), which had been founded by the Phoenicians in the ninth century; it was a powerful commercial rival to Syracuse with which it fought for control of the west Mediterranean trade, and survived long enough to become a challenge to Rome.

If we try to concentrate on the broader picture, ignoring the details, and looking only for the continuing threads which link our own culture with that of the ancient world, we have, I think, to recognise that from this point onwards for a thousand years, the peoples of western Asia—with one exception—had little further direct influence on western civilisation. Their direct contribution was very great—far, far more than was recognised before the development of scientific archaeology during the past century. Until about one hundred years ago it was assumed that our intellectual and material culture rested mainly on foundations laid by the Greeks. The Greeks themselves admitted owing a debt to the Oriental peoples, especially the Egyptians, but it has been left mainly to archaeologists and philologists to discover just how great that debt was—in science (especially mathematics), art, and craftsmanship.

But by 450 B.C., and even earlier, the Greeks were already in possession of most of this knowledge and skill, and with their agile, free-thinking minds, had adapted and re-used it to shape their own distinctive culture-pattern. The Greeks were the principal channel through which the achievements of those earlier civilisations have flowed down to us. From now on, therefore, we have to focus our attention mainly on them.

However, there is one important exception, or half-exception— Hebrew religious literature. Among all the peoples, from mighty kingdoms to petty states, who lived in Western Asia before the birth of Christ, one small nation, politically so feeble that it is hardly mentioned by the early chronicles of Egypt and Babylon, has had a more powerful influence on the growth of western civilisation than all the Oriental empires put together; an influence as great—some would claim even greater—as those of Greece and Rome. I use the word 'half-exception' because, although Judaism eventually reached Europe directly, via the Jews who travelled there, it remained an exclusive religion which had little or no

effect on the peoples among whom the Jews settled—except sometimes to arouse hostility. The main stream of Jewish influence, the
faith which was to become 'a light to lighten the Gentiles', flowed
through Hellas, when Hellenised Christians translated the Gospels,
and with them the Jewish sacred writings, into the Greek language.

That was not to happen for several hundred years, but it is
important to remember that in 480 B.C., when the Greeks were
celebrating their triumph over the Persians, the people of Jerusalem still guarded their ancient faith. Their misfortunes, though
considerable, had probably been no worse than those of other
small Semitic peoples who were unlucky enough to live in the path
of the rival kings of Egypt, Babylon, and Assyria. In 586 many of
the Jews were taken to captivity in Babylon—the second time this
had happened—but when, in 538, Cyrus took the city, such Jews
as wished to return to Jerusalem were allowed to do so. Not all of
them did. Many refused to return, preferring the great city.
Moreover, according to Glover, the Babylonian Jews considered
themselves superior to the returned exiles. They were probably
more sophisticated.

A Greek visitor to Judea in 450 B.C. would see nothing to
interest him; Jerusalem was an unimportant little town on a hill
with a ruined palace and a rebuilt temple (to which he would not
be admitted), and the country itself was the home of herdsmen and
small farmers, living a simple existence in the hills, along the
Jordan valley, and around Lake Galilee. No fine roads and high-
towered temples, as in Babylon; no pyramids, tombs, and obelisks,
as in Egypt. The Jewish heritage resided in two things, both
invisible to the Greek visitor. One was the blood and genius of the
Jewish race, which would one day be carried to the ends of the
earth. The other lay hidden in the archives of the temple. For
there, jealously guarded by the priesthood, were the texts[1] from
Moses to the second Isaiah; the Mosaic Law, the chronicles of
Judges and Kings, the Psalms of David, the teachings of the
Prophets, the songs of Deborah, of Miriam, of Solomon; epic
poems of war not inferior to the battlepieces of Homer; passionate
love-poetry; books of history, wisdom and prophecy; but no

---

[1] Though not all in the form in which we read them now.

philosophy which the Greeks would have recognised as such. For whereas the Hellenic thinkers reasoned their way to the idea of 'the one god', the Hebrew prophets, scorning reason, claimed direct Divine inspiration. They were monotheists by conviction, although it is true that the later teachers—e.g. the Second Isaiah —express their beliefs as speculative truths and not as dogmas.

But for centuries to come this treasure-house of literature and moral wisdom was locked from the rest of the world. For Jaweh, though no longer a mere tribal war-deity but a Lord of justice, mercy, and truth, was interpreted by the priesthood as a Jewish god, and a Jewish god only. Although the Psalmist had sung 'the Gentiles shall come to thy light and kings to the brightness of thy rising', our Greek, if he had approached the temple, would have been lucky to escape stoning.

We end this first part of our story with Athens. After the retreat of the Persians she became the acknowledged leader of the Hellenic world. Her leaders, not content with defeating the enemy, did not rest until they had broken Persian sea-power and freed all the Greek cities of the Aegean islands and Asia Minor. Their town grew rich, their fleet was powerful, and they organised a naval confederacy with headquarters on the island of Delos, with the purpose of keeping Hellas free of any further threat. But the Spartans, essentially a military people, took little interest, and retired to their 'barrack-state' in the Peloponnese.

Since men first achieved civilisation there has never been such a rich flowering of genius as occurred, *within one century*, in fifth century Athens. In a city no larger than, say Worcester, in England —a moderate-sized country town—only three generations produced such tragic poets as Aeschylus, Euripides and Sophocles, and the comic poet Aristophanes; philosophers such as Socrates, Plato, Aristotle, Anaxagoras; the sculptors Phidias and Praxiteles, and statesmen of the quality of Pericles and Themistocles. These were only the most distinguished. There were many others, who, in a less brilliant age, would have shone as brightly as Marlowe, Ford and Jonson might have done had they not lived in the age of William Shakespeare. As de Burgh remarks, 'It is as though the individuality of Greek civilisation strove for a brief period of its maturity to surpass the bounds of possible achievement.'

The character of the Athenian people at this period can best be appreciated by short extracts from two famous speeches which, like the symphonies of Beethoven, can never stale through repetition. The first was given by the greatest of Athenian statesmen, Pericles; it is part of his funeral oration on the men who fell in the war with Sparta.

'We admit anyone to our city, and do not expel foreigners from fear that they should see too much, because in war we trust to our own bravery and daring rather than to stratagems and preparations. Our enemies prepare for war by a laborious training from boyhood; we live at our ease, but are no less confident in facing danger. Indeed the Spartans have never ventured to attack us without the help of their allies. So with courage which comes from natural disposition rather than from laws, we have two advantages, for we avoid the preliminary labour, and are just as good as they when the test comes. We love the arts, but without lavish display, and things of the mind, without becoming soft. . . .'[1]

The second extract is from the speech of the Corinthian delegate to Sparta, when the Corinthians, jealous of the power of Athens and her leadership of the Hellenic world, had asked the Spartans to join them in a war against her.

'You have no idea what sort of people these Athenians are, how totally different from yourselves. They are always thinking of new schemes, and are quick to make plans and carry them out; you are content with what you have, and are reluctant to do even what is necessary. They are bold, adventurous and sanguine; you are cautious, and trust neither to your powers nor your judgment. They love foreign adventure, you hate it; for they think they stand to gain, you that you stand to lose something. When victorious they make the most of it: when defeated, they fall back less than anyone. They give their bodies to Athens as if they were public property: they use their minds for Athens in the most individual way possible. They make a plan: if it fails, they think they have lost something: if it succeeds, this success is nothing in comparison

[1] *The Greeks*—Kitto: Penguin Books, London.

with what they are going to do next. It is impossible for them either to enjoy peace and quiet themselves or allow anyone else to.'

When those words were spoken the first bars of shadow had already fallen across the sunlit courts of Hellas. For the defeat of the Persians did not bring the millennium. Greek individualism and self-interest, the stubborn pride which had beaten the barbarian, broke up, in the end, the precious unity which Athens had striven to create. War did not end. Greek fought Greek, for power, for possession of land or trade, or out of jealousy of Athens' dominance. Men fought and died bravely, but, year after year, the Hellenic world dissipated its wealth and strength in war, until finally it fell to another northern conqueror. That story belongs properly to another book, but, before we close this one, let us try to see Athens at the time when, in de Burgh's words, 'it seemed as though the individuality of Greek civilisation strove for a brief period of its maturity to surpass the bounds of possible achievement.'

The city stood on two levels. Above, on the crest of a high, steep-sided, jutting mass of rock—the Acropolis—stood the Parthenon, the white-marble Temple of Pallas Athene—and other sacred shrines. In Mycenean times the Acropolis itself had been the city, and fragments of its 'Cyclopean' walls could still be seen (as they can today). But in the time of Pericles it had become the sanctuary of Athene, the protecting goddess of Athens, and of Poseidon, god of the sea, with whom she was associated. Athene was the older deity, and had probably been worshipped in some form long before the Greeks came. But Poseidon had his place too, and the Athenians would point out the holes in the rock (still to be seen) which, they said, were made by the sea-god's trident. By this act Poseidon created a salt spring of water, from which sprang a horse. Athene also smote the rock with her spear, and from the spot grew an olive tree.

The symbolism of these two gifts is apparent. The Athenians, great seafarers and traders, lived by the sea. But their most valuable crop was the olive, the oil of which was then, as now, one of the most important products of the Mediterranean world.

Every year, at the time of the Panathenaic festival, a great procession wound its way up the steep hill to the Acropolis; priests and priestesses, youths and girls wearing garlands, some playing instruments, some carrying offerings, others driving before them beasts for sacrifice. At the top of the steep rocky approach the grand Propylea or portico rose above them. Entering, they passed on their right the delicate little temple of Athene Nike and then, climbing flights of steps flanked by fluted columns of Pentelic marble, came at last to the forecourt of the temple; not, as it is today, an uneven, empty expanse of bare rock, but thronged with statues of gods and heroes by the greatest sculptors of the age —indeed of any age.

A little to their left stood the Erechtheum, a smaller temple dedicated to Poseidon, with its rows of caryatids—columns sculptured in the form of girls. Ahead and slightly above them rose the Parthenon, sun-bright golden stone and black shadow against the deep blue of the sky; its pediment and friezes were alive with bas-reliefs[1] of horses and riders, youths and girls in procession, Amazons in battle, the Centaurs in combat with the Lapithae—all vigorous and glowing in the magical light of Hellas. And within the temple was the statue of the Goddess herself.

Beyond, a mile or so away, rose a cone of rock, Lycabettus. Below lay the city with its houses, its great Agora or market place, its public buildings, temples and gardens. Away to the right, glittering blue in the sunshine, was the Bay of Salamis with white-sailed ships, and the dim shape of the island where their fathers had taken refuge when the Persians burned their city. Yet Athens had risen again, lovelier and more splendid than ever.

Too much like the stereotype? Then let us descend the hill and mingle with the crowds in the city. The houses are comparatively small and unimpressive, but the public buildings where the citizens meet to discuss state policy, to hear their leaders speak (and heckle them if necessary) to hear and vote on motions, or to judge legal cases, are magnificent. So is the great *agora*, a ten-acre public square where you might meet anybody; captains and crews of ships newly-arrived at the Piraeus with news of other

[1] Some of which—the Elgin Marbles—can be seen in the British Museum.

parts of the world; Socrates in conversation with Plato; statesmen and soldiers, poets and philosophers; country-people at their stalls, selling onions, and figs, geese and ducks, pomegranates and clothing. Or maybe you prefer just to watch the young men and girls. There are two pretty girls coming towards us now, with their guardians. One is evidently a visitor from Sparta (we are not at war with them at the moment). How do we know she's a Spartan? Because, if you notice (as no doubt you have) her *peplum* or tunic, the single garment which women wear, is not sewn down to the hem like the tunics of the Athenian girls, but unsewn, so that it flies back to show the leg as she walks.

Some Athenians pretend to be shocked by this deliberately negligent manner of dressing. One poet, Ibycus, calls the Spartan girls 'the bare-thighed'. And Sophocles, when writing about Hermione, daughter of Helen of Sparta, has written:

> *And that young girl, whose tunic, still unsewn*
> *Lay bare her gleaming thigh*
> *Between its folds, Hermione. . . .*

Some of the Athenian matrons look askance, but the men don't seem to mind. A sailor with tanned skin who has recently been to Sparta, tells us that there the young girls even go naked in their ceremonial processions. Not only that, but they play games and even wrestle with the young Spartan men.

Shocking. Let us move on.

Still, it makes one reflect on the position of women in Greek society. They did not have a vote, of course, which proves that they were not free and emancipated, as our women are. Or does it? Scholars, especially those writing in the Victorian Age, told us that Greek women were treated by their men as inferiors; that they were deliberately kept within their homes to look after the children, while the men were free to indulge themselves with *hetairae* (courtesans). These scholars quote in support such lines as the following from Aristophanes, as translated by Jebb:

'*It is difficult for women to get out.*'

But Professor Kitto, writing in 1954, pointed out that what Aristophanes actually wrote was:

'*It is difficult for women to get out, what with dancing attendance on one's husband, keeping the servant-girl awake, bathing the baby, feeding it. . . .*'

Haven't we heard our own wives say something of the same kind; and are they slaves?

Now we'll go into the court-house near the Agora and hear a case being tried. Nerea, a courtesan, is accused of illegally marrying an Athenian and marrying off one of her daughters, also a prostitute, to an important Athenian official. The prosecutor is addressing the jury (all male):

'Gentlemen, if you acquit this woman, what will you say to your wives and daughters when you go home? They will ask where you have been. You will say, "In the courts". They will say "what was the case?" You of course will say "Against Nerea. She was accused of illegally marrying an Athenian, and getting one of her daughters, a prostitute, married to Theogenes the archon".'

'. . . you will tell them the details of the case, and you will tell them how carefully and completely the case was proved. When you have finished they will say, "And what did you do?" And you will reply "We acquitted her". And *then* the fat will be in the fire.'

This hardly indicates that Athenian women went in awe of their men-folk, as Victorian and Edwardian scholars suggested. Still, they did not have the vote—that is certain. Which means, does it not, that Greek men did not trust their womenfolk; or at least that the women did not possess minds worth considering. Dr. T. R. Glover, as late as 1932, makes Socrates say to his friend:

'*Is there anybody to whom you entrust more serious matters than to your wife—and to whom you talk less?*'

But Dr. Kitto, who belongs to the present generation of scholars, translates the same passage as:

'*Is there anybody to whom you entrust more serious things, and with whom you have fewer arguments?*'

—which puts an entirely new complexion on the matter. Could the tereotype of the Greek woman be false? Then we have the late Dr. Seltman, sometime Fellow of Queens' College, Cambridge, writing about the legendary huntress Atalanta:

'She was naturally both reluctant and ruthless; therefore the conditions for all suitors were "Outrun the girl, or pay with your life". The fairy-tale does not record how many died, nor is it consistent about the name of the splendid young man who at last won the race and the girl. Some call him Hippomenes, others Melanion, and they never forget that he won by the trick of throwing away gew-gaws to distract her. The girl was always the better runner . . .'

'. . . Atalanta is, in a sense, the feminine counterpart of those indefatigable heroes Herakles and Theseus, whose memory inspired every aspiring Greek athletic boy. The important point is that you only evoke, embroider, and recite legends about an imaginary athlete-heroine because your civilisation affords some scope for young females to be athletic. No medieval maiden ever stripped to wrestle with a troubadour; no virgin ever raced in the Hippodrome against a saintly deacon; no houri ever left a harem to hunt wild boar on foot. The answer is "no scope, no legend". But where there is legend there is, somewhere, scope. . . .'[1]

The sentimental Greek male probably felt as Sappho did about Kleis.

> *I have a child; so fair*
> *As golden flowers is she*
> *My Kleis, all my care.*
> *I'd not give her away*
> *For Lydia's wide sway*
> *Nor lands men long to see.*[2]

The child's mother probably felt equally tenderly about her; but she was far from being the tame household drudge, meekly obedient to her husband's will, which nineteenth century scholars liked to represent as the ideal of Greek womanhood. Take the heroines of Greek tragedy; Medea, Andromache, Antigone, Helen; they are vigorous intelligent women who speak their minds, not tame little slaves. And they must have been taken from life. As Kitto says:

[1] *Women in Antiquity*—Dr. Seltman: Pan Books, London, 1956.
[2] *The Oxford Book of Greek verse in translation*—Sir Maurice Bowra: No. 153. O.U.P., London, 1938.

'Euripides admittedly makes his women suffer at men's hands —which is a phenomenon not unknown today—but again and again he makes his men suffer from vengeful and uncontrollable women; e.g. Clytemnestra and Medea. There is one line in *Creon* when the old slave-woman says to her ill-used mistress:

> *Come, you must do something womanly!*
> *Take to the sword! Poison him!*'

In the writer's opinion Greek women were far nearer to their modern sisters than, for example, the pallid, lachrymose heroines of Shakespeare—the product of more than fifteen centuries of Pauline Christianity—with its emphasis on feminine chastity and obedience. Ask any contemporary actress of spirit whom she would rather play (other things being equal)—Desdemona or Clytemnestra; Ophelia or Medea? And note her reply.

Perhaps some will regard this as an unnecessary digression. On the contrary, it has been introduced deliberately. If we look back over the recorded history of the Egyptians, Sumerians, Babylonians, Assyrians, what does it tell us about the female half of the human race? Practically nothing. Men invented writing—and kept it to themselves. Men developed the techniques which made life easier and pleasanter for both sexes. Men made war, men made laws and statutes, created works of art, adventured on the seas, produced objects of beauty or utility for sale or consumption. Meanwhile women merely produced children; men to feed the armies, girls to become mothers—or so it would seem if one relied only on the earliest writings and did not use one's imagination.

Very occasionally a woman is allowed to come forward— Nefretiti, or the wife of Candaules, or the female admiral Artemisia who had a glorious time at the battle of Salamis; with typical feminine ruthlessness, she deliberately rammed and sank one of her own ships in order to fool a pursuing enemy into thinking she was on his side.... The truth is that there were women of character throughout history, though not all of them were lady admirals. But it is not until we come to the Greek writers that they are allowed a hearing; which is why they have been given prominence in this chapter.

S

One thing strikes us forcibly about fifth century Athens, particularly if we come from a northern country. Practically everything seems to take place out of doors. Houses are of little importance to the Athenian, except as places in which to sleep, feed, and entertain his friends. His home, his pride, is the city herself. As the Corinthian delegate said 'they give their bodies to Athens as if they were public property; they give their minds to Athens in the most individual way possible.'

Life centres around the *agora*, the streets and squares, public buildings and gymnasia where men meet and gossip, exchange news, listen to orators and poets, watch, or take part in the public games which play such a prominent part in Greek life. *Mens sana in corpore sano* is a Latin tag, but it was a Greek ideal. '*We love the things of the mind*,' said Pericles, '*without becoming soft*.'

There is, of course, another side of Athenian life which we find puzzling and perhaps distressing. There is a large slave-population, and these men and women are mainly Greeks, some of them of birth and rank in their own lands, but, taken prisoners in war, they are now compelled to work for their captors. But they bear no resemblance to the pitiful manacled captives which one sees in Egyptian and Assyrian temple and tomb reliefs. They wear the same dress as the free Athenians, enjoy some legal protection, and can purchase their freedom. Few are ill-treated, though conditions in the Laurion mines, where many slaves work, are said to be bad. Unhappily these unfortunates, like the concentration camp prisoners in the Second World War, are out of sight and mind of the ordinary citizens.

Many of the slaves are domestic servants.

'These added to the amenities of life, and to some extent promoted civilisation, just as the servants we used to have enabled middle-class women to play bridge in the afternoons, and professors to write books; but they were certainly not the basis of economic life in Attica. . . . Slavery helped, like an auxiliary engine; but to suggest that it was the mainstay of Athenian economy is a serious exaggeration and to say that it set the tone of society and estranged the ordinary citizen from hard work is ludicrous.'[1]

[1] H. D. F. Kitto, *The Greeks*: Pelican Books, London.

Looking around, we might ask ourselves from whence comes the wealth which makes possible all this richness and beauty—the temples and gymnasia, the theatres and magnificent public buildings? Part of it is revenue from land. Much of it is from trade; for Athens exports to other Greek cities and colonies large shipments of olive oil, and the produce of her craftsmen—those lovely figured vases, bowls, and other ceramics which have been found on sites as far apart as France and southern Russia, and of which examples are now shown in practically every Museum and Art Gallery in the western world. Keats's 'Grecian Urn' was probably made by slave-labour in an Athenian factory. In return for these manufactured goods Athens imports most of her grain from abroad, as Great Britain does today.

'We love the things of the mind.' . . . The Athenians enjoyed using their minds; not only the higher intelligentsia, the beautiful and high-born young men who sat at the feet of Socrates, Plato and Aristotle. The ordinary Athenians, men and women, who crowded the huge open-air Theatre of Dionysus, on the slope of the Acropolis, did not mind being asked to think. Not that they went there for 'culture'. They went to be entertained, as we do when we visit a cinema or watch television. In that theatre—the birthplace of western drama—they sat happily munching their figs and pomegranates, and saw played out before them the greatest tragedy in the world, the Oresteian trilogy, fresh from the pen of their poet Aeschylus, beside whom some of them might have fought at the Battle of Marathon, or at Salamis (for he was in that battle too). That particular tragic cycle was based on the Homeric story of Agamemnon, Clytemnestra, Orestes and the rest —stories they knew by heart; the interest lay in the significance which the poet drew from them. Then they could enjoy Euripides' topical satires on public men they knew well—for in fifth century Athens politicians were allowed no protection from the public barbs and lampoons. They had to 'take it'.

The Athenian theatre-goers also saw re-enacted for them the struggle with the Persians in which they themselves had taken part. And they roared at the comedies of Aristophanes—comedies of such outrageous, glorious, Rabelaisian wit that in many parts of the western world today they are not permitted performance, except in private theatres. Many of the situations were concerned with sex, but never in a sniggering, self-conscious way. The Athenians, being an adult people, did not think the frank representation of sex interesting or 'daring' in itself. They regarded it, like other human impulses and emotions, as a subject which could be treated, dramatically, in any way the author saw fit—tragic or comic. Aristophanes made it funny, which it often is.

Art, intelligence, beauty, courage—all the finest qualities and achievements of the human heart and mind seemed concentrated, for a brief period, in that little Greek city-state, two thousand four hundred years ago. In a way it might be regarded as the creaming-off of all that was best in the collective experience of mankind over three thousand years.

It did not last, of course. But when the bright light of Hellenic culture was dimmed (though never extinguished) the tragedy was brought about, not by the hand of a foreign invader, but through that spirit of jealous independence which had been the strength of the Greeks; but which, when turned inward, weakened and almost destroyed them. But that is another story.

Looking back over the long span of time we have covered, we see many peoples, but not all with equal clearness or equal understanding. The Ancient Egyptians, though they have told us more about themselves then any other civilisation of that far-off age, are attractive, but remote. As for the Sumerians, Babylonians, and Hittites one respects and admires their achievements, but again there is a barrier through which we cannot pass. We know the Jews because their religious literature has become part of ours. The violence and power of the Assyrians has less appeal for us than it had for the Victorians, who could afford to take a more romantic view than we can of 'the drums and tramplings of conquest'. The Cretans, much as we admire their art, remain strange and slightly sinister. With the Myceneans we are on firmer ground, for they have been speaking to us for years through the lips of Homer.

But when we reach the Ancient Greek world we are at home.

Here are people whom we can recognise, and who, in spite of certain differences, think, act and speak like us. One not only admires, but loves them—and despairs for them. They had all our faults; perhaps we have a few of their virtues—one hopes so. Therefore it is fitting to give to a Greek the last words in this book. They are a prayer to the goddess of Peace, from Aristophanes' play of that name. He wrote it when Athens, weakened and impoverished by warfare, looked back with longing to the days when life was free of the bitterness and privation which war brings. It expresses an emotion which millions of us experienced not many years back, and is as real today as it was to the Athenian audience of twenty-four centuries ago.

'Free us, then, Peace, from battle and evil deeds! Free us from our too subtle suspicions, which we hurl against each other! Mix us Greeks together as before, with the juice of friendship, and fill our minds with a milder forbearance, and fill our market with good and cheap wares, with onions and early figs, with apples and pomegranates and small warm clothes for slaves. And let us see the country-folk come to the market with geese and pigeons and sand-pipers . . .'

And a common soldier says:

'Ah, by Zeus! To live one's life in peace, and sit by the hearth with one's lass and rake up the coals!'[1]

[1] Frederick Poulsen, *Delphi*. Gyldendal, London, 1920.

Epilogue

In the Prologue I said that this book was 'in essence a quest; an attempt to clarify in my own mind some of the impressions I have received of these ancient lands'. A journey through such rich and varied territory inevitably implies a choice of route. One cannot hope to see everything; other voyagers might have set their course differently, or, even if they had covered the same ground, might have hurried through landscapes which I found interesting, or lingered in places which have less appeal for me. I can only say in extenuation that not all the omissions and abbreviations, which will no doubt be noticed, were due to lack of interest, but lack of space.

To take one example, I have said practically nothing about the music of the ancient world, which interests me much; but, apart from the fact that the subject is one for specialists, it is not possible—as with writing, sculpture and painting—to give practical illustrations. Judging from the types of instruments found in Egyptian and Babylonian tombs, and depicted on their walls, one suspects that oriental music, of say, 1500 B.C. was very similar to the monotonous twanging and banging one hears in eastern countries today. But the Greek mathematician, Pythagoras, by measuring the chords of the lyre, laid the foundations of musical theory, and discovered the mathematical properties which are called harmonic progressions. Examples of Greek musical notation have been found inscribed on the walls of the Treasury of the Athenians at Delphi. These Delphic hymns more than 2,000 years old, have been sung and recorded in modern times.[1]

Again I might have said more about the origin of drama, and the dance. Religious dramas were performed in Ancient Egypt, and as is generally known, Greek drama grew out of religious ritual. Our word 'tragedy' comes from *tragoidia*, meaning 'goat-

[1] By the Greek soprano Arda Mandikian.

song' and was part of the rituals performed in honour of the god Dionysus. At his festivals in the Greek countryside followers of the wine-god were impersonated by choruses of men dressed in goat-skins singing songs in his honour as they danced before the altar. Later an actor was introduced to fill the intervals with singing, mimicry and short dialogues with members of the chorus. From these rustic beginnings arose the true Greek drama from which ours is (very remotely) descended. We know far more about Greek dancing, which is described in their literature, and depicted on vases. There is one in the British Museum which shows a dancing-lesson, and others representing girls and men dancing to the sound of pipes. Most of us will recall the amusing episode in Plato's 'Symposium' in which a Syracusan girl plays a flute, another dances and performs acrobatics, and a boy dances and plays on the lyre. All this, incidentally, took place before one of the most profound philosophical discussions ever recorded, though that did not get thoroughly into its swing before one of the guests did a ridiculous imitation of the boy's dance, and Socrates had informed them all that though he was too old to dance, he still did physical exercises. It is rather difficult to imagine flute-girls and acrobats at a meeting of Oxford or Harvard dons. . . .

If, perhaps some readers think that I have introduced too many human and occasionally frivolous illustrations of this kind, I can only reply, with respect but without apology, that it has been my aim to break the stereotype which so often falsifies history and destroys our enjoyment of it. There is no phrase more misleading than 'this modern age'. All 'ages' have been modern at one time, and many of the things we say, do, and think, today, are no more modern than Socrates (many are a lot more old-fashioned).

Many readers will have seen, or I hope will see, the great monuments of the peoples whose achievements I have tried to describe in this book. They will admire the 5,000-year-old Step Pyramid of Djoser, the oldest large stone building in the world, explore with wonder the deep-hewn tombs of the Pharaohs at Luxor, ponder over the ruined walls of Babylon, watch the waves creaming against the jetties of Byblos (Gebal) which Ribbadi defended and from which the Phoenician galleys set sail. They will see the treasures which Woolley found at Ur, the papyri and the cuneiform tablets on which men first recorded the joy and grief of battle, the ecstasy and pain of love, or the mundane fact that A has married B, or that B owes C a certain sum of money. They will see the shores of Cyprus, where Aphrodite rose from the waves, Mount Olympus, where Zeus reigned with the Immortals, Mycenae, from which Agamemnon set out for Troy, or from the heights of the Athenian Acropolis they will look down on the Bay of Salamis, where a few thousand Greeks saved Europe from the Oriental invader.

But if we see these things only as relics of a dead past, we shall miss the point. The past is not dead. We carry it within us, even if we never read a page of history and call archaeologists 'bone-merchants'. It is with us in the things we use: the steel of our motor-cars is refined from iron, the secret of smelting which was first discovered three thousand years ago in Anatolia; the coins which jingle in our pockets were invented, nearly three thousand years ago, in Lydia. Every time we write a letter, or read a newspaper, we are making use of the symbols which can be traced back through the Romans and Greeks to Phoenicia; perhaps as far back as Ancient Egypt. Every time we look at our watches, with their dials divided into sixty minutes, we owe a debt to the ancient Babylonian mathematicians, who, though they had no mechanical clocks or watches, adopted sixty as a unit of measurement.

The past is with us in the things we like doing. We are moved or amused by watching other human beings act out a drama for our entertainment. So were the Greeks. We enjoy watching horse-racing, boxing and wrestling matches, rowing contests, running and jumping. So did the Greeks and the Myceneans.

The past is with us in the things we hate doing. When we send our cheque to the Income Tax Inspector, we share the gloom and resentment of Ancient Egyptians, Sumerians, and most other ancient peoples who also had to pay taxes. When we feel ill we usually visit a doctor, as they did; and if he gives us a drug containing for example, castor beans, or sodium bicarbonate, sulphur, anise, or nitre (the name is Egyptian) we have to swallow the same substances which the Ancient Egyptian doctors gave their patients—and probably for the same ailments.

The past is with us every day in the language we speak and write; even apparently modern words like *aerodrome* and *mechanic* have a Greek origin. When we ask for a bunch of hyacinths we are using a word which may have been spoken in the Palace of Minos in Crete. Such words as *ocean, rower, elephant, lion, crocodile, hippopotamus*—to name only a few, have an ancestry which goes back more than three thousand years.

Finally, the past is present even in the way we think. When we accept, unquestioningly, established usages in religion, politics, business or social life, merely because they *are* established, we are thinking as most Ancient Egyptians thought. When we allow our imagination to relish the thought of laying waste enemy cities, we are thinking as the Assyrians thought. When we wonder if, perhaps, reason is not infallible, and that truth may be revealed to us by inspiration, that in spite of our rational scepticism, there may be a 'Divinity which shapes our ends' we are feeling as did the Jews. And when we toss on our beds at night (reasoning with that extraordinary clarity which only comes at about two in the morning), and ask ourselves '*why* should I believe that the Rector, or the Sales Manager, or the Premier, is right, when I can clearly see that he is wrong?'—then we are thinking like the Greeks.

Glossary

Agora. Public square or market-place in a Greek city.

Amulet. A charm.

Animism. The attribution of living spirits to inanimate objects or natural phenomena.

Artefact. A product of human workmanship.

Carnelian (or Cornelian). Red chalcedony, much used by the Egyptians and Mesopotamian peoples for jewellery and decorative inlay, etc.

Complex. An arrangement of buildings, e.g. 'the temple complex' —all the buildings comprising the temple and its adjuncts.

Cult. System of religious worship; hence 'cult-object', 'cult-sign', 'cult-centre', etc.

Culture. People following the same customs and using similar objects—e.g. tools, weapons, pottery, are said to belong to the same 'culture' though they are not necessarily of the same race. Cultures are usually named after the 'type-site' on which such objects were found for the first time, e.g. 'Halafian', from Tell Halaf on the river Khabur. Hence 'culture-spread'—indicating the area over which objects of a common culture have been found.

Cuneiform. System of writing with wedge-shaped characters incised on clay tablets. Originating in Sumer *circa* 3000 B.C., it spread throughout Western Asia.

Dynastic. Belonging to the period during which *known and named* kings ruled. There were kings in pre-dynastic times but their names have not survived. In Egypt the First Dynasty begins with Menes (3200 B.C.). The last Dynasty, the Thirtieth, ended in 321 B.C. The history of the Hittite, Assyrian, and Babylonian kings can also be chronicled dynastically.

Dynasty. Line of hereditary rulers, e.g. in Egypt the Eighteenth, Nineteenth Dynasties, etc.

Glossary

Faience. Glazed clay, usually green or green-blue.

Graffito. Crude writing scratched on a wall or potsherd. Pl. *graffiti.*

Hattusas (Boghaz Keiu). Capital of the Hittite Empire, in Asia Minor.

Hellas. The ancient name for the Greek world.

Hellenes. Greeks.

Helot. Slave.

Hieroglyph. Literally 'sacred sign'. Name given by the Greeks to the Ancient System of 'picture-writing'. Hence 'hieroglyphic(s)'.

'Historical Horizon'. On an archaeological site which has been occupied for several millennia B.C. the 'historical horizon' is the level at which objects dating from the beginning of 'historical' time are found.

Jaweh (or Yaweh). Jehovah, god of the Hebrews.

Ka. Ancient Egyptian word whose exact nature is disputed. Some believe it to have been the double of the dead man or woman, others a protecting presence. 'Spirit' is only a very rough definition.

Lapis-lazuli. A blue stone much used by the Egyptians and Sumerians for jewellery, decorative inlay, etc.

Malachite. A green mineral (hydrous carbonate of copper) which can be given a fine polish.

Mastaba. Arab word meaning 'bench'. Used by archaeologists to describe the rectangular tombs of the Old Kingdom of Ancient Egypt, which in shape resemble the mud-brick benches which stand outside some Arab houses.

Megaron. Hall or palace.

Memphis. Capital of Ancient Egypt during the Early Dynastic Period (3200–2800 B.C.) and Old Kingdom (2800–2100 B.C.).

Millennium. One thousand years. Hence, 'the beginning of the second millennium B.C.' was 2000 B.C.

Neolithic. 'New Stone Age.' Belonging to the later stone age, when ground or polished stone implements were used.

Nomarch. Governor of a *nome,* or province.

Nome. In Ancient Egypt, a district, or province.

Occupation layer. On an archaeological site, occupied during a long period, objects, e.g. pottery, belonging to one defined period of

Glossary

time form an 'occupation layer', which can be dated absolutely and/or relatively.

'Palace-style'. In Ancient Egypt, an architectural style, found in both mud-brick and stone, of which the principal feature is rectilinear panelling. Found in monuments of the Old Kingdom.

Paleolithic. 'Old Stone Age'. An era marked by the use of primitive stone implements.

Papyrus. (a) An aquatic plant of the reed family which, in Ancient Egypt, grew beside the Nile. (b) Ancient Egyptian writing material made from this plant. (c) A document written on such material.

Philology. The science of language. Hence 'philologist'.

Pictograph. A pictorial symbol. Hence 'pictographic' writing, a system using such symbols, e.g. the Egyptian *hieroglyphs*.

Polis. Greek city-state.

Potsherd. Broken scrap of pottery.

Pre-Dynastic. In Egypt, the period before the founding of the first Egyptian Dynasty by Menes in 3200 B.C.

Prehistoric. Literally, the period before the beginning of recorded history. In Egypt and Mesopotamia, before *circa* 3000 B.C. In other countries, e.g. Asia Minor and Greece, the 'historical' period begins later.

Pylon. In Ancient Egypt, a monumental gateway leading to a temple. Usually there were several pylons.

Rhyton. Ritual vessel used in religious ceremonies.

Satrap. A Persian military governor.

Stele. Upright slab of stone, usually inscribed and/or sculptured. Pl. *stelæ*.

Tell. Arab word meaning 'mound'. On sites which have been continuously occupied for many centuries, the accumulated material forms a high mound, called a 'tell'; e.g. Tell-el-Amarna.

Thebes. Greek name for *No-Amun*, capital of Ancient Egypt from the Eighteenth to the Twentieth Dynasties (1555–1090 B.C.).

Trireme. Galley with triple row of oars.

Vizier. Prime Minister. Chief official under the king.

Glossary

Wattle and daub. A lattice-work of twigs bound together by mud. Primitive method of building walls.

Ziggurat. A tiered tower. Remains of many have been found on Mesopotamian sites such as Ur, Nippur, Babylon, etc.

Bibliography

*The following books will be helpful to readers wishing
to study in more detail the civilisations described in
this volume. The list does not claim to be comprehensive;
the majority of the works selected can be enjoyed by the
'general reader'.*

GENERAL

Childe, Gordon, *What Happened in History*, Pelican Books,
London 1942.
——, *Man makes himself.*
Dawson, Christopher, *Enquiries into Religion and Culture*, New
York 1933.
de Burgh, W. G., *The Legacy of the Ancient World*, London 1947.
Fraser, Sir James, *The Golden Bough.*
Glover, T. R., *The Ancient World*, Cambridge University Press
1936.
Maspero, Sir G., *The Struggle of Nations*, S.P.C.K. London and
New York 1925.
Muller, H. J., *The Uses of the Past*, The New American Library
1954.
Myres, J. L., *The Dawn of History.*
Read, Winwood, *The Martyrdom of Man*, London 1872.
Rowse, A. L., *The Use of History*, London 1946.
Schweitzer, Albert, *Civilisation and Ethics*, London 1929.
van Loon, H. W., *The Home of Mankind.*
——, *The Story of Mankind.*
Wells, H. G., *An Outline of History*, Cassell & Co., London 1931.
Woolley, Sir L., *Digging up the Past*, Penguin Books, London 1940.

EGYPT

Baikie, J., *Egyptian antiquities of the Nile Valley*, London 1932.

Bibliography

Breasted, J. H., *Ancient Records*, University of Chicago Press.

——, *History of Egypt*, New York and London.

Carter, H., *The Tomb of Tutankhamun*, London 1925.

Cottrell, L., *Life under the Pharaohs*, Evans Brothers, London.

——, *The Lost Pharaohs*, Evans Brothers, London 1950.

——, *The Mountains of Pharaoh*, Rinehart, New York, and R. Hale, London 1956.

Drioton & Lauer, *Sakkarah; the monuments of Zoser* (Institut de l'Archeologie Orientale).

Edwards, I. E. S., *The Pyramids of Egypt*, Penguin Books, London 1947.

Erman, A., *A Handbook of Egyptian Religion*, London 1907.

——, *Life in Ancient Egypt*.

Erman: Blackman, *The Literature of the Ancient Egyptians*, London 1927.

Gardiner, Sir A., *The Attitude of the Ancient Egyptians to Death and the Dead*, Cambridge 1935.

Glanville, S. R. K. (editor), *The Legacy of Egypt*, Oxford University Press 1953.

Goneim, Z., *The Buried Pyramid*, Rinehart, New York and Longmans Green, London 1956.

Grinsell, L., *Egyptian Pyramids*, Gloucester 1947.

Herodotus, *History*.

Lucas, A., *Ancient Egyptian materials and industries*, London 1934.

Maspero, Sir G., *The Dawn of Civilisation*, S.P.C.K.

Murray, Dr. M., *The Splendour that was Egypt*, London.

Newberry, P. E., Presidential Address to the British Association (Anthropological Section) 'Egypt as a field for Anthropological Research'. *Annual Report of the British Association*, London 1923.

Pendlebury, J. D. S., *Tell el Amarna*, London 1935.

Petrie, Sir Flinders, *Naquada and Ballas*, 1924.

——, *Royal Tombs of the First and Second Dynasties*, Egypt Exploration Fund, London 1901–2.

Pritchard, J. B. (editor), *Ancient Near Eastern Texts relating to the Old Testament*, Princeton University Press 1950.

Reisner, G., *The Development of the Egyptian Tomb down to the Accession of Cheops*, Harvard University 1936.

Bibliography

MESOPOTAMIA

Buckingham, J. S., *Travels in Mesopotamia*, London 1827.

Budge, E. A. W., *By Nile and Tigris*, London 1920.

Delgougaz, P., *The Temple Oval of Khafajah*, Chicago 1940.

Gadd, C. J., *Stones of Assyria*, London 1936.

Hilprecht, H. V., *Exploration in Bible Lands*, New York, and Edinburgh 1903.

——, *The Excavations in Assyria and Babylonia*, Philadelphia 1904.

Koldewey, R., *The Excavation at Babylon*, London 1914.

Kramer, S. N., *Sumerian Mythology*, Philadelphia 1944.

Layard, A. H., *Autobiography and Letters*, 2 vols., London 1949.

——, *Discoveries in the ruins of Nineveh and Babylon*, 2 vols., London 1853.

——, *Nineveh and its Remains*, London 1849.

——, *Early adventures in Persia, Susiana, and Babylonia*, London 1887.

Musil, Alois, *The Middle Euphrates*, New York 1927.

Rassam, H., *Asshur and the land of Nimrod*, New York 1897.

Rawlinson, G., *A Memoir of Major-General Sir Henry Creswicke Rawlinson*, London 1898.

Rich, C. J., *Narrative of a journey to the site of Babylon*, 2 vols., London 1939.

Sayce, A. H., *Religions of Ancient Egypt and Babylonia*, Gifford Lectures 1902.

Woolley, Sir L., *Ur Excavations*, 3 vols., London 1934–39.

——, *Ur of the Chaldees*, London 1929.

——, *The Development of Sumerian Art*, London 1935.

——, *The Sumerians*, London.

SYRIA-PALESTINE

Allbright, W. F., *The Archaeology of Palestine*, Penguin Books, London 1949.

Bates, Sutherland, (editor), *The Bible designed to be read as Literature*, London 1938.

Bevan, E. R. and Singer, C., *The Legacy of Israel*, Oxford 1927.

Bibliography

Hogarth, D. G., *The Hittites of Syria*, Cambridge Ancient History, Vols. 3 and 6, Cambridge 1929.

Moore, G. F., *History of Religions*, Vol. 2. Judaism-Christianity-Mohammedanism, New York 1919.

——, *Judaism*, London.

Oesterly *and* Robinson, *History of Israel*, London.

Parkes, J., *Judaism and Christianity*, Chicago 1948.

Pritchard, J. B., *Ancient Near Eastern Texts relating to the Old Testament*, Princeton University Press 1950.

Smith, W. R., *The Old Testament in the Jewish Church*, London.

——, *The Prophets of Israel*, London.

——, *The Religion of the Semites*, London.

Wade, G. W., *Old Testament History*, London.

ASIA-MINOR

Ainsworth, W. F., *Travels and researches in Asia Minor, Mesopotamia, Chaldea and Armenia*, London 1842.

Bittel, K. *and* Campbell, H., *Boghazkoy* (English guide to the site), Istanbul 1951.

Blegen, C. W., *Troy*, 3 vols., University of Princeton 1950.

Bossert, H. Th. *and* Campbell, H., *Karatepe*, First report 1946, second report 1947, Istanbul.

Ceram, C. W., *Narrow Pass, Black Mountain*, London and New York 1956.

Garstang, J., *The Hittite Empire*, London 1929.

——, *The Land of the Hittites*, London 1910.

Gurney, O. R., *The Hittites*, Penguin Books, London 1952.

Sayce, A. H., *The Hittites. The Story of a forgotten Empire*, London 1910.

Schliemann, H., *Troy and its remains*, London 1875.

——, *Ilios, The city and country of the Trojans*, London 1880.

Schmidt, E. F., *Anatolia through the ages. Discoveries at the Alishar Mound 1927–29*, Chicago 1931.

——, *Aishar Huyuk. Season 1928–29*, Parts 1 and 2, Chicago 1932–33.

Schuchardt, C., *Schliemann's excavations*, London 1891.

Wainwright, G. A., *Asiatic Keftiu*, American Journal of Archaeology, LVI., 4 (1952).

CRETE

Apollodorus, Loeb Classical Library, Vol. 2.

Bury, J. B., *History of Greece*, Macmillan, London.

Cottrell, L., *The Bull of Minos*, Evans Brothers, London 1953.

Evans, Joan, *Time and Chance* (Biography of Sir Arthur Evans), London 1943.

Evans, Sir Arthur, *The Palace of Minos*, Macmillan, London.

Forsdyke, Sir John, *Minoan Art*, British Academy Vol. 15, Humphrey Milford, London.

Hawes, B. M. *and* Hawes, H. W., *Crete the forerunner of Greece*, London.

Homer, *The Iliad*.

——, *The Odyssey*.

Myres, J. L., *The Dawn of History*, London.

Pendlebury, J., *The Archaeology of Crete*, London.

Thucydides, *History*.

GREECE

Aeschylus, *The Oresteia* (Trilogy).

Blegen, C. W., *Troy*, Vols. 1–3, Princeton University Press 1940–1953.

Bury, J. B., *A History of Greece*, New York 1937.

Cottrell, L., *The Bull of Minos*, Evans Brothers, London 1953.

Dickinson, G. L., *The Greek view of life*, New York 1925.

Glotz, G., *The Aegean civilisation*, London 1925.

Glover, T. R., *The Ancient World*, Cambridge University Press.

Greene, W. C., *The Achievement of Greece*, London 1923.

Hall, H. R., *The Civilisation of Greece in the Bronze Age*, London 1923.

Herodotus, *History*.

Homer, *The Iliad*.

——, *The Odyssey*.

Kitto, H. D. F., *The Greeks*, Penguin Books, London 1951.

Lang, A., *The World of Homer*, London 1910.

Livingstone, Sir R. W., *Greek ideals and Modern Life*, Cambridge 1935.

Livingstone, Sir R. W. (editor), *The Legacy of Greece*, Oxford 1928.

Lucas, F. L., *Greek poetry for Everyman*, London 1950.

Ludwig, E., *Schliemann of Troy*, London 1931.

Murray, G., *The Rise of the Greek Epic*, London 1924.

Nilsson, M. P., *Homer and Mycenae*, London 1933.

Rose, H. J., *A Handbook of Greek Literature*, London 1934.

Schliemann, H., *Mycenae and Tiryns*, London 1878.

Seltman, C., *The Twelve Olympians*, London 1952.

——, *Women in Antiquity*, London 1956.

Thucydides, *The Peloponnesian War*.

Index

Abednecho, 195

Abraham, 59, 96, 99, 120, 123, 126, 145

Abydos, 40, 42, 56, 68, 69, 72, 73

Achaeans, 138, 141, 182, 183, 185, 228

Achilles, 206

Acropolis, 252, 253, 259, 264

Adjib, 69

Adonis, 217

Aeschylus, 214, 218, 219, 233, 250, 259

Aesculapius, 78, 82

Agade, 98

Agamemnon, 74, 259, 264

Agriculture, birth of, 21, 22

Aha, 69

Ahiyawa (Ahhiya), 182, 228

Ahmosis, 130

Akhetaten. *See* Tell-el-Amarna

Akhnaten, 123, 130, 146–51, 159, 163, 165 *et seq.*, 172, 174, 180
    art in his reign, 167
    Foreign Office, 162, 164

Aki-Izzi, 164

Akkad, 60 *et seq.*, 98, 104
    cities in, 63 *et seq.*
    development of the civilisation, 60 *et seq.*
    their civilisation compared with Egyptian civilisation, 65–7
    language, 62
    origins of, 61
    religion, 62, 64
    union with Sumer, 65, 66, 98
    way of life, 63–5

'Al Ubaid', 94

Alcaeus of Mytilene, 224

Alexander the Great, 247

Alexandria, 46

Amélineau, E., 56, 69

Amenemhet I, 145

Amenemhet II, 90

Amenemhet III, 90, 92

Amenemope, 131–3

Amenophis II, 146

Amenophis III, 145–7, 151, 164

Amenophis IV. *See* Akhnaten

Amorites, 100

Amun and Amun-Re, 27, 71, 72, 74, 134–6, 143, 148, 159, 165, 217, 221

Anatolia, 113, 159

Anaxagoras, 203, 250

Ancient Near Eastern Texts (Kramer), 60

Ancient World, The (Glover), 231

Animals, as gods, 27
    pack, 25, 31, 61

Ankhesnamun (Ankhsenpaaton), 160, 170–2, 174

Anu (Huni), 80, 83, 94, 217

Anubis, 85, 217

Anzety, 72

Ape't, 71

Aphrodite, 213, 214, 217–9, 264

Apollo, 213, 214, 220, 221, 242

Apollodorus, 107, 108

Archaeology of Crete (Pendlebury), 112, 156, 157

Archaeology, Victorian, 192

Archilochus, 202

Ares, 213, 215, 218

Argos, 142

Aristagoras, 232, 233
Aristeides, 243
Aristophanes, 250, 254, 259, 261
Aristotle, 173, 203, 205, 250, 259
Armenia, 61
Artaxerxes I, 187, 247
Artaxerxes II, 187, 247
Artaxerxes III, 247
Artemis, 221
Artemisia, 257
Arvad, 125
Ashmolean Museum, 55, 109
Ashtoreth, 129
Ashurbanipal, 122, 228, 231, 234
Ashurnasirpal, 193
Asia, Hither, 30
    Western, 22
Assuan, 49, 77
Assyria, 61, 63, 101, 103, 159, 178,
    179, 186–8, 190, 193, 194,
    199, 228, 232, 235, 246, 260,
    265
    cities in, 191
    cruelty in, 188, 191, 192
    sculpture, 192, 193
Atalanta, 255, 256
Atenism, 146–51
    end of, 167–9
Athens, 215, 234, 247, 253
    description of, 253
    National Museum, 221
Attarisiyas, 182
Ay, 148, 171
Aziru the Amorite, 164–6

Baal, 221
Babel, Biblical Tower of, 198
Babylon, 34, 36, 63, 101 *et seq.*,
    178, 179, 186, 188, 190, 193,
    194, 198, 199, 211, 228, 260,
    263, 264
    achievements of, 194–5
    aerial impression of, 35, 36

culture, spread of, 195
discovery of, 196–8
Hanging Gardens of, 197
literature of, 194–5
rise of, 101
Tower of, 93
writing (cuneiform), 147, 162,
    195
Baikie, James, 167
Basra, 36, 191
Before Philosophy (Frankfort,
    Wilson and Jacobsen), 28
Belshazzar, 195, 196
Belzoni, 175
Bes, 71
Birs Nimrud, 198
Bismayeh, 94
Blackman, 52
Blegen, Professor, 154, 155, 206
Boghaz-Keui, 128, 162, 170, 176
Book of the Dead, 144, 145
Boston Museum of Fine Arts, 221
Botta, Paul Emile, 190, 191, 196
Bowra, Sir Maurice, 256
Boyd, Miss, 112
Breasted, Professor J. H., 144–6
Brick making, 20
British Association for the Ad-
    vancement of Science (P. E.
    Newberry), 41, 46
British Museum, 188, 191–3, 221,
    253, 263
Bronze, 20, 31, 61, 207
    Age, 138, 140, 210
Brugsch, Emil, 125
Bubastis, 71
Buckingham, James Silk, 94, 196
Budge, E. A. W., 144
Bulis, 237
Bull of Minos, The (Cottrell), 115
Burgh, de, W. G., 16, 234, 250,
    252
Burnet, Professor, 203

Index

Byblos, 125, 161, 263
Byron, Lord, 188, 196

Cadmus, 140
Callimachus of Cyrene, 226
Cambyses, 186, 232
Candaules, 229, 230
Carmel, Mount, 21
Carnarvon, Lord, 171
Carter, Howard, 168, 171
Carthage, 180, 208, 247
Chadwick, J., 206
Champollion, J. F. 53
Chapman, G., 222
Chariot, horse drawn, 124, 161, 162
Charlemagne, 56
Cheops (Khufu), 75, 77, 83, 84, 88, 89, 92, 93, 104, 135, 160
Chephren (Khafre), 89
Childe, Gordon, 16, 19, 22, 25, 26, 62, 160, 162, 163, 173, 194, 230
Christ, 74
Churchill, Sir Winston, 173
Civilisation, influence of geographic and climatic conditions, 24
Cleomenes, 232, 233
Clytemnestra, 257, 259
Cocalus, 108
Code of Laws (Hammurabi), 101, 102
Coinage, 230, 264
Copper, 20, 26, 29, 31, 39
Corinth Canal, 227
Corinthian Order, 227
Cory, William (Johnson), 226
Cottrell, Leonard, 27, 73, 90, 115, 147, 165
Creon, 257
Crete, 44, 92, 105 et seq., 142, 151, 159. See also Minoans

Croesus, King, 230, 231
Cronos, 216
Cult-signs, 44, 113, 114
Cybele, 129
Cyprus, 98, 264
Cyrus, 187, 199, 231, 232, 249

Daedalus, 107, 108
Dance, the, 262, 263
Daniel, 195, 196
Danube, 137
Daphne, 213
Darius I, 187, 233, 234
Darius II, 187, 247
Darwin, 204
Dashur, 90
David, King, 31, 122, 124, 187
Dawn of Conscience, The (Breasted), 144
Dead Sea, 35, 59
Delphi, 204, 214, 215, 220, 221, 230, 242
Delphi (Poulsen), 261
Deluge, the. See Flood
Demaratus, 238–41
Democritus, 203
Den, 69
Derby, Lord, 222
Desdemona, 257
Deutsch-Orient Gesellschaft, 94
Development of the Egyptian Tomb down to the Time of Cheops (Reisner), 79
Diomedes, 183
Dionysus, 217
    Theatre of, 259
Djer, 69, 76
Djeserti-ankh, 81
Djet, King, 46, 69, 76
Djoser, King (Neter-khet), 77–82, 99, 135, 263
Don Juan (Lord Byron), 196
Dorian Greeks, 178, 183, 186, 207

Doric Order, 227
Drama, 262–3. *See also* Egyptian, Greek, etc.
Dudu (or Tutu), 166
Dumuzi, 94
Dungi, 99
Dunne, J. W., 29
Dur Sharrakin, 191

Ea, 94
Economy, mixed, 21, 22
Edel, Herr E., 171
Eden, Garden of, 36
Edwards, I. E. S., 85, 91
Egypt, 21, 22, 31, 63, 103, 104, 124 *et seq.*, 174, 186, 190, 199, 232, 248
  aerial impressions of, 34–6
  Amratean culture, 38, 39
  Badarian culture, 38, 39
  civilisation, compared with Sumerian and Akkadian, 65–67
  culture of, 47
  Delta, people, 39 *et seq.*
    their houses, 47, 48
    their origins, 44
  pre-Dynastic, 22, 23, 37 *et seq.*
    their graves, 38–40
  Dynastic, 23
  1st Dynasty, 37, 38
    architectural styles of, 46
    use of timber in, 45, 46
  everyday life in, 86, 87
  Gerzean culture, 38, 39
  hieroglyphs, 41–3, 106. *See also* writing
  Hittites, defeat of, 133
  Kingdom, Old, 38, 55, 68, 72, 73, 84, 85, 87–9, 91, 101, 130, 161, 199
    collapse of, 89

Kingdom, Middle, 72, 90, 101, 104, 115, 124, 130, 137
  art in, 161
  land transport in, 161
  trade in, 159–62
  weapons of war in, 163
Kingdom, New, 90, 136, 161
Lower, 40, 41, 80
  religion, 68 *et seq.*, 89
  scientific achievements, 50, 51
  sculpture, 91, 92
  temperament, 70, 71
  territory extension, 125, 126
  trade, 66, 67. *See also* Kingdom, Middle
  union of Lower and Upper, 40, 41, 54, 55
Upper, 39, 41, 42, 73, 80
  war, attitude to, 54, 55, 130, 131
  writing, 82, 87, 88. *See also* hieroglyphs
Egypt as a Field for Anthropological Research (Newberry), 41
Elamites, 100, 101
Elephantine island, 49
Elgin marbles, 221, 253
Ellil, 62
Embalming, 69
Emery, Professor Walter, 38, 69
Engelbach, Rex, 70
Enki, 217
Enlil (Ki), 94
Ephialtes of Trachis, 240, 241
Epicurus, 203
Erech, 62
Erechtheum, 253
Eridu, 62, 66, 99
Erman, A., 52, 136
Eshnunna, 93
E-temen-anki, Temple of, 197
Etruscans, 208
Eumenides (Aeschylus), 214

Index

Euphrates, 24, 32, 57, 59 *et seq.*, 93
  annual flooding of, 60
Euripides, 216, 218, 224, 250
Europa, 140
Europe, 137
Eurybiades, 243
Evans, Sir Arthur, 108 *et seq.*, 140, 142, 152–4, 205
Ezarhaddon, 190, 193
Ezekiel, 221

Fairman, Professor H. W., 147, 150, 167, 169
Flood, the, 59, 63, 120, 123
Ford, J., 250
Forrer, E., 182
Forster, E. M., 198, 199
Foundations in the Dust (Seton Lloyd), 94, 95, 193
Frankfort, Professor, 28, 48
Fraser, Sir James, 216

Galilee, Lake, 249
Gardiner, Sir Alan, 82
Gawra, 30
Geb, 73
Gebel el Araq., 45
Gelo, 238
Genesis, Book of, 59
Gideon, 187
Gilgamesh, 120
Gilliéron, 111
Giza, 44, 77, 83
Glanville, Professor, 50
Glover, Dr. T. R., 231, 249, 255
Goneim, Zakaria, 81, 82
Gournia, 112
Grant's Tomb, 222
Graves, Robert, 216
Grebaut, M., 163
Greece, 138, 200, 264, 265
  art and sculpture, 221, 222
  character, 201, 203

'classical', 201 *et seq.*
colonies, 208
culture, 205
Dorian. *See* Dorian Greeks
drama, 250, 259–60
economy, 209, 259
pre-Hellenic, 22, 205
influence of geography on, 227, 228
language, 204
literature, 205, 219 *et seq.*
mythology, 213 *et seq.*
physical appearance, 201
poetry, 222 *et seq.*
religion, 213 *et seq.*
scientific knowledge, 203, 204
slave population, 258
war with the Persians and defeat of, 233 *et seq.*, 243
way of life, 258
women, 254–7
Greeks, The (H. D. F. Kitto), 202, 214, 220, 244, 251, 258
Greek Poetry for Everyman, 226
Grote, G., 205
Grotefend, 94
Gurney, O. R., 128, 129
Gyges, 228, 229, 230

Hagia Triadha, 112
Halbherr, Frederico, 111, 112
Hammurabi, 101 *et seq.*, 115, 144, 173, 179, 193, 194, 231
Hassan, Beni, 137
Hassuna, 95
Hat-hor, 85, 91
Hattusas, 194
Hattusilis III, 162, 177, 179
'Heb-sed' ceremony, 31, 56, 57, 76, 147
Hebrews. *See* Jews
Hector, 202, 206
Helen, wife of Menelaus, 141

Index

Helen of Sparta, 254
Heliopolis, 71, 72, 85, 175
Helladic period, late, 138
Hellas. *See* Athens
Hellespont, 228, 235, 236
Hephaestus, 213
Hera, 219, 221
Heracles, 216, 231
Heraklion, 109
Herculaneum, 247
'Heresy Period', 146–51, 167–9
Hermes, 214, 215
Hermione, 254
Hermopolis, 168
Herodotus, 36, 37, 44, 63, 91, 114,
    188, 197, 198, 202, 203, 210,
    211, 229, 230, 234–7, 239, 243
    244
Hierakonpolis, 40, 42, 55
Hillah, 196
Hipponax of Ephesus, 223
Histories, The (Herodotus), 91,
    198, 211, 230, 235
History of Egypt, A, (Breasted),
    145
*History of the English-Speaking
    Peoples* (Churchill), 173
Hittites, 119, 126 *et seq.*, 159, 164,
    176, 177, 180, 182, 183, 194,
    199, 228, 260
    defeat by Egyptians, 133
    extension of territory, 130
    physical appearance, 129
    religion, 129
    unification of, 129
Hittites, The (Gurney), 128, 129
Holocene period, 21
Homer, 63, 107, 109, 141, 142,
    152, 155, 163, 176, 181–4, 202,
    205, 213, 214, 216, 218, 220,
    222, 223, 249
Horemhab, 171, 174
Hori, 159, 162

Horus, 71–4, 85, 91, 199
Housman, A. E., 244
Howards End (Forster), 198, 199
Huni. *See* Anu
Huxley, T. H., 204
Hyksos, 124, 126, 128, 140, 158
Hypostyle Hall, 175

Ibycus, 254
Icarus, 107
Ice Age, 21
Ida, Mount, 116, 216
Iliad, 141, 142, 163, 176, 183, 202,
    205, 206, 218, 222
Imhotep, 78, 79, 82, 99, 173
Inanna, 94, 99
Indus Valley, 19, 24, 32
Ineni, 70
Ionia, 231, 232
Ionic Order, 227
Iraq, 23, 30, 35
Iron, its effect on mankind, 180,
    181
    working, 160
Isaiah, 145, 193
Ishtar, 129, 217
    Gate, 197
Isis, 71–3, 85, 91, 94, 199
Israel, 21, 59

Jacob, 145
Jacob-her, 124
Jason, 183, 205
Jaweh, 177, 180, 217, 218, 221,
    250
Jebb, 254
Jemdet Nasr, 48, 94
Jephthah, 159, 187
Jericho, 35
Jerusalem, 249
Jews, 92, 120 *et seq.*, 126, 158, 177,
    190, 195, 211, 218, 248, 249,
    265

Index

Jews—*cont.*
  birth of their nation, 187
  religious literature, 248, 249
Jonson, Ben, 250
Jordan, 35
Joseph, 26, 145
Judah, 31, 47
Judea, 59

Ka, 69, 79
Kadesh, 133
Kamose, 126
Karnak, 30, 175
Kassites, 193
Kenya, Mt., 30
Khaba, 80
Khasekhemui, 40, 77
Kheta. *See* Hittites
Khorsobad, 190
Khufu. *See* Cheops
Ki, 217
Kikuyu, 30
Kingdom, Old, Middle and New.
  See Egypt.
Kish, 93, 94, 98
Kitto, H. D. F., 202, 204, 214,
  215, 220, 244, 251, 254, 255,
  256, 258
Kizwadana, 180
Knossos, 109, 116, 128, 140, 152–
  157, 167, 205
  fall of, 113, 154–7
  Palace of, 110, 111, 152, 157
Koldewey, Dr., 94, 196, 211
Kramer, S. N., 60, 100

Labarnas, King, 129
Labyrinth, 108, 110
Lagash, 62, 93, 98, 99
Langdon, S., 94
Larsa, 62, 66, 99
Lauer, M. Jean-Philippe, 79, 82

Layard, Austen Henry, 94, 191,
  192, 193, 196
Lebanon, 45, 125
Legacy of the Ancient World (de
  Burgh), 16, 234
Leonides, 238, 241
Libya, 44, 67, 85, 114, 179, 186,
  235
Life, 192
Life under the Pharaohs (Cottrell),
  27
'Linear A and B' tablets, 116, 140,
  154, 155, 206
Literature of the Ancient Egyptians
  (Erman and Blackman), 52
Lloyd, Seton, 94, 95, 192, 193
Lost Pharaohs, The (Cottrell), 73,
  90, 147, 165
Louvre, the, 99, 188, 221
Lucas, F. L., 222, 226
Luxor, 35, 46, 263
Lycabettus, 253
Lydia, 129, 186, 228, 230–2, 264

MacNeice, Louis, 222
Macedonia, 228
Maduwattas, 182, 228
Magic, 27, 29, 30, 144, 151
Mahomet, 74
Mahu, 87
Mallia, 112
Mandikian, Arda, 262
Manetho, 38, 56, 68, 78, 80, 81,
  82, 124
Marathon, 233, 259
Mardonius, 244
Mareotis, Lake, 48–9
Marlowe, Christopher, 250
Marseilles, 247
Martyrdom of Man (Winwood
  Reade), 16
Masai, 30
Maspero, 192

Mastabas, 77, 83, 84, 85, 86, 143, 160

Medea, 256, 257

Medes, 190, 232

Medinet Habu, 175, 182

Mediterranean, 137

Melville, Herman, 173

Memphis, 23, 68, 71–3, 77, 78, 84, 85, 135

Menelaus, 141

Menes, 38, 39, 40, 45, 47, 55–7, 65, 66, 68, 69, 72, 73, 75–8, 98, 130, 160, 199
  ceremonial palette, 55, 56
  conquest of the Delta kingdom, 55, 56
  macehead, 55, 56, 76

Menkaure. *See* Mycerinus

Mereneptah, 177, 179

Meritaten, 168

Mesach, 195

Mesopotamia, 19, 21, 22, 26, 37, 48, 53, 60 *et seq.*, 92 *et seq.*

Metropolitan Museum of Art, 221

Midas, 231

Miletus, 182

Millennium, Second, 101, 103, 112, 119, 129, 137
  everyday life in the, 160–2
  Third, 19, 54, 65
  Fourth, 31

Mimnermus of Colophon, 224

Minoans, 134, 159, 175, 217
  civilisation, its beginnings, 112, 113
  cult, 153
  culture, 138, 142, 143
  development of, 116
  frescoes, 152
  maritime trade of, 117
  origins of, 113–5
  Period, Early, 115
  Period, Middle, 115, 128

  physical appearance of, 106
  writing, 109, 116, 205

Minos, King, 107, 108, 110, 140
  Palace of, 265

Minyan pottery, 138

Mittani, 119, 130, 135, 176

Moby Dick, 173, 174

Moeris, Lake of, 90–2

Mohl, 191

Monumental Architecture in Egypt (Frankfort), 48

Moral values, 145

Moses, 145, 151, 177, 180, 221

Mursilis III, 228

Museum, British. *See* British Museum

Music, 262

Myceneans, 63, 108, 119, 138, 140, 142, 143, 154–6, 159, 163, 175, 176, 181–6, 205, 208, 209, 215, 246, 264
  art, influence of, 207
  culture, 207
  writing, 53, 154, 155

Mycerinus (Menkaure), 89, 135

Myres, Sir John, 109

Nagada, 39, 42, 77, 115

Nahum, 190

Naram-Sin, 98

Narmer. *See* Menes

Nebuchadnezzar, 187, 195, 197, 231, 234

Nefer-ka, 80

Nefretiti, 147–51, 168, 169

Neith, 114

Nekhen, 41

Nelson's Column, 222

Nephthys, 73

Neptune, 113

Nerea, 255

Nestor, 183

Newberry, Professor Percy, 41–4, 46, 56, 72, 113
Nicolson, Sir Harold, 129
Nile, 135
First Civilisation of, 37
aerial impressions of, 34, 35
annual flooding of, 37, 50, 51, 76
Nile Delta, 39, 40, 55, 71, 124
Nile Valley, 19, 24, 32, 34, 39, 62, 63, 74, 199
Nimrud, 94
Nineveh, 95, 186, 187, 190, 191, 193
Nineveh and its Remains, 191
Nippur, 59, 62, 93, 98, 99
No-Amun. *See* Thebes
Noah, 59
Nubia, 49, 66, 85, 90, 126, 179, 186, 235
Nut, 73

Occupation layers, 19
Odysseus, 183, 184
Odyssey, 141, 152, 183, 184, 205, 206, 218
Omphale, Queen, 231
Ophelia, 257
Oresteia (Aeschylus), 218, 233
Orestes, 74, 259
Orpheus, 217
Osiris, 71–4, 85, 91, 94, 135, 199
Outline of History (H. G. Wells), 16, 37
Oxford Book of Greek Verse in Translation, 256

Palace of Minos (Evans), 152–4
Palestine, 21, 124, 158
Pallas Athene, 215
Temple of, 252
Parnassus, Mt., 221
Parthenon, 252, 253
Paul, St., 218

Pendlebury, J. D. S., 112, 113, 115, 146, 147, 150, 151, 154, 156, 167, 169
Per-Re, 168
Pericles, 234, 250, 251, 252, 258
Persephone, 94
Persia, 231 *et seq.*, 246
Empire, 199
Navy, defeat by Greeks, 242–44
war with Greeks, 233 *et seq.*
Persian Gulf, 98
Petrie, Sir Flinders, 39, 40, 47, 48, 56, 69, 83, 147, 180, 192
Phaestos, 111, 112, 116, 128, 152, 154
Pharaohs, absolute power of Old Kingdom, 84, 85, 89
absolute power of Middle Kingdom, 90
Phidias, 250
Phoenicians, 119, 120, 125, 186, 194, 199, 208, 235
Phrygia, 231
Pictographs, Cretan, 109
Piraeus, 253
Plato, 173, 205, 216, 218, 220, 250, 254, 259, 263
Poseidon, 113, 214–16, 252
Potter's wheel, 20, 25, 31, 61
Poulsen, Frederick, 261
Power, through military prowess, 29–31
Praxiteles, 250
Prehistory, 19
Priests, 29
and magic, 30
Pritchard, James B., 60
Prometheus, The (Aeschylus), 233
Promised Land, 59
Pylos, 206
Pyramids, the, 75 *et seq.*, 143
construction of, 77–9, 83, 84
furnishing of, 79–80

Pyramids—*cont.*
  religious significance in shape, 85, 86
  sculptured scenes in, 86, 87
Pyramid, Great, 75, 77, 83, 84, 88, 92, 93, 104, 180
  Step, 77–80, 83, 263
Pyramids of Egypt, The (Edwards), 85, 91

Qu', 69
Queequeg, 174
Quibell, J. E., 40, 55

Ramesses, 122
Ramesses II, 162, 163, 174, 175, 177, 178
Ramesses III, 174, 175, 179, 182
Ramesses VI, 171
Ras Shamra, 140, 175
Rassam, Hormuzd, 94, 196
Rawlinson, Henry, 94, 196
Re, 71, 72, 74, 85, 86, 91, 134, 135, 143, 146, 199
Reade, Winwood, 16
Red Sea, 34, 35
Reisner, Dr. George, 78, 79
Rekhmire, 134
Religion and kingship, 30, 31
  coming of priests, 29, 30
  female deities in, 28
  understanding of, 26–8
  See also Egyptian, Greek, etc.
Republic (Plato), 216
Rhea, 216
Ribbadi, 165, 263
Rich, Claudius, 94, 196
Rieu, E. V., 184
Romans, 51
Rossetti, Dante Gabriel, 225

Sa'id, 71, 72
Sais, 41, 48, 55, 113, 114, 199

Sakkara, 68, 69, 77, 79, 82, 83, 87, 89
Salamis, 244, 257, 259, 264
Samson, 187
Samuel, 31
Sa-nakht, 80
Sappho, 225
Saqqara, 38
Sargon, 98, 99, 101, 104, 158, 160, 173, 188, 193, 231
Schliemann, Heinrich, 108, 109, 114, 141–3, 163, 182, 205
Scribes, 25
Sculpture. *See* Egyptian, Greek, etc.
Seager, R. B., 112
Sekenre, 125, 126, 130
Sekhem-khet, 81, 82
Sekhmet, 27, 71, 217
Seltman, Dr., 255, 256
Semerkhet, 69, 76
Semonides of Amorgos, 225
Sennacherib, 187, 188, 193
Senusret, 49
Senusret II, 90
Senusret III, 90
Seth, 71, 73, 74
Sethe, K., 43
Sethi I, 174, 175
Seven against Thebes (Aeschylus), 233
Shadrach, 195
Shakespeare, William, 205, 250, 257
Shalmaneser, 193
Sharona, 43
Shatt Charraf, 93
Shepherd Kings. *See* Hyksos
Sheshonk, King, 187
Shinar, 36, 59
Ships, sailing, 20, 29
Shubbuliliuma, King, 159, 165, 177

Index

Sidon, 125, 178
Sinai, 67, 85
Smenkhkare, 168, 169
Smith, George, 94
Snofru, 83, 88
Sobek, 27
Social Life in Ancient Egypt (Petrie), 47, 48
Socrates, 250, 254, 255, 259
Solomon, 122, 187
Sommer, F., 182
Sophists, 220
Sophocles, 218, 250, 254
Spartans, 202, 208, 209, 232, 233, 237, 239, 240, 241, 243, 251, 254
Sperchias, 237
Stone Age, 20, 27, 37
Stone, Egyptian working of, 75, 78-80
    use of as building material, 66
Story of Gilgamesh, 63
Stubbings, Dr. Frank, 138, 140
Sudan, 42. *See also* Nubia
Sumer, 36, 59 *et seq.*, 92 *et seq.*, 158, 193, 217, 260, 264
    cities of, 63 *et seq.*, 93, 94
    development of civilisation, 59 *et seq.*
    language, 62
    physical appearance, 103
    origins of, 61, 62
    religion, 62, 64, 93, 94
    trade, 66, 67
    union with Akkad, 65, 66, 98
    way of life, 63-5
    writing (cuneiform), 53, 63, 101, 106
Sumerian and Akkadian civilisation, comparison with Egyptian, 65-7
Sumerian-Akkadian culture, development of, 94

Sumerian Mythology (Kramer), 100
Susa, 101, 232
Sybaris, 247
Symposium (Plato), 263
Syracuse, 247, 248
Syria, 21, 23, 45, 90, 113, 158, 159, 164

Tanta, 71, 72
Tarshish (Cadiz), 186, 208
Taylor, J. E., 99
Tehenu-land, 56
Tell-el-Amarna, 147, 151, 159, 162, 163, 165, 167-70
Tell-el-Amarna (Pendlebury), 150, 151
'Tells', 23, 30
Testament, Old, 31, 100, 120, 126, 128, 145, 188, 190, 193, 195, 211
    influence of, 122-4
Thammuz, 94, 217
Thebes, 34, 71, 72, 90, 133-5, 143, 146-8, 162, 168, 169, 171, 175, 182, 190
Themis, 214
Themistocles, 202, 233, 234, 242, 243, 250
Theognis of Megara, 223
Thermopylae, 227, 239, 244
Theseus, 107, 155, 157
This (Thinis), 68
Thoth, 85, 217
Thoueris, 85
Thrace, 228
Thucydides, 117, 188, 235, 243
Tiglath-Pileser, 193
Tigris, 24, 32, 59 *et seq.*, 95, 159, 178, 179, 186
    annual flooding of, 60
Tiryns, 140
Tiyi, Queen, 146, 147

Tombs, archaic period of, 76, 77
  Egyptian, 69, 70
    significance of two tombs of Old Kingdom Pharaohs, 72–4
  rock-cut, 143
Tools, stone, 20
Transport, wheeled, 20, 25, 29, 31
Trojan War, 141, 142, 181
Troy, 141, 142, 163, 176, 182, 183, 205, 228, 264
Tunip, 164, 165
Tushratta, 164
Tutankhamun, 160, 168, 169, 171, 172, 180
Tuthmosis I, 70
Tuthmosis III, 49, 122, 133–6, 143, 144, 146, 159, 164, 234
Tuthmosis IV, 146
Tyre, 125, 178

Ubaste, 71
Udimu, 40
Umma, 93, 99
Underworld, 143
Ur, 36, 62, 65, 66, 93, 96 *et seq.*, 120, 264
  Royal graves at, 96, 97
  Sack of, 100, 101
Ur of the Chaldees (Woolley), 65
Urban Revolution, 19, 24, 82
Ur-Nammu, 99, 104

Uruk, 36, 62, 66, 93, 98

Ventris, Michael, 117, 138, 154, 155, 206
Venus de Milo, 221
Vinci, Leonardo da, 82

Wace, Professor Alan, 155, 205
Wadji, 40
Warka, 94
Warner, Rex, 235
Weigall, Arthur, 167
Wells, H. G., 16, 37, 176
What Happened in History (Childe), 16, 19, 22, 162, 173, 194, 230
Women in Antiquity (Seltman), 256
Woolley, Sir Leonard, 36, 65, 94, 95, 96, 98, 99, 264
Writing, 120, 121
  development of, 51–3
  earliest forms of, 19
  hieratic, 54
  hieroglyphs of, 41–3
  See also Egyptian, Minoan, etc.

Xenophanes of Colophon, 204, 226
Xerxes, 187, 234 *et seq.*, 247

Zazamonkh, 88

by Cyrus (553)	(621)	600
ylon (539)	597 Babylonian Conquest (1st deportation)	
	586 Final captivity of Judah	500
	538 Restoration under Cyrus	
	PERSIAN DOMINATION	475
		450
		425
		400

in a br
sible. I
e liable

LEONARD COTTRELL

Babylon & Assyria	Egypt	
	11th Dynasty (2100–2000)	
	12th Dynasty (2000–1790)	1900
Hammurabi (c. 1792) of Babylon		1800
	13th Dynasty (1790–1700)	1700
Sack of ... Babylonian ...	HYKSOS PERIOD (1700–1555)	
		1600
	New Kingdom begins (...1555)	
		1500
RISE OF ASSYRIAN POWER (c. 1360)	18th Dynasty (1555–1350)	1400
	Thutmosis III—1480–1450	
	Maximum expansion of Egyptian Empire	
Shalmaneser I (1270)	Ramesses II signs treaty with Hittite king Hattusilis III (1269)	1300
Babylon under Assyrian ...	Ramesses III defeats coalition of invaders (c. 1190)	
	20th Dynasty (1200–1090)	
		1200
Tiglath-Pileser I (c. 1110)		1100
	21st Dynasty (1090–945)	
Decline of Assyria		1000
REVIVAL OF ASSYRIAN POWER		900
Adad-nirari II (911–891)		
Shalmaneser III (859–824)	22nd Dynasty (945–745)	
Shamshi-adad V (824–810)		800
Adad-nirari III (810–783)	23rd Dynasty (745–718)	
Tiglath-Pileser III (745–727)	24th Dynasty (718–712)	
c. 750 HEIGHT OF ASSYRIAN POWER	LATE EGYPTIAN PERIOD	700
Sennacherib invades Judah (...)	25th Dynasty (712–663)	
Death of Esarhaddon (c. 668)	26th Dynasty (Saites) (663–525)	
Ashurbanipal (669–626)		600
Fall of Nineveh (612)		
Nebuchadnezzar reigns from 605–562	PERSIAN DOMINATION (525–332)	500
Cyrus conquers Babylon (539)		
PERSIAN DOMINATION		475
		450
		425
		400